THE VEGETABLE GARDENER'S HOW BOOK

THE MACMILLAN COMPANY
NEW YORK · BOSTON · CHICAGO · DALLAS
ATLANTA · SAN FRANCISCO

MACMILLAN & CO., LIMITED
LONDON · BOMBAY · CALCUTTA
MELBOURNE

THE MACMILLAN COMPANY
OF CANADA, LIMITED
TORONTO

The Vegetable Gardener's How Book

By

CHESLA C. SHERLOCK

❦

New York

THE MACMILLAN COMPANY

1941

PRINTED IN THE UNITED STATES OF AMERICA
NORWOOD PRESS LINOTYPE, INC.
NORWOOD, MASS., U.S.A.

To

MY WIFE

KATHLEEN

WHOSE GARDEN ENTHUSIASM

IS A

CONSTANT INSPIRATION

CONTENTS

PART I

THE GENERAL VEGETABLE GARDEN

CHAPTER I

vii

CONTENTS

CONTENTS

Chapter XXIV

Chapter XXV

Chapter XXVI

Chapter XXVII

PART II

THE SALAD GARDEN

Chapter XXVIII

CONTENTS

CONTENTS

Chapter XXXVI

Chapter XXXVII

Chapter XXXVIII

Chapter XXXIX

Chapter XL

Chapter XLI

Chapter XLII

CONTENTS

PART III

THE FRUIT GARDEN

CHAPTER XLIII

CHAPTER XLIV

CHAPTER XLV

CHAPTER XLVI

CHAPTER XLVII

CHAPTER XLVIII

Chapter XLIX

Chapter L

Chapter LI

Chapter LII

Chapter LIII

Chapter LIV

Chapter LV

CONTENTS

Chapter LVI

Chapter LVII

ILLUSTRATIONS

xvii

ILLUSTRATIONS

PART I

THE GENERAL VEGETABLE GARDEN

CHAPTER I

ASPARAGUS

The Eternal Fitness of Things

"What is the greatest satisfaction you get out of your garden?" a friend asked the other day.

I was stumped for a moment. But, do you know, I believe the biggest thing I get out of my garden is a sense of the eternal fitness of things? One cannot witness the riddle of the seasons, the unfolding of seeds into marvelous plants, the might and mystery of sunshine and rain upon senseless dust without coming closer to the Author of all Creation. Our strivings and our sense of importance fade when we dig in our gardens, for we turn up grains of pure gold and get back to the elemental things. With Emerson we come to say: "All things matter, but nothing matters much"—except that there is Order back of it all and the highest attribute of intelligence is to know that it all matters some!

—CHESLA C. SHERLOCK in
Better Homes and Gardens.

CHAPTER I

ASPARAGUS

1. Preparation of Bed. Select a plot at one side of the garden which is fairly well drained. Preparation of the bed should begin the fall before planting, especially if the soil is heavy and hard to work. Spade or plow to a depth of nine or ten inches; for small beds it is best to spade. Trenching is the best method (see Sec. 585) because the subsoil can be broken up and enriched. Place two inches of well rotted manure or compost at the bottom of the trench. Allow the soil to remain in large chunks so that the frost can work on it during the winter.

In the spring, work over the soil thoroughly, breaking up the chunks into fine particles. Work in more well rotted manure. Asparagus is a rank feeder and must have plenty of plant food at hand. Dig trenches at least nine inches deep where the rows are to be, placing well rotted manure in the bottom. These trenches (rows) should be five feet apart.

2. When to Plant. The proper time to start an asparagus bed is in the spring. Plant as soon as the roots can be secured, or the soil can be worked. When planting seed, wait until frost is over.

3. Type of Roots to Buy. Some growers advocate buying two-year-old roots, others one-year roots. We prefer the latter. In either case, select only strong, healthy roots. All weaklings should be discarded. Buy only rustproof types. Mary Washington seems to be the best. Many growers claim different varieties but unbiased growers think

3

that all rustproof varieties are one and the same. The older varieties all seem to be subject to rust.

4. How to Plant. We prefer to plant roots about nine inches deep, as noted in Sec. 1. Some growers, however, advocate trenching to a depth of eighteen inches. Still others prefer shallow planting. Deep planting makes deep cultivation safer, as one is not so likely to strike the crowns; on the other hand, the shoots will be slower coming up in the spring. This is the only advantage of shallow planting, and where this is followed the shoots are likely to be smaller.

In planting, point the eye up and spread out the roots carefully. The bottom of the trench should be at least eight inches wide to facilitate this. Work the soil carefully and compactly around the brittle, fleshy roots. It can be best settled by copious applications of water. Place the roots from ten to twenty-four inches apart in the row. The wider distance will give longer life to the bed, provided supplementary feedings are made each season. Crowded plants do not last so long or produce quality shoots.

Cover the crowns with only two inches of dirt at first. This is gradually filled in during the first season as the tops grow. By fall the soil should be level around the tops.

5. Care the First Season. The bed should be carefully and continually cultivated during the first season. Keep down all weeds between the rows and hand-weed in the rows between the plants. Be careful not to injure the crowns or roots. At each cultivation, a little dirt can be worked into the trenches. A well set asparagus bed should make a top growth of about three feet the first season. If it is not coming as it should, follow directions in Sec. 7.

6. Cultivation. Small plots and beds can best be cultivated by hand tools during the season. A small bed is best handled with an ordinary garden rake. The sharp teeth will break up the top crust and keep down weeds before they

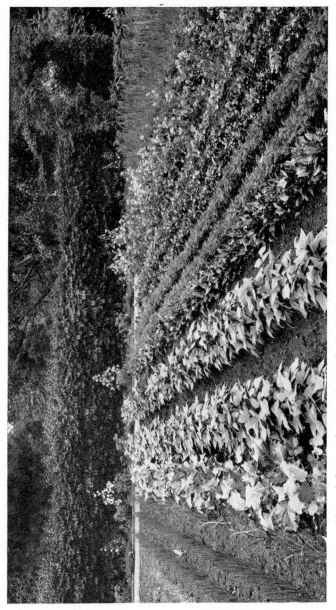

Nature's bounty is never better realized than in the well-kept home vegetable garden.

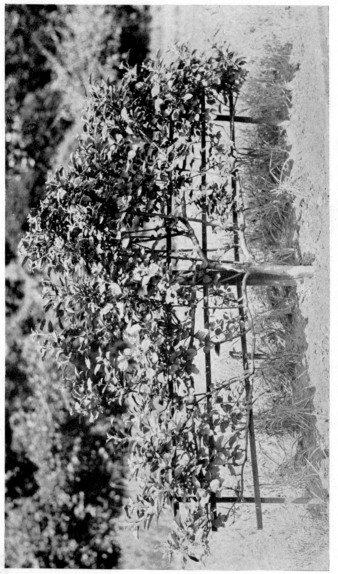

Dwarf apple tree as trained in Shaw's Garden, St. Louis, Mo.

get started, if used with sufficient frequency. If weeds get a start, use a hand hoe, then rake. Larger beds and plots can be handled with a wheel hoe. Commercial plantings will have to be cultivated with horse cultivators or garden tractors.

A good rule is to cultivate as soon as possible after every rain. If a good dust mulch is kept on the surface through frequent cultivation weeds will never get a start. Do not attempt to cultivate between the rows with large tools; the danger of injury is too great.

7. **Use of Manures and Fertilizers.** Asparagus needs a great deal of humus, which is semi-decayed vegetation. Manure is the principal source of this, but it may be purchased in commercial form. Humus is not, in a strict sense, a fertilizer or plant food. Its value lies in the fact that it contributes the necessary bacteria to break up the soil particles and render the plant foods and mineral fertilizers in it available. Manure, of course, contains fertilizing elements in addition to providing humus. It is almost impossible to have too much humus in the asparagus bed.

As soon as the planting has been completed, add 5–8–7 fertilizer or a commercial plant food to the rows. In the former case, use from five to ten pounds to one hundred feet of row; in the latter case, follow the manufacturer's directions. If you prefer, an inch covering of rotted manure or compost can be spread along the row.

Poultry manure, if available, makes an excellent fertilizer for asparagus. No manure of any kind should be spread directly over the crowns, as this encourages the production of short shoots. The best time to apply commercial fertilizers is after the cutting season is over. Manures can be used as a mulch in the fall and spaded under in the spring.

If the tops are not growing as well as they should, nitrate of soda, applied at the rate of five pounds to one hundred feet of row, will be beneficial. But do not apply nitrate of soda and poultry manure at the same time.

8. Salt and Its Use. It is an old axiom among gardeners that salt is beneficial for asparagus. Whether that be true or not, salt will aid in keeping down the weeds. It seems to do no harm to the asparagus plants, and if you wish to apply it do so early in the spring. The more advanced opinion among experts is that it has no particular value, except as noted. If your fertilizers are lacking in potash, it may even have value.

9. Mulches. The problem of weeds can be largely solved in the home garden by using mulches. Six or eight inches of clean straw or marsh hay will keep down the weeds and conserve the moisture content of the soil. The application in the fall of heavy mulches of manure will not only protect the plants from the "heaving" action of frost, but supply plant food and humus when spaded under in the spring. Mulches will have to be renewed in late summer or early fall.

10. Winter Protection. In the fall, when the tops die, they should be cut off a few inches above the ground and removed from the bed. The best disposal of them is burning. This precaution will destroy such insect pests as may be present.

The first season or two, the crowns need mulching of clean material (avoid manure here in the row) to protect them against "heaving" during winter thaws.

11. Harvesting the Crop. Commercial growers usually do not attempt to harvest any crop until the third spring, feeling that it is best to get the plants thoroughly established. Other experts claim that shoots may be cut out for three weeks the second spring provided the top growth reached three feet the first year; if it grew five feet high, then cutting of shoots may be continued for five weeks.

This is an arbitrary yardstick that may not always work

out to the best advantage. The safest rule is to wait until the third spring for any heavy cutting.

In harvesting shoots, use a long, sharp knife and make the cut as deep down as possible. Do not allow the shoots to get too high above the ground before cutting. Cutting may last until July 10th in established beds; the third year it is best to stop cutting the latter part of June.

12. Diseases and Pests. Rust is the most common disease and the worst. It will not bother the average gardener if rustproof varieties like Mary Washington are planted. Badly infested plots should be destroyed and the plants burned.

The asparagus beetle is the most serious pest and seems to be especially fond of new plantings. Everything should be cut clean during the cutting season and the plants sprayed with lead arsenate. In the case of new plantings, spray as soon as the beetles appear.

CHAPTER II

BEANS

> *To see a world in a grain of sand,*
> *And . . .*
> *Hold infinity in the palm of your hand . . .*
>
> —WILLIAM BLAKE.

BEANS

13. Soils, Preparation. Beans are popularly supposed to thrive in any soil, however poor. It is true that they will grow in some poor soils, but they do best in a warm, sandy loam. Lima beans, particularly, demand a warm soil, and even with this condition present should not be planted as early as snap beans.

Light, sandy soils should have humus added to increase the moisture-holding content. Heavy soils should be broken up by the addition of humus. Generally, a good friable loam will give the best results. Soils too rich will produce an indifferent crop; so avoid excessive fertilization.

14. When to Plant. Wait until the soil is thoroughly warmed up before planting beans. When cold, wet weather is in prospect the planting should be postponed, as the seed will rot in the ground. The proper time varies with each latitude, and the gardener will have to use his own judgment. Usually it is safe to plant the middle of April in the latitude of Philadelphia and St. Louis—earlier some years, later others. Lima beans should not be planted until frost is definitely past and the season has turned to the warm side.

15. Sowing for Succession. If snap beans are planted at intervals of two weeks until midsummer, a succession of tender, succulent beans can be supplied for the table throughout the summer. The main crop can be planted so as to come on in late summer, and the surplus allowed to mature. These beans may be shelled and stored in bags or jars for winter use. Only one planting of navy beans or pole beans should be made per season, which provides the whole crop.

16. How to Plant. Most gardeners plant beans too close together. Snap beans, whether green or wax, should run three or four plants per foot in the row, and main crops and bush limas at the rate of about two plants per foot. They will produce more beans than if crowded, and spraying is made easier. Plant snap beans one inch deep. Lima beans are planted one inch deep, with the eyes down. Pole beans, whether snap or lima, are planted four to a hill at the base of the pole, and covered one inch.

17. When to Cultivate. Cultivation should, of course, be kept up throughout the growing season. Weeds must be kept down, and the surface crust broken up. There is one caution to observe in cultivating beans: Do not hoe or cultivate when the plants are wet from rains or dew. Wait until dry, to prevent rust.

18. When to Harvest. Beans should be picked as soon as they are large enough to eat, if of the snap variety. Daily pickings must be made to prevent any of the pods maturing. If this happens, the plant will cease producing, wither, and die. Daily pickings will prolong the life and productivity of the plant. Main-crop beans, such as navy and limas, should be allowed to mature. Pick when thoroughly dry in the pod and just before the pods shatter. If green lima beans are desired, they can be picked when the beans have reached sufficient development.

19. Pole Varieties. Snap beans and the old-fashioned lima bean may both be grown in pole varieties (see Sec. 21). Some gardeners contend that pole varieties produce a greater quantity of beans than the bush types. This is perhaps due to the fact that the bush beans have been crowded, whereas the pole varieties seldom are.

20. When to Set Poles; Type of Poles to Use. Poles should be set at the time of planting, if not before. Place

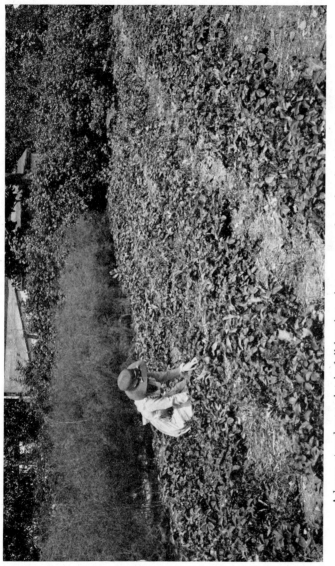

A home strawberry plot in full bearing. Asparagus and raspberries in the background.

This matured cherry orchard was successfully transplanted many miles by the use of proper care.

Barrel-type sprayers enable one to cover all parts of the tree with ease.

Potatoes properly hilled up. A corner of the author's vegetable garden.

the poles so that the plants can readily make use of them as soon as they commence to grow. Many types of poles can be used. The light cedar poles sold by many seedsmen and lumber dealers are good and will last many years if given reasonable care. Any light saplings or branches from a wood lot may be used. One gardener, hard put for something to use one season, nailed laths together and set them up wigwam-fashion. He got along very well.

21. **Diseases and Pests.** Bean spot, or anthracnose, is a fungous disease of the pods. This is best prevented by not disturbing the plants when they are wet, either by cultivation or by picking. It is best to avoid them until they are thoroughly dry.

If black aphids are seriously affecting the tender growth, spray with nicotine sulphate.

The Mexican bean beetle is often a serious pest, eating the leaves. Two broods a season come on. They are controlled by spraying with pyrethrum soap. Large plantings may be dusted or sprayed with magnesium arsenate.

The bean weevil is an old-time pest. The eggs are laid in the pod, and the weevils will destroy the dry seed. The weevils in the dried beans may be killed by heating in an oven, but if the temperature rises over 150 degrees Fahrenheit, the value as seed to plant will be impaired. Weevils may be killed by placing two fluid ounces of carbon disulphide in a shallow dish on top of a barrel of seed which is tightly covered. Leave for thirty-six hours. This will not injure beans for planting or for food.

Chapter III

BEETS

More grows in the garden than the gardener has sown.
　　　　　　　　　　—Proverb.

BEETS

22. Soil Requirements. Beets demand a rich soil, and it will pay to build up the plant-food content before planting. As in all proper garden practice, this is best done the fall before planting. Incorporate in the soil all the manure, compost, or humus that seems necessary. Beets respond to supplementary feedings during the growing season.

23. Fertilizers and Plant Foods. Ten to twelve pounds of stable manure per square yard of soil should be applied for beets. If poultry manure is available, one pound should be applied to the same amount of ground. The stable manure should be applied before spading or plowing, and the poultry manure afterwards.

Commercial fertilizer of 2–8–4 type may be applied at the rate of two ounces to a square yard of soil. A 2–8–4 fertilizer contains two per cent nitrogen, eight per cent phosphoric acid, and four per cent potash.

Nitrate of soda may be applied along the row after the tops have reached six inches in height.

24. When to Plant. Beet seed may be sown in the greenhouse or hotbed the latter part of February in the latitude of New York City. The young plants should be transplanted in frames the middle of March and to the open garden during the first ten days of April, as a rule. Seed may be sown in the open garden early in May. The proper time to plant in other localities will depend upon whether they are north or south of New York; earlier to the south, later to the north.

25. How to Plant. Beet seed should not be covered

more than half an inch. A simple way to mark the rows in
the seed bed is to use the blunt handle end of a hoe or rake.
Make the depression half an inch deep. About three plants
to the running foot is proper; but many gardeners drill the
seed in close together because the germinating qualities of
beet seed are notoriously poor. The surplus plants are
thinned out, and the tops used for early greens. The rows
may be from one to three feet apart. The latter distance
makes easy field culture possible.

26. **Thining.** Where beets are thickly sown, they should
be thinned out as soon as possible. If it is put off too long
the quality of the roots will be impaired. If you like beet
greens, wait until the tops have reached the correct size;
then thin down to three good plants per foot. Remember
that beets like plenty of plant food, and the thinning process
insures that the main stand will have every opportunity to
mature properly. Thinning is best done by hand, the entire
plant being pulled out.

27. **Use as Greens.** Beet tops make excellent greens.
As soon as the leaves have attained proper size, the plants
may be thinned and the leaves used in cooking for greens.
Usually the plant will be at least six inches high before they
are harvested for this purpose; but do not allow them to
remain too long, for the roots' sake.

28. **Sowing for Succession.** Beets may be sown three
weeks apart from early May until late July in order to
provide a succession of tender roots for table use. The main
crop is usually sown in July. As a rule two or three sowings
will insure a continuous supply, especially where the small
varieties are planted.

29. **Best Varieties.** Egyptian and Early Globe are the
best early varieties, while Edmand's is a satisfactory late
variety.

Chapter IV

BRUSSELS SPROUTS

My garden, with its silence and the pulses of fragrance that come and go on the airy undulations, affects me like sweet music. Care stops at the gates, and gazes at me wistfully through the bars. Among my flowers and trees, Nature takes me into her own hands, and I breathe freely as the first man.

—ALEXANDER SMITH.

BRUSSELS SPROUTS

30. Plants or Seed? For ordinary garden culture it would be best to buy plants, because the bother of growing the few from seed would not be worth the slight saving in cost. These plants should be ready to transplant about the middle of June—sometimes a little later. Seed may be started, however, in the greenhouse or hotbed. This is advisable where large plantings are to be made.

31. When to Transplant. The latter half of June is the best time to transplant Brussels sprouts plants in the latitude of New York.

32. How to Space. The plants should not be placed closer together than fifteen inches in the row, and it would be better to allow from twenty to twenty-four inches. The more room, the better the chance they have and the greater ease in cultivation. The rows should not be closer together than twenty-four inches; and if more room can be given, so much the better.

33. Care and Cultivation. Brussels sprouts are, in the main, grown like cabbage (see Chapter V). Good cultivation should be practiced as with other garden crops. Weeds are an abomination in any garden; keep them down. Watch for cabbage pests and dust or spray as recommended in Sec. 591.

Many gardeners have an idea that the leaves should be broken off in order to encourage the formation of the small sprouts at their base. This is not necessary, as this characteristic is inherent in the plants.

34. Fertilization and Plant Foods. Brussels sprouts

require reasonably fertile soil. Ordinary preparations for good garden culture will suffice. Ten to twelve pounds of manure applied in the fall to a square yard of soil and then turned under in the spring will supply reasonable fertility. A pound of poultry manure to the same area of ground may be applied after spading or plowing.

Instead of stable or poultry manures, a commercial fertilizer containing five per cent nitrogen, eight per cent phosphoric acid and four per cent potash may be applied at the rate of two ounces per square yard of soil. Where branded commercial plant foods are used, follow the manufacturer's directions.

35. **When to Harvest.** Brussels sprouts mature in sixty to eighty days. Since they may be transplanted from April to August, the growing season computed will give the beginner the proper time to harvest.

CHAPTER V

CABBAGE

A garden of vegetables is a beautiful thing, if it is a good garden.

—J. HORACE McFARLAND.

CABBAGE

36. Plants or Seed? The easiest way to start with cabbage is to purchase plants from the seedsman or local greenhouse. They can be started from seed, however, in the hotbed or greenhouse in February. They may even be planted in "flats" or shallow boxes and started in the house. Late cabbage should be started in March. Cover the seed one-half inch.

37. When to Transplant. The early crop may be transplanted to the open garden late in March or early in April. If there is danger of hard frosts, the young plants should be protected at night by paper caps or jars. Late cabbage should be transplanted to the open garden the early part of July.

38. Soil Requirements. Cabbage is a gross feeder and requires heavy fertilization even on fairly rich garden soils. The soil should be in good condition, friable, and easily worked. It can hardly be too rich for a heavy crop. See Sec. 34 for directions in fertilizing.

39. Fertilizers for Early Maturity. About three or four weeks after transplanting, an application of nitrate of soda will hurry the plants along to early maturity. This is especially valuable for the early crop. Use at the rate of one ounce per square yard, and work into the soil around the roots. Keep it off the foliage of plants.

40. Spacing in Garden. Early varieties which do not grow as large as the late, or main-crop, varieties, should be spaced twelve to fifteen inches apart in the rows. Rows should be from twenty-four to thirty inches apart. Late cabbage is spaced from eighteen to twenty-four inches in the row and the rows are twenty-eight to thirty-six inches apart.

41. Mid-Season Culture. Sudden rains often cause cabbage to grow so quickly that the heads burst. This may be prevented by cutting some of the roots so that growth is not so rapid. Some gardeners accomplish the same result by pulling up the head sufficiently to break a few of the roots.

The early crop should be hurried along as rapidly as possible. Commercial plant foods can be added, mixing in soil around the roots, and continual cultivation should be kept up. Watch closely for pests.

42. Late Varieties. Savoy, Flat Dutch, Surehead, and the like are all good varieties. You can start your own plants by sowing seed the first two weeks in May; the seedlings are transplanted to the permanent location in the garden the last two weeks of June. (See Sec. 40 for spacing.) Late varieties are most likely to be bothered by pests. Keep a sharp lookout for them, and apply remedies as recommended in Sec. 45.

43. When to Harvest. Early cabbage may be harvested from the time the heads become hard, and used as needed. A surplus may be saved by making into canned sauerkraut. This is done by cutting up and placing in ordinary fruit jars. Screw tops on, but not down tight. Allow to remain until it has stopped working, then screw the lids tight. It will keep perfectly until used.

Late cabbage need not be harvested until just before freezing weather, when it is gathered.

44. How to Store Late Crop. All root crops may be stored in old-fashioned outdoor pits. Cabbage is one of these. Select a well-drained spot in the garden and dig a shallow pit, covering the bottom with a layer of straw that,

Proper cultivation is easy labor with a good wheel hoe.

Swiss chard growing in a home garden.

Strawberries planted in the single-row system in a commercial test plot.

Fifty strawberry plants have just been started in this back-yard garden.

A commercial planting showing the double-row system, heavily mulched with straw.

when packed down under the weight of the vegetables, will be from six to eight inches thick. The cabbage is pulled up in the garden, roots and all, and placed heads down in long, narrow piles. It is then covered with a layer of thick straw, and on top of this is a layer of dirt. When severe weather approaches, the mound is covered with sufficient manure to prevent the vegetables from freezing. It is well to remember that cabbage, like other root crops, requires a cool, moist situation but will not tolerate freezing. Only salsify and parsnips, among the root crops, will withstand freezing.

Where the late cabbage is to be used up within a reasonable time, it should be cut in heads in the garden, stored in barrels or deep boxes filled with earth or moist sand, and placed in a cool cellar.

When supplies are needed from the outdoor pit, a hole is opened on one side of the mound sufficiently large to enable one to reach in and pull out the vegetables needed. This is closed up by wadding straw in the opening and covering with earth and manure as before.

45. Diseases and Pests. Cabbage worm is the most common insect pest. It feeds on the leaves throughout the growing season. If the plants are unheaded, spray with lead arsenate. If headed, dust heavily with insect powder, or spray them with pyrethrum soap.

The cabbage looper often feeds on the leaves in late summer and then bores into the heads. It is controlled by spraying with pyrethrum soap.

Plant lice (aphids) often infest the underside of the leaves. Dust the underside, or spray with nicotine sulphate.

The cabbage maggot is a pest that infests the main root or stem near the surface of the ground. Tarred paper discs placed around the stems are a control measure, and a 4 per cent Calomel gypsum dust may be applied. When the ground becomes infested, avoid growing cabbage on the same location the next season, and practice rotation.

The larvae of the diamond-back moth often eat round holes in the leaves. Lead arsenate spray will keep them under control. The zebra caterpillar is controlled in the same manner.

Yellows is a fungus disease that causes the base of the stalk to rot. The only remedy worth while is to use resistant varieties.

Other fungus diseases, such as blackleg and black rot, are controlled by treating the seed with corrosive sublimate and by rotation. It usually is not safe to use the soil again for three years. Suspend the seeds in a 1–1000 solution of the corrosive sublimate in a cheesecloth bag for from twenty to thirty minutes. Then rinse in clear water, plant immediately, or spread out to dry.

46. **Chinese Cabbage.** Grown in much the same manner as late cabbage, Pe-Tsai and Wong Bok should be planted at the same time and in the same way. Space nine to twelve inches apart in the row, and space the rows from eighteen to twenty-eight inches apart. They can be planted as late as the latter part of July and still make a crop. Harvest when full size has been attained or before frosts, and store in boxes or barrels of earth or moist sand in a cool place until used.

CHAPTER VI

CARROTS

Nature never did betray
The heart that loved her

—WORDSWORTH.

CHAPTER VI

CARROTS

47. How to Sow Seed. Carrot seed should be planted in finely prepared soil at a depth of not more than one-fourth inch. As a rule the seeds are not especially vigorous, so shallow planting must be followed. The general culture of carrots is very similar to that recommended in Chapter III for beets. The seed should be sown rather thickly to insure a good stand. The best way to make the "furrow" for carrots is to draw the blunt end of a rake or hoe handle along the string used to mark the row; do not press down too deep. Cover by drawing the dirt of only one side over the seed and tamp down lightly with the rake or hoe.

48. When to Plant. The first planting in spring can be made at the same time that radishes are planted; in other words, about the time frosts are over. (See Sec. 51.)

49. Soils and Fertilizers. The usual garden loam, well prepared, is best for carrots. Carrots, like all root crops, need a well worked and easy tilled soil. One tending to the light side is better than one that packs down hard in mid-season. Hard soils can be broken up with sufficient humus.

Contrary to a widely prevalent opinion, carrots do not require nitrate of soda. Most soils will carry a sufficient amount of nitrogen to secure a good crop. The ordinary types of garden fertilizers are quite sufficient. A reasonably good soil with proper cultivation during the season will produce a good crop.

50. When to Thin Plants. Just as soon as the seedlings

are large enough to pull, the thinning process should begin. Even as small as one inch high is not too soon. Thinning means that better development will be secured in the plants remaining in the row, and is a process that really never quite ends until the entire crop is harvested, as carrots should be pulled and used on the table right along once they have attained sufficient size.

The better carrots are produced if the tiny plants are thinned out so that they are two inches apart in the rows. Rows should not be closer than eighteen inches apart.

51. Sowing for Succession. The first planting, as stated in Sec. 48, can be made very early in the spring. A succession can be provided for by making several additional plantings—say, the second in the latter part of May, additional plantings three weeks apart until the final, or main, crop is planted the latter part of July. The late crop is important as it is the one to be stored, and must be given careful attention. Cultivate continuously and promptly as soon after rains as possible. Above all, do not allow weeds to get a foothold. An additional application of a good plant food will help to bring them along properly.

52. Fertilizing Late Crops. For this purpose I prefer a good "complete" plant food of the commercial sort, which should be on hand in the garden tool shed at all times. It acts quicker than manures and is not so dangerous, if directions are faithfully followed. Poultry manure, however, is good and may be used at the rate of one pound per square yard of soil.

53. How to Store. Carrots may be stored in the home cellar, in pits, or in an outside storage cellar. Harvest and allow to remain on the ground a few hours until surface moisture has evaporated. Cut off tops within an inch of the crowns. If you have a cellar storage room walled off from the furnace, they may be placed there either in slatted bins

or in boxes. They may also be stored in slightly moist sand to advantage. (See Sec. 44 for pit storage.)

54. Best Types to Grow. The smaller varieties are the best to grow as they excel in flavor and structure. We like the Danvers Half Long and Oxheart best.

Chapter VII

CAULIFLOWER

Fie on 't! oh fie! 'tis an unweeded garden.

—SHAKESPEARE.

CHAPTER VII

CAULIFLOWER

55. Special Care Needed. Cauliflower is considered a difficult crop to grow by many gardeners for the reason that they do not understand its peculiarities. It is true that it requires more care than cabbage, a crop customarily referred to when its culture comes up. In spite of many experts, cauliflower cannot be dismissed by saying that its culture "is similar to that of cabbage." It requires constant care to keep it growing; the least check or setback in its development results in disappointment.

Furthermore, it should be borne in mind that cauliflower requires a moist atmosphere for the best development. It does not succeed in dry-air climates. For this reason, plantations along the seacoasts always produce better heads than those at higher altitudes. If such regions afford plenty of rain during the growing season, good heads will be produced. This may explain why it does well one year and does not succeed another.

56. When to Start Seed. Seed should be started a week or two later than cabbage seed (see Sec. 36). The seed are started in the same manner as cabbage, indoors in "flats" or shallow boxes, or outdoors in the hotbed. The important thing is to see to it that there is no check in the growth, and to so "time" them that they can be set outdoors before becoming overdeveloped or "leggy."

57. When to Transplant. Seedlings or plants should be transplanted outdoors ten days or two weeks later than the

37

early cabbage crop would be transplanted. This will usually be around the middle of April.

58. How to Plant. Plants are transplanted to the garden in the same manner that cabbage plants are.

59. Late or Main Crops. The main crop is planted at the same time that the late crop of cabbage is. (See Sec. 37 and Sec. 42.)

60. Soil Requirements. Cauliflower requires an even richer soil than cabbage; that is, its demands are more catholic. It is a lush grower, a rank feeder, and it is almost impossible to have too much plant food of the proper sort present.

61. Lime, Manures, and Fertilizers. Cauliflower requires plenty of lime in the soil. This may be supplied by adding agricultural gypsum or ordinary slaked lime. An abundance of rotted stable manure should be incorporated into the soil and, in addition, a complete commercial fertilizer or plant food added. Keep the plants growing and give supplementary feedings of liquid manure just as the heads begin to form.

62. Cultivation. Keep down the weeds, but do more than that. Cultivate frequently, but do not cultivate deeply. Always stay on the shallow side. This plant needs all the rootlets possible to insure quick and uninterrupted growth.

63. Continuous Growth Essential. The point that continuous and rapid growth is essential cannot be overemphasized. Any check in the growth will cause imperfect or poor heads to be formed. Pay close attention to the needs of this plant, for neglect will result in failure.

64. Special Care; Tying Heads. When the curds appear, tie the leaves over the head in such a manner as to shut out the light. This must be done if white heads are to be produced. Be sure you have the worms under control before doing this, however. In mid-season, the heads will be ready within a week. Later, when it is cooler, a longer time will be required.

65. **When to Cut Heads.** Heads should be cut before the curd begins to separate.

Chapter VIII

CELERY

He who enters the Garden's gate
Is never afraid or desolate.
On little paths that wind and wind
He shall unwearied pleasures find.
He shall learn beauty's last secret
And he shall forget, he shall forget.

—Louise Driscoll.

CHAPTER VIII

CELERY

66. Seed or Plants? Celery may be started from either seed or plants. For the small home garden it is generally the best practice to buy plants from the seedsman or local greenhouse supplying garden plants. This often has a disadvantage in that the gardener cannot be sure of getting the variety he wishes to grow. Then, again, if a large planting is to be made in succession, plants often cannot be obtained at the time they are desired. It will then be best to grow one's own plants from seed.

67. When to Sow Seed. Celery requires from 120 to 150 days of growing season. It is true that it can be kept in the open garden later in the fall than most vegetables, with proper care; but it will not tolerate hard freezes. The gardener, then, can estimate approximately the exact time when the plants should be started. Some varieties, especially in the North, will require 170 days from the time the seed is sown until a marketable crop is produced.

Celery must be transplanted from the original seedbed or flat to coldframes before being transplanted to the open garden. On the average, thirty-five days must be allowed from the time the seed is sown originally before the first transplanting can take place. The seedlings seldom appear until twenty days after sowing, and an additional two weeks is necessary before they are large enough to transplant. The young seedlings require heat for the best growth, and this means that they must be grown either in a hotbed or in a greenhouse. The seed is sown early in March for

43

the early crop, and late in April in open ground for the main crop.

68. **How to Sow Seed.** The richest sort of soil, well-prepared, is required for celery at all stages of growth. The seed is very small, almost microscopic, and needs merely to be pressed into the surface. This must be kept moist to insure germination at all, and the approved way is to cover the surface with burlap which is kept moist. This also insures that, when moisture is applied, it will not disturb the seed.

Germination is very slow, and usually twenty days elapse before the tiny seedlings begin to appear. Be sure that there is sufficient moisture to prevent the surface from drying out, but do not supply so much that diseases and rots are encouraged. Seed may be sown either broadcast or in rows. The latter method is to be preferred, to make pinching out or transplanting easier. Remember that heat is essential as long as the seedlings are less than one inch in height.

69. **When to Transplant.** Seedlings are not ready to transplant to the open garden until they are from three to five inches in height. In order to encourage vigorous and uniform growth it is, therefore, necessary to transplant them at least once from the original seedbed before taking them to the garden. Sometimes, this may have to be done twice. The point is, keep transplanting as often as necessary to keep them growing properly and to prevent crowding. The first transplanting should be about thirty-five days after planting the seed, or when they are over one inch in height. This will usually be the middle of April for the early crop; if development is proper they can go into the open garden the third week of May.

70. **Soil Requirements.** No ordinary vegetable is the gross feeder than celery is. It is impossible to have too much plant food present in the soil. Several years ago a success-

ful northern commercial grower, who had then had twenty-two years' experience with this single crop, told me that he applied twenty wagonloads of well rotted manure to the acre each year. In addition, he was growing his crops in the black muck of drained-out lake beds!

71. **Supplementary Feeding and Fertilizers.** Celery is a crop that requires plenty of lime, humus, and commercial fertilizer in the average home garden. It will be noted that too much well rotted manure *cannot* be applied to an otherwise rich soil. In addition, applications of a complete plant food should be made along the side of the row *every three weeks* during the growing season. A pint of this for each twenty-five feet of row is not too much. Three and even four of such applications will be made for the main, or late, crop.

72. **How to Transplant.** Celery plants, when slightly more than one inch high, are transplanted to the coldframe or to specially prepared beds in the open ground, depending upon the season. They are "pinched out," as the expression is, and spaced far enough apart each way at each transplanting to prevent overcrowding.

They should be from three to five inches tall when transplanting to the permanent location in the open garden or field. They may be placed two feet apart in rows for the early crop, and six inches apart in the row. The late, or main, crop is usually planted in rows six feet apart where blanching is done by hilling up the earth.

73. **Cultivation and Care.** Cultivation must be kept up continuously throughout the season. No weeds are to be tolerated, and hand weeding will be necessary between the plants in the row. Continuous cultivation is necessary to conserve as much of the moisture in the soil as possible; it is, therefore, imperative to keep it up whether weeds are present or not.

74. When to Start Late Crop. Seed is started for the late crop the first of May, and the seedlings should be ready to transplant to the open garden the latter part of June.

75. When to Start Blanching. For the early crop, blanching can start when the plants have attained a height of one foot. The late crop should be allowed to make as much growth as possible, the blanching to be done only in time to save it from disastrous freezes. It requires at least three weeks, often longer, to do this properly. Since the celery should not be allowed to remain in the open garden later than late October or early November, the gardener can govern himself accordingly.

76. Various Methods of Blanching. For small plantings, wide boards may be set on edge on each side of the row and held in place by nailing cleats across the top. Building paper may be used, rolling it around each plant and fastening with clips or twine to hold it in place.

The approved method for large plantings is to hill up around the plants with soil scraped up on each side of the row. Allow the upper leaves to extend above the mulching material, whatever it is.

77. When to Harvest. The early crop may be harvested and used whenever it is properly blanched. The late crop must be gotten out of the ground in time to avoid hard frosts.

78. How to Store. Celery may be lifted, roots and all, late in October and placed in soil in the cellar. It may also be stored in trenches in the garden. It is covered over with straw and will, if protected from freezing and given sufficient ventilation, keep a long time. Storage in the cellar is the most practicable for the usual home usage, however.

Chapter IX

CHARD

I like to see a man proud of the place in which he lives. I like to see a man so live in it that his place is proud of him.

—ABRAHAM LINCOLN.

CHARD

79. General Culture. The general culture of chard is similar to that of beets. In reality, chard is a beet—the Silver Leaf Beet. The plants are thinned out more than in the case of beets, however, one for every foot in the row being sufficient.

80. When to Plant. Plant in the open ground early in May, or as soon as the ground is warm and the season has settled down. Seed may be sown earlier in the greenhouse or hotbed, for an earlier crop. As a rule, one crop for the season is sufficient. See Sec. 24.

81. How to Plant. Cover the seed not more than one-half inch deep. If drilled in, the plants must be thinned out later, as noted in Sec. 79. Make the rows from one to three feet apart, the latter distance being for field culture.

82. Soil Requirements; Fertilizers. Chard requires a rich soil, just as beets do. Incorporate all the rotted manures, humus and plant food possible. It responds to supplementary feedings of commercial plant foods during the growing season, and nitrate of soda may be applied as suggested in Sec. 23. Supplementary feedings induce the quick, succulent growth so desirable in this plant.

83. How to Harvest. The outside leaves of chard are removed, the blade being used as pot herbs and the stem cooked like Asparagus. Sometimes it is used in combination green salads, at certain seasons being very desirable for this purpose.

CHAPTER X

SWEET CORN

I learn with great pleasure the success of your new gardens at Auenay. No occupation can be more delight or useful.

—THOMAS JEFFERSON, to
Madame de Tessé.

CHAPTER X

SWEET CORN

84. Types to Grow. The nature of sweet corn is such that it does not remain edible more than a week or ten days. In order to have it available for the table over as long a portion of the growing season as possible, the gardener should select types that will permit this.

The "early" varieties mature in sixty-five to seventy-five days; the mid-season varieties, in eighty to ninety days; and the late, or main, crop varieties in ninety to one hundred days. Theoretically, a sowing of the three types at the same time would give one a succession of edible sweet corn for thirty-five days, ranging from sixty-five to one hundred days after planting. This does not always work out in practice, however, because of variation in seasons. The difference in growing habit of the various types can be depended upon, though, to prolong the normal period.

Another method is to sow corn in succession (see Sec. 89) in order to achieve the same purpose.

While early varieties of corn may be canned, the usual purpose of them is solely for table consumption. The late varieties are the ones most commonly canned commercially, although the popularity of Golden Bantam corn (an early variety) in recent years has caused it to be canned commercially on a widespread scale.

85. Soil Requirements. Good average garden soil is best for success with sweet corn. It should have a good supply of humus and plant food, but an overly rich soil will result in poor yields. The soil should be in good tilth, easily worked, and friable. Humus is necessary in order to give it

moisture-retaining properties and to prevent it from becoming hard and baked in mid-season.

Ten or twelve pounds of rotted stable manure to a square
yard of surface, applied before plowing or spading—preferably during the winter—is sufficient for corn. If this is
not available, one pound of poultry droppings can be used
for the same area after spading. A commercial fertilizer
should be applied according to the manufacturer's directions just before planting.

86. When to Plant. The time-honored rule in planting
corn is to wait "until oak leaves are the size of squirrel's
ears." This applies to sweet corn as well. It means that the
soil is warm and the season is definitely under way. Usually
in the North this will not be before May 10th. The dividing
line runs through Philadelphia and St. Louis. See Sec. 89.

Seed may be tested to save disappointment later by the
simple expedient of the old "rag doll" tester. Take a piece
of stout cloth and mark it off in large squares with a heavy
crayon or pencil. These squares should be numbered to
correspond to numbers placed upon the seed packets or lots
to be tested.

Select a few representative kernels from each packet or
lot and place them in these squares. Then roll up the entire
cloth carefully in order not to misplace the seed. Soak the
whole "rag doll" after it is securely tied and keep it moist
and in a warm place until the seed have sprouted. One can
judge the germination ability of the seed by the character of
the sprouts. If they are numerous and vigorous it is safe to
plant that particular lot; if weak or poor and a low percentage germinate in any given lot, do not plant, but secure
other seed to replace it.

87. How to Plant. Sweet corn should be planted from
one to two inches deep. Four plants should be allowed to
grow in each hill, and in order to insure strong ones six or

Onions grown from sets in an Iowa back yard.

Onions grown from seed in a Minnesota garden.

Celery being blanched with wide planks.

Showing method of blanching celery by hilling up the soil around the stalks.

eight kernels should be planted, and the weakest plants thinned out later.

The hills should be from thirty to thirty-six inches apart in the row and the rows a similar distance apart. This is for the late varieties, which are ranker and more vigorous in growth. The earlier and smaller-growing varieties may be crowded closer together, but there is no point in this unless space is at a premium.

88. How Many Rows to Plant. Instead of planting one long row at a time, if you are following succession planting, it is better to group your plantings in a number of short rows side by side. This is done in order to insure better fertilization. Pollen will not be successfully carried from the plants in one long row and, therefore, a better crop is to be expected from a number of rows parallel to each other.

89. Planting for Succession. Within ten days to two weeks after the first planting is made, another should be made in order to provide a succession of edible corn for the family table. Additional plantings can be made every ten days to two weeks thereafter throughout the growing season, the last planting to be made in time to mature a crop before frost. The last planting can be of the quick-maturing "early" varieties, if desired. Or, if one prefers these to the larger main crop types, they can be planted in succession throughout the season just as well. It all depends upon individual preference. In figuring the last planting allow a minimum of sixty-five days, dating from the time when frosts are to be expected in your locality.

90. Care During Season. Cultivation must be kept up at all times, not only to keep down the weeds but to conserve as much of the moisture present in the soil as possible. Try to cultivate as soon as possible after every rain, especially in midsummer when moisture is at a premium. This can easily be done with an iron rake; care should be taken,

however, not to work too close to the hills so as to injure the
roots. The rake attachment on the wheel hoe is also fine
for this work. If weeds are kept down, the rake will break
up the crust of the soil and tend to decrease evaporation.

When the plants are approaching maturity it is a good
idea to hill up the soil around them to a depth of four or
five inches in order to conserve moisture and to aid in pre-
venting the plants being blown over in high winds. Take
care, again, not to work too close to the roots with the hoe
or rake. Corn roots are close to the surface and easily injured by careless work.

91. Late Crops. Late crops come on in ninety to
one hundred days and are usually planted to provide corn
for home canning. The favorite variety for this purpose is
Country Gentleman, although the White Evergreens of
various names are also popular.

Late crops have to contend with all the unfavorable
factors, such as droughts, heat waves, and pests. They
should, therefore, be given every aid possible by the gardener. Keep up cultivation whether it seems to be necessary or not. In time of drought, especially when the tassels begin to appear, irrigate if you are so fortunate as to
possess the means. This does not mean simply spraying
with the garden hose of an evening; it means digging a
slight trench to the side of the rows (far enough away not
to injure the roots) and flooding this trench several times
twice a week. After each period of irrigation cover over the
trench with dry soil. This effort will be well repaid in a
better crop.

92. Diseases and Pests. The corn ear worm is a frequent
pest. It eats the immature kernels at the tip of the ear. To
control, dust the silks with equal parts of sulphur and
powdered lead arsenate.

The European corn borer is becoming a serious pest in

several parts of the country. It infests dahlias, beets, beans, gladiolus, and the like in addition. It bores into the stalk above ground. It hibernates in the dry stalks and the only effective control seems to be to burn all infested plants *before* May 1st each year.

Smut is the most common disease. It is a fungus disease that causes black, spongy growths on stalks, tassels, leaves, and ears. It winters in the soil or manure. Remove all smut balls found. Where it persists, year after year, the best control is to dust young plants with copper lime dust.

93. Best Varieties. Country Gentleman remains the best canning variety. It matures in about 100 days. Golden Bantam, as an early variety, is still popular, but is being rapidly displaced by its crosses, such as Improved Golden Bantam. Stowell's White Evergreen and Metropolitan, old favorites, still lead the list of white corns, in my estimation.

Chapter XI

CUCUMBERS

*Do the thing yourself! I would set that down
as the mintage of wisdom in making a real home.
Not because you have to do it—but because you
like to do it. The fact that you have a check book
is no release from the joy of doing. Many a home
would be saved if the check books were used in
starting the furnace fire, and the whole family
went to work with their hands!*

—Chesla C. Sherlock, in
Better Homes and Gardens.

CUCUMBERS

94. Where to Grow. Contrary to an old opinion, cucumbers can be grown *anywhere* in the garden. It is not necessary to keep them separated from melons. Repeated experiments have demonstrated that cucumbers do not have an injurious effect upon melons, or vice versa. Some experimenters have even directly cross-pollinated the two with no result. Therefore, do not feel that one or the other must be sacrificed in the small garden.

95. Soil Requirements; Preparation. Cucumbers require an abundance of rotted manure in the soil in order to make a satisfactory growth. They are like celery in this respect, and it may be safely said that too much rotted manure cannot be used.

This should be thoroughly worked into the soil before planting time arrives. It can be spread over the ground during the fall and winter and turned under in the spring; it should at least be spread over the ground before plowing. Fresh manure should be avoided unless it can be spread during the fall and winter.

The better the preparation of the seed bed, the better the results. Thoroughly incorporated in the soil, such rotted manure will add greatly to the moisture-retaining qualities, which may be one of the principal sources of benefit.

96. Fertilizers. It is well known that manures are chiefly valuable for the humus they add to the soil. No one will deny that they do not have certain fertilizing properties also, but their main contribution is that noted. Cucumbers not only thrive best on soil having this desirable quality,

61

but demand an abundance of plant food too. Humus aids in releasing the natural plant foods locked in the soil, but the addition of commercial plant foods will richly repay the expense and effort.

Cucumbers especially respond to nitrogen, which is best supplied by nitrate of soda. It has also been demonstrated that lime is beneficial. Supplementary feedings of fertilizer or nitrate of soda, especially just before the vines commence to run, will be well worth while.

97. When to Plant. Cucumbers should be planted as early as possible, but they will not tolerate cold, wet soils or frosts. Growers usually overcome this by planting a few seeds in each hill late in April and protecting them with "hot caps." These are paper cones which may be purchased from seedsmen. One is placed over each hill and kept there until the plant is sturdy enough to maintain itself. The hot caps must be ventilated (lifted up) on good days.

98. How to Plant. Hills may be from four to six feet apart each way. Another way to plant is to space the rows six feet apart and the plants twelve inches apart in the row. Cover the seed one inch deep. The plants require from sixty to eighty days to mature.

99. Seasonal Care. Plants must be kept growing without interruption if a good healthy production is to be obtained. Lagging growth is usually caused by lack of sufficient humus or decayed manure in the soil. One old-fashioned yet good method is to put a forkful of this material at the bottom of each hill. The roots will grow deeply in order to tap this rich supply. Supplementary feedings, as recommended in Sec. 96, will help to keep them producing. Remember that the crop must be kept picked; to allow a cucumber on a vine to ripen is to lose that vine as a producer.

100. Cultivation. Cultivate only until the plants start to vine. After that, they should be hand-weeded. Be careful not to injure the vines by rough handling or by stepping on them. Since cultivation is possible only for a short period, it should be kept up faithfully during that time in order to have the soil in good tilth when the hoes and cultivators must be laid aside.

101. Growing Habits. The plants start to grow upright, and during this period the gardener should keep up cultivation and supplementary feedings. As soon as the plants fall over and start to vine, the die is cast, and the crop to be obtained will depend upon how faithfully the ground was prepared and kept in condition.

102. Pests and Their Control. Keep a sharp lookout for squash bugs, striped beetles, mildew, and wilt. They may be controlled either by spraying or by dusting with a combined lead arsenate and Bordeaux mixture. Nicotine dust is beneficial in keeping insect carriers of certain bacterias off the plants. Slug shot and land plaster are also used in controlling pests, but I have found the combined lead arsenate and Bordeaux mixture to be the most effective "cure-all" for cucumber pests.

103. When to Harvest. Cucumbers can be harvested at any stage of growth, depending upon the purpose for which they are desired. For canning or pickling, select the size you prefer and pick them when they have attained it. Go over the vines every day, because they make rapid growth. Daily and constant picking also has the advantage of encouraging continual production. To allow the cucumbers to get too large, or ripen, is to discourage further production.

Chapter XII

EGGPLANTS

The Garden of Eden is a place where there is just one man and one woman—one family. And they are the real Chosen People who work to make this whole glorious dream a living reality.

—Chesla C. Sherlock, in
Ladies' Home Journal.

EGGPLANTS

104. When to Plant Seed. Eggplants must have warm weather in order to succeed, and the seed should be started in the greenhouse or hotbed as recommended for tomatoes or peppers. See Sections 173 and 342. Seed is started in March, under protection, sowing in flats or small boxes. Cover not more than one-half inch deep.

105. When to Transplant. Transplant to the open garden when the season has thoroughly settled down and danger of frost is past. A safe rule to follow is that they may be transplanted when tomatoes may. Usually this will not be before late April and early May in the average season.

106. How to Plant. The little plants are set two feet apart in rows that are three feet apart. Ordinarily half a dozen plants will supply the average home table with all the eggplants that will be required, a dozen at the outside. Transplant in the same manner as tomato plants.

107. General Requirements. The general culture of eggplants is similar to that of peppers and tomatoes. Cultivation is necessary, and a sharp lookout must be kept at all times for pests.

108. Fertilizers. Ten to twelve pounds of stable manure, thoroughly rotted, should be applied before plowing or spading the soil. This quantity will cover a square yard. One pound of poultry manure applied after turning the soil will answer the same purpose. Commercial fertilizers may be applied just before planting in accordance with the manufacturer's directions.

109. Diseases and Pests. The most common pest is the

Colorado potato beetle. It is controlled by applying powdered lead arsenate. Wilt is a common disease. No control
is known for it, and all the gardener can do is to pull the
infected plants and burn them. Phomopsis blight is a fungus
disease causing leaf spot of the foliage. It is borne by the
seed and can be controlled by treating the seed before planting with corrosive sublimate. Use a 1–1000 solution for
ten minutes on the seed, rinse in running water, dry slightly,
and plant at once. During the growing period the plants
should be dusted regularly with copper lime dust.

110. **Best Varieties.** Black Beauty and New York improved are the two best varieties. Ivory and Long Purple
are novelties some people like.

Chapter XIII

KOHLRABI

Hope is the way we feel when morning is here, and the sun is shining.

—Anon.

CHAPTER XIII

KOHLRABI

111. General. Kohlrabi is a bulb-shaped vegetable which combines the flavors of turnips and cabbage. In recent years it has largely replaced turnips, especially early in the season. The general culture is similar to that of cabbage except that the plants are spaced closer together. People who dislike the flavor of cabbage or turnip often find they have a decided liking for this dependable vegetable.

112. When to Sow Seed. Seed should be sown as early in the spring as possible. This means not later than April, as a rule, even in the North. Successive plantings can be made at intervals of ten days until real hot weather (August) arrives. The seed should be used at the rate of one-quarter ounce per one hundred feet of row. Cover about one-half inch deep. The seedbed should be well prepared, and a light rich soil gives the best results.

113. When to Transplant. As soon as the plants are well established they should be thinned out to stand four to six inches in the row. The rows are eighteen to twenty-four inches apart. The plants thinned out can be transplanted to other rows, if desired. If they have been originally sown in rows out of doors, no transplanting is necessary as they may be thinned as noted above. This is, of course, necessary where plants are started in frames or seed boxes.

114. How to Space. In transplanting, space the plants as noted in Sec. 113.

115. Types. Two types of kohlrabi are commonly grown. They are green and purple. Market gardeners inform the author that there is slight difference in demand between the two types the country over.

116. Late Plantings. Most home gardeners overlook the advantages of late plantings of most vegetables. The best gardeners keep up a succession all season, taking note of course of the length of the growing season and the time necessary to bring the crop to maturity. Sometimes, accidents of the season cause disappointment in the earlier plantings; this can be remedied by planting in succession. In a normal season in the North kohlrabi can be planted until early August.

117. When to Harvest. The crop through the season should be harvested when small and tender, as kohlrabi is more edible at this stage.

118. How to Store. The late crop can be stored for home use well into the winter by cutting off the stems and leaves and storing the bulbs in sawdust, dry peat moss or similar material. Medium-sized boxes are better containers than barrels.

Chapter XIV

MELONS

> *Insult not nature with absurd expense,*
> *Nor spoil her simple charms by vain pretense;*
> *Weigh well the subject, be with caution bold,*
> *Profuse of genius, not profuse of gold.*
>
> —HUMPHREY REPTON.

Chapter XIV

MELONS

119. How to Start Seedlings. Unless otherwise noted the directions given in this chapter are for muskmelons. Generally, watermelons require the same care and culture except that a great deal more room is needed for them; they are rampant growers, producing much vine.

Seed may be started in pots, flats, or frames about four weeks before they are to be planted outdoors. For the average home garden enough seed can be planted in one pot to furnish all the seedlings necessary for use. For this small planting ten or twelve seed in a six-inch pot will suffice.

120. When to Transplant. Seedlings grown as recommended in Sec. 119 must not be transplanted outdoors until the weather is absolutely settled. Determine when this period normally arrives in your locality, then make the indoor plantings accordingly. Usually this will not be before May 10 or 15 in the North. Seed sown directly in the garden should be planted as recommended for cucumbers, in Chapter XI.

121. Soil Requirements. See Sec. 95, the recommendations for cucumbers.

122. Fertilizers and Manures. See Sec. 96, the recommendations for cucumbers.

123. Growing under Hot Caps. Seed may be sown earlier than usual outdoors if a hot cap is used over each hill. This is a conical paper cover which increases the heat in the soil, hastens germination, and affords protection against sudden drops in temperature. A few hills of melons so grown in the home garden will well repay the cost.

124. Seasonal Care. See Secs. 99 and 100. Plants must be kept growing as in the case of cucumbers.

125. Pests. See Sec. 102.

126. Watermelons. Watermelons require the same general care and culture as cucumbers and muskmelons, with one or two exceptions. One is that a great deal more room is necessary for the vines. Another is that a warm, sandy soil is desirable. Be sure to select early varieties and start as early as possible in order to insure a crop. They require from 100 to 120 days to mature and should average ten feet apart in the row, while muskmelons may be grown six feet apart.

127. Where to Grow. Some people believe the old superstition that melons should not be planted near squash or pumpkins. This has long been exploded through the practical failure of scientists to cross them with melons. Melons may be grown at any suitable place in the garden without reference to other crops, aside from convenience.

128. When to Plant. See Sec. 97.

129. How to Judge Ripeness. This is a question that has divided experts as well as amateur growers. The ancient test for judging ripeness of a melon, especially a watermelon, is to thump it with a finger. When it gives forth a dull, hollow ring, it is said to be ripe. Of course, if you have plenty of melons and are in doubt, you can "plug" them by cutting out a small *V* section with a long knife and examining the interior. Yellow-fleshed muskmelons are usually ripe when the blossom end becomes soft, or the veining becomes a golden color. Green-fleshed varieties when they become soft.

130. Best Varieties. Emerald Gem is the favorite early yellow or orange-fleshed variety for home use. Honeydew is the best green-fleshed variety. Rocky Ford is an old favorite in this class. In Watermelons, Cole's Early and Harris' Earliest are best for home use.

CHAPTER XV

ONIONS

> The nearest approach to tears that should be
> shed in gardening are drops of honest sweat,—
> and these are good for us.
>
> —JULIA H. CUMMINS.

ONIONS

131. Seed or Sets? This question will have to be settled by the preference of each gardener. I have long since settled it in favor of "sets." These are small onion bulblets grown from seed planted the previous season. They may be procured from any seedsman or dealer. They usually come in white or red sets, the color determining the color of the matured onion. They are easy to handle, and for an ordinary family one quart of sets will provide all the onions necessary. Where certain varieties are desired, one will have to plant seed to be surer of what one is getting.

132. When to Plant Seed. Onion seed should be planted in April or May in the North, as early as possible, for they require a growing season of 130 to 150 days.

133. How to Plant. Cover seed one-half inch deep. They should be drilled one to two inches apart in rows twelve to eighteen inches apart. One ounce of seed is sufficient for 100 feet of row.

134. Soil Requirements. Onions succeed in ordinary good garden soil, well prepared.

135. Fertilizers and Supplementary Feeding. Stable manures may be used in soil preparation before plowing or spading. Commercial plant foods are good. As a supplementary feeding when the tops are six inches tall, use sixteen ounces nitrate of soda per 100 feet of row. If poultry manure is available, it may be substituted for the nitrate of soda.

136. When to Plant Sets. Onion sets can be planted as early in the spring as anything can be planted. In the home garden they can be placed two inches apart in the row. Rows should be twelve to eighteen inches apart. One quart of sets will ordinarily plant 100 feet of row.

137. **Thinning.** As the young onions develop, they may be thinned by pulling up the entire plant and using as green onions on the family table. Thinning out in this manner will provide more room in which those remaining may develop.

138. **Cultivation and Care.** Onions must be constantly cultivated and weeded. Hand weeding is necessary in the row, whereas the rake, hand-hoe, or wheel-hoe may be used between the rows. Do not allow weeds to get a start. If the surface of the soil is constantly stirred, a rake will usually suffice. Only when protracted wet spells give the weeds a chance will the hoe be needed.

139. **Scallions.** In common parlance any onion which retains a thick stem and does not bottom out is a scallion. That is, it retains the shape and form of the leek. The Egyptian Tree Onion is the distinctive scallion, however.

140. **When to Plant.** Plant scallion sets late in August or early in September as you would large ordinary sets; in other words, as close together as possible. The rows are twelve inches apart. Each set must stand perfectly upright in order to produce a perfect stem.

141. **Care.** Give the same care during the fall growing season as you would give to any other onion crop, keeping in cultivation and well weeded.

142. **Winter Protection.** During the winter protect the tops with a light covering of straw or other similar light material.

143. **Supplementary Feeding.** As in the case of onions, it is beneficial in late March or early April to give a light application of nitrate of soda.

144. **When to Harvest.** Scallions should be harvested when from eight to nine inches tall. Green onions may be

A simple way to support raspberries.

For field culture of grapes, allow plenty of room for horse or tractor.

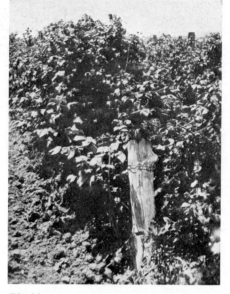

Blackberries growing along a garden fence.

Three-year-old vines bearing their first crop in the author's vineyard.

harvested at any time during the growing season, the medium-sized being the best. Mature onions from sets are usually ready to harvest in August. Onions from seed that fail to reach sufficient size may be harvested and used as sets the following season.

145. How to Store. When harvesting, pull up in the garden and allow to remain in windrows, or in wire-bottomed shallow trays in a cool shed, for several days in order to dry out thoroughly. The tops may then be removed and the onions placed in a well ventilated spot to cure.

146. Growing Your Own Sets. You may grow your own sets, but this practice is to be discouraged for the home gardener. It is not worth the cost or bother. The onion maggot is, besides, a serious menace beyond the bother of the average gardener.

147. How to Keep through Winter. Onions may be conveniently stored in a dry, well ventilated storage place in the home cellar or basement. Slatted crates or porous sacks are best.

148. Diseases and Pests. Two pests are common. The most serious is the onion maggot which feeds upon the bulbs of young and growing onions. Crop rotation must be practiced, and weekly sprayings with sodium arsenate followed. Use it at the rate of one-fifth ounce to one pint of molasses and one gallon of water.

The onion thrip is a very small insect which feeds upon the tops, giving them a whitish character. Burn all infected tops and spray the remainder with nicotine sulphate.

149. Best Varieties. Ebenezer is the best variety of onion sets to buy and the least likely to be infested with maggots. It is an excellent keeper through the winter and matures in ninety days. Southport Red Globe is excellent for home gardens, and Yellow Dutch is widely used.

Chapter XVI

PARSNIPS

Cultivate your garden!

—Voltaire.

CHAPTER XVI

PARSNIPS

150. Habit of Growth. Parsnips are a whole-season plant and must be sown as early in the spring as possible to insure proper development of the roots. The seed is slow to germinate, like that of parsley, and of weak vitality. Parsnips do best in a loose, rich sandy loam, but may be grown in garden soil that will produce other root crops, if care is used. Heavy clay soils must be thoroughly broken up by incorporating humus in some form, and it is also wise to sow radish seed in the rows to assist the parsnip seed in breaking through.

151. When to Plant. Plant as early in the spring as possible, certainly before the spring rains set in. Parsnip seed require abundant and continual moisture in order to germinate at all.

152. How to Plant. Cover the seed one-half inch deep. Plant in rows twenty-four to thirty inches apart.

153. Early Care. If the season is dry, keep the surface moist in order to promote germination. This may be best accomplished by covering with burlap and wetting. In sprinkling otherwise one is likely to wash out the seed. If the ground is sufficiently moist to insure germination, keep the surface between the rows broken up with an iron-toothed rake.

154. How to Space; Thinning. When the plants have appeared, thin out to about five inches apart in the row. Small seedlings thus thinned out may be transplanted to spots where seed has failed to germinate. For large plants, one should further thin out to about ten inches apart in the row.

155. Seasonal Care. As young plants make a weak growth, it is best to disturb them as little as possible until they have become established, after which they are sturdy in habit. Cultivation may, of course, be kept up. No addition of garden or other plant foods and fertilizers is necessary during the growing season, as parsnips seem to succeed without extra feeding.

156. Lifting in Fall. The roots may be lifted in the fall when they seem to be matured. This work can be put off until the last minute before heavy frosts. Use a spading fork and take care not to break off the roots.

157. Wintering in Garden. Some of the roots may be allowed to remain in the row all winter. Indeed, many people contend that parsnips should not be harvested until the spring. Freezing does not seem to injure them seriously; however, a few plants are always lost every winter.

158. How to Store. The roots may be stored, after the tops have been cut off, in the same manner and place that any root crop may be so handled. Small boxes are best. Pack in sawdust or dry peat moss.

159. Value of Frost. Freezing seems to increase the sugar content of parsnips, which is the reason many gardeners advance for leaving them in the open ground all winter. Parsnips so treated may be dug up in March or April, as soon as they can be lifted.

160. When to Harvest. You may harvest either in the fall or in the spring, depending upon your preference. Most modern gardeners harvest and store part of the crop in the fall and part of it in the spring, thus prolonging the season when parsnips may be enjoyed on the family table.

Chapter XVII

PEAS

To have worked is to have succeeded—we leave the results to time. Life is too short to gather the harvest—we can only sow.

—Elbert Hubbard.

PEAS

161. Types. Peas are variously classified as Early and Late, Dwarf or Tall-Growing. These terms are self-explanatory. When one understands these types, and the fact that all types overlap generally, one may have a continuous supply of green peas for two months in a normal season.

The smooth-seeded type are not injured by light frost and may, therefore, be sown as early in the spring as the soil warms up. They grow to various heights, but for these I prefer to stick to the dwarf types for quick results.

All varieties growing over eighteen inches tall will produce a better crop if staked in some way, or provided with supports. Some growers plant double rows in order to aid the plants themselves to remain upright. This will succeed for the medium-tall varieties, but wire netting staked along the rows, birch brush, or some other support will give the best results. The Telephone types will grow as high as eight feet in normal surroundings.

Wrinkled peas should not be planted when there is any danger of light frosts. They are the main-season or late peas and should not go into the ground until the weather is thoroughly settled.

162. When to Plant. Peas can be planted from March to June, according to the type and variety. They are a cool-weather plant, generally, and will not succeed in hot weather. Planted in the months noted, a crop can be expected from June to August.

163. How to Plant. Cover from three to four inches deep, depending upon season. The rows should be from two and one half to three feet apart. The plants may be spaced an inch apart in the row. It will require from one to two quarts of seed to plant one hundred feet of row.

164. Supports. Wide-mesh chicken wire securely tacked upon sturdy stakes is the most satisfactory support for peas requiring such assistance. The busy gardener can dispense with this bother by growing dwarf types entirely, and this is especially recommended for the very small garden. Birch brush is an old favorite kind of support in the country where it can be procured. These supports should be cut in the spring before the buds open. Stakes with strands of wire strung between them may also be used.

165. Soil Requirements. Peas are great lovers of alkaline soils, and it seems that the soil cannot be too sweet. They produce disappointing crops on sour soils. Be sure that the garden is in good tilth, that the seed bed has been carefully prepared. They will give a good account of themselves on almost any type of soil, except very light, if it is not acid.

166. Fertilizers and Plant Foods. Manures may be used before plowing or spading, but the simplest fertilizer is a good general garden plant food. The chief delight of peas is lime, and it is a good idea to make an application, incorporating it in the soil where the rows are to be, at the time of planting the seed. Commercial plant foods will give the best account of themselves if applied after the plants are about two inches tall; then it should be drilled along the sides of the rows.

167. Sowing for Succession. Sow peas every ten days to two weeks from March to late June for a succession. Abnormalities in the seasonal weather will often tend to delay maturity of one planting and to speed up another, but the safer course is to have a continual succession, in order to be sure of having fresh peas.

168. How much to Plant. One hundred feet of row

Grapes grown on a hillside by a Western dairy farmer.

The same scene in winter, showing the manner of spacing posts for wire supports.

The second season for a young cherry tree.

Remnants of the old orchard at John Alden House, Duxbury, Mass.

will provide the average family with sufficient green peas for the main crop varieties—half this amount for the early sorts. As noted before, one to two quarts of seed will be required for one hundred feet of row, depending upon how close they are planted together in the row.

169. Seasonal Care and Cultivation. Peas, like all garden crops, should be continually cultivated to keep down weeds and to conserve the moisture supply in the soil. Hand weeding will be necessary in the row. If supports are used, examine them after storms and high winds to be sure that they have not toppled over.

170. Pests and Their Control. Cutworms are a particular pest when the plants are young and tender. Keep a close watch to see that they are not working on the plants. They are especially likely to be present in new soil, or soil that has been heavily manured. The approved control is poisoned bran made with the following ingredients and proportions: wheat bran, 5 pounds; white arsenic, 4 ounces; juice of 1 lemon; molasses, 1 pint; water, 7 pints. Mix bran and poison together when dry. Squeeze lemon juice in water and cut up peel in small bits and add to water; then mix in molasses and stir. Add this syrup to the bran and mix thoroughly. The crumbly mass should be sprinkled over the ground just before dark, preferably a few days before planting, but may be used at any time when needed. For smaller quantities, reduce the ingredients in proportion. This is also an effective control for grasshoppers. Plant lice are sprayed with nicotine sulphate.

171. Best Time to Harvest. Pick the peas before they become too far developed. Allowed to remain too long on the vine, they will cook up hard and will further decrease the productivity of the vines. Some people prefer the very small peas for the table. Watch your vines, and you can harvest your crop at the proper time.

172. Best Varieties. Alaska is the best dwarf early smooth-seeded variety. There are many variations of it listed in the catalogues according to dealer. Gradus, Thomas Laxton, Laxtonian, and Telephone come on later and in mid-season. Champion of England and Improved Stratagem are good late varieties.

CHAPTER XVIII

PEPPERS

This rule in gardening ne'er forget,
To sow dry and set wet.

—Proverb.

PEPPERS

173. When to Plant Seed. Seed should be planted in frames or hotbeds from six to eight weeks before the plants can be transplanted to the open ground, which is usually in May. Seed should be covered about one-half inch.

Since only a few plants, from six to twelve, are needed to supply the average family with all the peppers it will require, the most economical practice is to buy the plants from the seedsman or local market gardener. In most localities they are now readily obtainable because the increased use of green salads in recent years has caused the pepper no longer to be a rarity in the home garden.

The seeds and plants of the pepper require a higher temperature than does the tomato—otherwise the culture is practically the same.

174. When to Transplant. Transplant to the open garden at the same time you would transplant tomatoes. This means after danger of frost and usually around the middle of May. "When oak leaves are the size of squirrel's ears," is the olden-time rule.

175. Soil Requirements. Peppers will succeed in the average garden soil. They make no special demands.

176. How to Space. The plants should be eighteen inches apart in the row and the rows two feet apart.

177. Fertilizer Requirements. Peppers do not require heavy feeding. However, when the plants are eight inches tall a moderate dressing of poultry manure or complete garden plant food worked into the soil around the roots will be beneficial. On the latter, follow the manufacturer's directions.

178. Types to Grow. Peppers have been divided into two types in common parlance, the "sweet" varieties and the "hot" varieties. These classifications have largely been determined by their usages in cooking. The "hot" varieties are chiefly used in relishes, pickles, and condiments. They are smaller and finer-fleshed than the "sweet" varieties, and usually the smaller they are, the "hotter." The "sweet" varieties are large-fleshed, of mild flavor, and are used for stuffing, in green salads, or combined with other vegetables or meats in cooking. The catalogues usually divide them according to the above classifications.

It will be easy for the gardener to decide what type to grow when the purpose for which they are intended has been decided.

179. Seasonal Care. Peppers require only sufficient cultivation to keep down the weeds.

180. When to Harvest. Peppers should be harvested at maturity for the "hot" varieties (fall), whereas the "sweet" varieties can be used during the season as they attain sufficient size to serve the purpose intended.

Chapter XIX

IRISH POTATOES

> *The Book of Life begins with a man and a woman in a garden.*
>
> —OSCAR WILDE.

Chapter XIX

IRISH POTATOES

181. Soil Requirements. Good, well drained garden soil is essential for successful potato production. Potatoes are heavy feeders, requiring not only liberal quantities of commercial plant foods, but an abundance of humus or well rotted manures as well.

Good drainage is imperative. Potatoes will not succeed in wet and boggy ground. The soil should be in good tilth —what is called "friable." That is, it is open and contains sufficient humus to be crumbly. Hard clay soils must be well prepared, as they will not produce abundant crops.

182. When to Plant. There are all kinds of old adages as to when to plant potatoes. These are pure bunk, except in so far as they happen to coincide with the season. Early potatoes should be planted as early in the spring as the ground can be worked. This holds for all localities. The late or main crop is planted late in May or during June, depending upon the length of the growing season in your locality.

183. How to Plant: Potatoes or Eyes? Personally, I prefer planting medium-sized whole potatoes to cutting them in pieces. The latter method is widely followed in order to reduce the cost of seed, especially in large plantings. It has seemed to me, and I am frank to confess that I was taught this by a grandfather who never failed with his "spuds," that whole potatoes insure a sturdy hill that will produce a maximum crop.

Where eyes are planted, care should be taken to cut the pieces so that at least two strong eyes remain on each seed-piece. Furthermore, cut the pieces in as large blocks as possible; avoid niggardly wedge-shaped pieces.

Whole potatoes can be planted deeper, as a rule, than seed-pieces, thus gaining some advantage if the season turns dry and hot.

Seed-pieces should be planted three inches deep in hills or rows for the early crop, and five inches deep for the main crop. The rows should be two to three feet apart, and the seed pieces fifteen to eighteen inches apart in the row. Where whole potatoes are planted in the home garden, plant in hills two to three feet apart each way.

184. **Planting Systems.** There are two planting systems in vogue in potato growing: the hill system and the row or furrow system. Rows may be laid out in the home garden with a hoe; in field planting it is usually done by opening a furrow with a plow, which is closed in the same manner. Hills may be planted either with a hoe or with a spading fork.

185. **Fertilizers and Plant Foods.** Manures should not be added to soils for potato growing except when well rotted, and then should be used only before the seedbed is prepared, preferably in fall plowing or preparation. Manures induce scab and other parasites.

High-grade commercial fertilizers (complete) and commercial plant foods can always be used advantageously. Follow the manufacturer's directions on the latter. The former should usually be applied at the rate of 15 to 25 pounds per 100 foot of row.

Poultry manure, if available, can be used at the rate of one pound per square yard of soil.

186. **Care and Culture.** The young shoots will begin to appear above the surface in three or four weeks after planting, depending upon the season. Even before they begin to appear the surface of the soil should be broken

Grapes growing on the Sagamore Hill estate of the
late Theodore Roosevelt.

The ancient grapevine over the back door at "Home, Sweet Home."

Laying mulching paper along the rows is excellent for small plantings.

Mulching strawberries with marsh hay.

up with an iron rake to prevent a hard crust forming. Cultivation should be given every week throughout the growing season, not only to keep down weeds, but to conserve the moisture supply in the soil and keep the soil particles broken up so that the tubers can develop normally.

In the early part of the season, when the shoots are tender and weak, the soil should be hilled up along the sides of the row, and around the hills, to support them. Later in the season this can be leveled, if desired.

187. **Diseases, Pests, and Their Control.** The principal disease is blight, of which there are two kinds: early and late. Early blight shows brown spots, with concentric rings on the leaves. It thrives in moist weather. Late blight has dark brown spots without concentric rings. The remedy for both is the same: Spray with Bordeaux mixture when the plants are six inches high. Repeat in two weeks and again in another two weeks. Remember that the whole question of producing tubers and bringing them to maturity is to keep the tops healthy and growing. If they fail, your crop fails.

The worst pest is the Colorado potato beetle, the common potato bug which devours the leaves. Spray with arsenate of lead when it appears, and as often as necessary. The blister beetle is another leaf-eater, a long black potato bug. Spray with arsenate of lead. The flea beetle is a small jumping beetle that also eats leaves. Use arsenate of lead.

188. **When to Harvest.** The early crop can be harvested as soon as the potatoes reach sufficient size. Usually the first potatoes may be eaten on the table by the Fourth of July. The main crop is harvested at any time after the tops have thoroughly matured. They may be left in the ground until late in the fall, but watch out for gophers, moles, and field mice!

189. **How to Store.** When digging potatoes, allow them to remain on the ground for several hours before gath-

ering. They should be further cured before storing permanently.

In the fruit and vegetable cellar boxes or bins of open slats can be built, in which the potatoes may be kept for winter use. Sand sprinkled on the floor and kept moist will aid in keeping them in good condition, provided a ventilation system of some sort is introduced. Moist dank air minus circulation is dangerous in that it induces many rots which destroy the tubers. See Sec. 588.

Chapter XX

SWEET POTATOES

As is the garden such is the gardener.

—Hebrew Proverb.

SWEET POTATOES

190. **Soil Requirements.** A warm, moderately deep sandy loam is required. Sweet potatoes require a growing season of 150 days in which a relatively high temperature is constantly maintained. For this reason, they succeed best in the South, although they are grown in home gardens as far north as southern New York. A deep loose soil has a tendency to produce stringy roots and should be avoided. Good garden loam in good tilth will grow a profitable home crop.

191. **Causes of Failure.** The chief causes of failure are improper soil, lack of adequate drainage, and poor quality of plants. The sweet potato requires less moisture than any other garden vegetable and is totally unlike the Irish potato in cultural requirements. Hard soils will prevent the formation of tubers, and improper drainage will defeat the gardener's purpose in growing them.

192. **How to Start Your Own Plants.** The average small garden will require such a small number of plants that it is much more economical and less bothersome to buy the plants needed from the seedsman or dealer. However, you can grow your own plants, if you wish. Six weeks before apple trees in your vicinity normally blossom, start a hotbed. Place six inches of sand over the manure, and on top of this lay medium-sized, sound sweet potatoes. Cover these with about two inches of sand and keep it moist. Before long sprouts will begin to appear and to send out roots. When they are four inches tall they may be pulled away from the tubers and set in small pots for further development,

or you may wait until time to transplant to the open garden.

193. When to Transplant. Sweet potatoes are transplanted to the open garden when all danger of frost is past.

194. Preparation of Seed Beds. Work up the seed bed thoroughly, being sure that all hard lumps are broken up. It should then be drawn up in ridges eighteen inches high and five feet apart. This can be done by pulling the soil from each side of the ridge up to the center with a hoe. The chief purpose of the ridges is to insure complete drainage throughout the growing season. Make broad ridges.

195. Systems of Culture. Sweet potatoes will also succeed when planted in individual hills ridged up in the home garden. Ridging is not necessary in well drained soils in climates where rainfall is light during the growing season.

196. How to Plant. Set the plants fourteen inches apart in the row or center of the ridges. They are transplanted like any other garden plant, preferably on a cloudy day, and the soil should be firmly packed around the roots. This may be done by generous applications of water to carry the soil down. Cover over the surface with dry soil. Set the plants deeper than the roots seem to require, in order to encourage additional root development.

197. Seasonal Care. As the vines begin to grow, see that they do not take root. This can be prevented by twining them around one another so that the rootlets cannot come in contact with the soil. Keep the crust of the ridges broken up by light cultivation until the vines cover the ridges. Any weeds that appear thereafter should be pulled by hand.

198. When to Harvest. As soon as the vines have been nipped by the first frost, the tubers or roots must be harvested. Use a spading fork and take care not to bruise or injure them in lifting out of the soil. Do this work on a bright, sunny day, and expose them to the sun for three or four hours.

Then take them to a well ventilated room to cure for about ten days in a temperature ranging between 80 and 90 degrees. After this they are to be stored in a temperature of 55 degrees. They may be placed in shallow boxes or slatted crates. Handle carefully and as little as possible after curing. If desired, each tuber may be wrapped in a piece of old newspaper.

CHAPTER XXI

PUMPKINS

> *Fie on 't! oh fie! 'tis an unweeded garden,*
> *That grows to seed . . .*
>
> —SHAKESPEARE.

CHAPTER XXI

PUMPKINS

199. Where to Plant. Pumpkins should be planted only in the large garden. They require too much room for the small place and for their relative importance in the family garden; the ground they occupy can be more profitably employed in other crops. In the large garden, however, they can be planted to advantage. They can follow some other early crop, such as potatoes or corn, and will mature a profitable crop.

200. When to Plant. Pumpkins are affected by both cold and heat and should not be planted until settled weather arrives. They require from 100 to 140 growing days and may therefore be planted late in May or early in June with safety.

201. How to Plant. Cover the seed one inch deep. Pumpkins may be planted in hills to themselves, or in rows with other crops. The hills should be spaced ten feet apart each way. In rows with other crops, the practice is to space eight to ten feet apart in the row, planting seed in every fourth or fifth row. Plant several seeds to each hill to insure a good stand; they may be thinned later by pulling out the weakest plants.

202. Types Best Adapted for Home Garden. Grow the smaller and improved pie pumpkins in the home garden. (The old-fashioned field pumpkin has long since been superseded.) Many of these are now available. Sugar and Winter Luxury are recommended.

203. Care and Culture. Pumpkins require no special culture except to keep pests in control while the plants are

111

young and tender. In working around them care must be taken, of course, not to step on or otherwise injure the vines.

204. Diseases and Pests. Pumpkins are subject to the same diseases and pests as the cucumber. See Sec. 102.

205. When to Harvest. Harvest before danger of hard frosts. Light frosts which merely nip the vines are not injurious to the pumpkins.

206. How to Store. Pumpkins may be successfully stored in the average cellar. They require a dry, warm, and well ventilated spot. I have found that a shelf under the ceiling in the furnace room is ideal. They do best where the temperature is slightly above 50 degrees all the time. Pumpkins stored in this manner have kept for me until the following spring without difficulty.

Chapter XXII

RADISHES

> *Make for the shortest path, which is that of Nature.*
>
> —Marcus Aurelius.

Chapter XXII

RADISHES

207. When to Plant. Radishes are hardy and can be planted as early in the spring as the ground can be worked. Indeed, radishes and lettuce are as true harbingers of spring as the first birds.

208. How to Plant. Cover the seed one-half inch deep. The seedbed must be thoroughly prepared and finely pulverized to encourage quick growth. The rows are twelve to eighteen inches apart—whatever is a convenient width to make cultivation easy.

209. Planting for Succession. Plant radishes every ten days to two weeks to insure a continuous crop. They do not produce as good quality in hot, dry weather, but may be planted at any time up to and including September. With due reference to the planting of proper varieties (see Sec. 215), there is no reason why there should not be a continuous supply of radishes on the family table during the growing season.

210. Thinning. As soon as the plants begin to appear they should be thinned out so that only one radish remains each two inches. Some gardeners drill in the rows when planting and allow the natural thinning that occurs when radishes are picked each day for the table to take care of this problem.

211. Fertilizers and Plant Foods. Radishes do best where there is a quick, steady growth to maturity. This means that supplementary feeding will pay good returns. Commercial plant foods, used in accordance with the individual manufacturer's directions, may be applied. Complete commercial fertilizers may be used at the rate of two ounces per square yard of surface. This should be applied just before planting.

212. Seasonal Care. Cultivate continually, and do not allow the weeds to get started. Keep the surface in good tilth to conserve moisture. Thin out spots in the row where the radishes are so crowded that the formation of good roots is hindered.

213. Pests. The maggot is the most serious pest; it is similar to the one attacking the onion and cabbage. Sprinkled with 4 per cent calomel dust from May 1 to May 5, as this pest appears early in May. Subsequent plantings should be treated as soon as they break through the surface. One or two applications are generally sufficient.

214. Winter Types. These radishes are larger and sturdier than the regular types. In reality, they are better described as late-season sorts in that they are planted in mid-season and mature by fall. Unlike the ordinary radish, they seem to do best in hot weather. A list of good varieties is found in Sec. 215. The roots of this type keep well when properly stored for winter use.

215. Best Varieties. Early Scarlet Globe is the favorite for early planting. The name describes the type. White Icicle is the favorite long white; Stuttgart, or Early White Giant Summer, is the favorite main-season white variety. Cincinnati Market is the best long red type.

In the so-called "winter" varieties, the best are: Scarlet China, Chinese White Winter, Long Black Spanish, and Round Black Spanish.

Chapter XXIII

RHUBARB

> *No mystery is involved in the making of a garden;*
> *only the learning of a few of Nature's laws, and*
> *of the likes and dislikes of the plants.*
>
> —Thomas R. Best.

RHUBARB

216. Best Varieties. Victoria is probably the best variety for the home garden. It is a good producer and hardy. Crimson Winter is a good variety for the garden, but more commonly used in commercial production.

217. When to Plant Roots. Although rhubarb can be started from seed, the best practice is to buy roots for the home garden. Four to six hills will provide all the stalks necessary for the average family. The best time to plant is in the spring.

218. Best Location. The best location for the rhubarb bed is the most convenient spot in relation to the kitchen door. I have found that the clumps can profitably border the main garden path. Seldom are they planted in the center of the garden; it is better to place the bed at one end or the other of the garden. Rhubarb is not changed from one location to another, but is permanently located for years at a time. Select a convenient place, therefore.

219. Soil Preparation. Well drained fertile soil is essential for successful rhubarb culture. This must be carefully prepared because rhubarb is a gross feeder and since it is to remain in a more or less permanent position, an abundance of plant food must be provided.

The soil should be spaded to a depth of eighteen inches and well rotted manure, leafmold, compost, leaves, sod, or the like thoroughly mixed with the subsoil. A generous handful of bonemeal in the bottom of each hole will prove beneficial in seasons to come. It is almost impossible to have too much decayed vegetation and manure incorporated in the soil.

220. How to Plant. Set the plants so that the crowns will be two inches under the surface of the soil. The plants are set three to six feet apart each way, if more than one row is planted. Rhubarb is a rank grower when established and requires plenty of room. Thoroughly settle the soil around the roots by generous applications of water, and cover the surface over with dry soil.

221. Fertilizers and Plant Foods. Where manure is available, little other plant food or fertilizer will be required. Applications of fresh horse manure to the crowns early in the spring will "force" early growth and provide the needed plant food. Manure may be used either spring or fall, or both.

If manure is not readily available, a good handful of complete commercial fertilizer or commercial plant food applied according to the manufacturer's directions in the spring will give the plants the push they need. In many respects, rhubarb needs about the same treatment peonies do.

222. Care First Season. Rhubarb should be given every care during the first season. Above all, do not cut the stalks for table use. Let the plant get firmly established; therefore all possible strength should be conserved to go back into the roots for future seasons. The first season careful cultivation should be given to keep down weeds and to conserve the moisture content of the soil. When established the plants require cultivation only to the extent of weed extermination.

223. When to Cut; When to Stop. When the plants are established, the stalks may be cut as soon in the spring as they are large enough to use. This may be continued until July, after which it is best to give them a rest, so that energy may be stored in the roots for the next season.

224. Growing in Cellar. In November, surplus clumps may be dug up and stored in a coldframe for use in winter forcing later. In January or February, bring them into the cellar and place them in some convenient warm place away from the light. It is not necessary to set them in soil, at least any more than naturally adheres to the clumps. Do not allow to dry out. Before long you will have nice succulent shoots to use for making sauce or pies.

Chapter XXIV

SPINACH

Every clod feels a stir of might....

—Lowell.

Chapter XXIV

SPINACH

225. Types and Varieties. The chief differences in types is found between ordinary spinach and the so-called New Zealand spinach. The latter is not a spinach at all, but has desirable qualities which makes it valuable in the garden. It is usually planted to bridge the gap during the hot summer. It has a branching habit of growth, small leaves, and the advantage that the more leaves are cut from it the more it branches.

Good varieties to grow in the home garden, for ordinary usage, are: Prickly Seeded, Bloomsdale, and Virginia Savoy —the latter best adapted to regions where blight is common. Bloomsdale should not be planted late in the Spring, as it does not succeed in hot weather.

226. When to Plant. Spinach can be planted as early in the spring as possible, and every two weeks thereafter until the middle of September—with due regard to type and variety. See Sec. 228.

227. How to Plant. Cover seed one to two inches deep. Drill seed in row twelve to eighteen inches apart, the plants eventually to be thinned as they grow. Space the seed two to three inches apart in the row.

228. Planting for Succession. Plant smooth-leaved sorts for very early crops; follow with the crinky-leaved sorts such as the Savoys, then New England or Long Standing Bloomsdale, then Prickly Seeded or Yellow Resistant Savoy for fall. Crops should be planted every two weeks to maintain continuous succession. A very small row will keep the average family supplied.

229. Fertilizers and Supplementary Feeding. Spinach is a great lime-lover, and a generous amount should be incorporated in the soil before planting. Nitrate of soda is necessary when the first leaves are forming and ten days thereafter. Apply when the foliage is dry, and take the extra precaution of keeping it off the foliage. Apply at the rate of one ounce per square yard and work well into the soil.

230. How to Gather. Where it is desired to obtain the maximum yield from the plants, care should be used in cutting the leaves so as not to injure the plant or to take too much from a given plant at the start. Do not "riddle" them; later pickings will be larger.

CHAPTER XXV

SQUASH

> *Surely there is something in the unruffled calm of Nature that overawes our little anxieties and doubts.*
>
> —EDWARDS.

Chapter XXV

SQUASH

231. New Varieties. Recent years have seen a constant refinement in the squashes offered by the hybridizers for the home garden. Personally, I have become a great booster for Des Moines, or, as some would have it, Table Queen. The latter name is probably more expressive of its chief characteristic, but the squash originated in Des Moines. It is small, just right to be served in halves on the table. Most of the old squashes, with the possible exception of the Bush Scallops, or Patty-Pans, so prized in the South, are too large to be brought to the table except after being cut up.

Summer Crookneck is probably still the favorite for the average home garden. It is a bush type, and the fruit average about two pounds each in weight.

The old, old favorite was, of course, the Hubbard, which runs up to fourteen pounds in weight. A newer Hubbard is the Golden Hubbard. These are main crop varieties.

232. When to Start Seed. Seed may be started in the hotbed or even a coldframe in April. Bush types require from 60 to 80 days to mature, while the main-season types require from 120 to 160 days. Des Moines is intermediate, maturing in about 100 days. The time to plant seed can be determined from the number of days necessary to mature a crop. Squash are sensitive to frost, but somewhat hardier than melons or cucumbers; they should not, as a rule, be planted out-of-doors before May.

233. When to Transplant. To be on the safe side, especially if you are growing the bush types, do not transplant until early May. They may be transplanted earlier if it is possible to provide protection when frost is threatened.

234. Where to Plant. Squash may, if space is limited, be planted as pumpkins often are, with other crops such as corn or potatoes. If plenty of room is at hand, best results are obtained by giving them a plot to themselves. Bush types will require this, anyway, as only the late or main-season types will do well with other crops. The bush types require from three to four feet of space each way, while the late varieties should have from seven to nine feet.

235. Training on Supports. Sometimes, squash can be grown along a wire boundary fence, if given the opportunity. This will require extra attention and some support, especially as the fruits develop in weight.

236. Seasonal Care. The only care once they are established is to keep down the weeds. Cultivation, as with most vine crops, must cease as soon as the vines commence to grow. The chief anxiety about squash is to keep pests in control until the vines get established. See Sec. 238.

237. Fertilizers and Plant Foods. Rotted manure or some form of humus such as compost should be placed in each hill. Commercial plant foods should also be given in order to hurry them along. A complete commercial fertilizer should be applied at the rate of about two ounces per square yard.

238. Pests and Their Control. The striped cucumber beetle is a serious pest when the plants are young and tender. The remedy is to use powdered arsenate of lead as a dusting agent. Late varieties are also bothered by the squash bug and the squash borer. The best remedy for the former is to place a few boards on the ground near the hills. In the morning, lift the boards and kill your bugs.

The borer is a more serious problem. A common method of control is to cover the plant with soil at the point where the vines branch out. Further precautions consist in weighing down with soil the base of each leaf. Roots are thrown out by these knots, and even though a borer destroys a section of vine, the plant can still carry on and mature a crop.

239. **When to Harvest.** The early varieties are thin-skinned and should be harvested while tender, when you can puncture the skin with the thumbnail. The late varieties have tough skins and therefore are better keepers in storage. Harvest them before a hard frost.

240. **How to Store.** Squash should be stored in the same manner that pumpkins are. See Sec. 206. Under proper conditions it will not be at all difficult to keep them until midwinter.

Chapter XXVI

TOMATOES

He who enters the garden's gate
Is never afraid, or desolate.

—Louise Driscoll.

TOMATOES

241. Soil Requirements. Good garden loam such as will produce a good crop of potatoes, for instance, will produce tomatoes satisfactorily for you. Humus is the principal requirement, so far as consistency of soil is concerned. Manures should be added before plowing, preferably the fall before. Have the soil in good tilth before the plants are transplanted.

242. When to Start Seed. Seed should be planted from five to seven weeks before plants are required in the open garden. These may be planted in a hotbed, coldframe, or in a flat box indoors where there is sufficient warmth and light to insure germination and growth. As a rule, enough plants may be started in a window box to supply the average home garden. Unless one wishes to be certain of securing a specific variety, or a large planting is to be made, it is much more economical to buy the plants from the local seedsman or dealer.

243. Buy Plants? For small plantings, buy plants by all means. As a rule, dealers will accurately label the varieties. Now and then there may be mistakes and disappointment, but, unless you have a large planting to make, we unhesitatingly recommend buying the plants.

244. When to Transplant. Transplant to the open garden when all danger of frost is past. Tomatoes are sensitive to frost and, as a rule, should not be put outdoors until the middle of May.

245. How to Transplant. Tomatoes growing "on the ground"—that is, not staked—should be planted from two and one-half to three feet apart in the row. The rows should be from three to four feet apart. Select medium-sized plants, plants that are not tall and "spindly," for the best results. A medium, stocky plant with a good root system is best. For the small garden planting, a dozen potted plants of the sort described will be best, because as a rule they will have the best root systems.

Dig a generous hole in the ground with a garden trowel and put compost or well rotted manure in the bottom. Set the plant deeper than it grew before. The deeper you set the plant (see Sec. 249) the more of a root system will be developed. Roots form from the portion of the stalk that is underground, to the infinite advantage of the gardener in dry, hot weather.

Work the soil firmly around the roots; this may be done by generous applications of water to settle the soil. Do this work, if possible on a still, cloudy day. Potted plants give less trouble in transplanting than the usual sort, because it is not necessary to disturb the root systems.

246. Deep Planting for Better Crops. I am in favor of deep planting for better crops. I learned the lesson when experimenting to find the best way to insure a crop by staking and rigid pruning. If I had an eight-inch plant, for instance, I would remove all the side leaves, allowing only the two top leaves to remain on the stem. I would then set the plant in the ground so deep that only the two top leaves extended above the surface. The entire portion of the stem that is underground will form rootlets. A plant so treated will be slow in making top growth, because it is busy forming a gigantic root system, but in the productive midsummer days it will render a better account of itself than a plant that is transplanted in the ordinary manner.

247. Pinching and Pruning; Suckers. Tomato vines are rank growers and have an ever-present tendency to go

Various fruit trees trained to a trellis in Shaw's Garden, St. Louis, Mo.

Dwarf peach tree trained to supports.

A young berry plot grown without support by pruning the canes low.

A berry patch on a suburban hillside which returned excellent profits
to the owner.

more to vine than fruit. They must be rigorously pruned back to insure that the strength shall go to fruit, no matter what system of culture is followed. Side shoots may be stopped in growth by pinching the tips after one or two leaves have formed. Suckers are branches that form in the intersection between the main stem and the side or lateral branches. At first they are tiny and innocent-appearing, but before long they become vigorous and rank, sapping strength from the true lateral on which the fruit are produced. They must be pinched or cut out, if fruit is to be developed. Go over your plants, no matter what system of growth is employed, and cut out all suckers.

248. Fertilizers and Plant Foods. Soils well manured and given an application of commercial plant foods at the time the plants are transplanted ordinarily will not need further fertilization. One thing must be avoided: the use of poultry manure and other fertilizers or plant foods having a large content of nitrogen, as this causes tomatoes to go largely to vine rather than to fruit.

249. Use of Stakes and Supports. I would not think of growing tomatoes in my home garden without stakes or supports. The two terms are not synonymous as I use them: A staked plant is one that is pruned to a single, central stem; a supported plant is one that is permitted to form several main stems but is supported from contact with the ground by a framework of lath or other light material.

I prefer the staked tomato plant. A dozen plants on stakes will supply any ordinary family with all the tomatoes it can consume, except for canning on more than an ordinary scale. The advantage of staking is that it enables the gardener to produce quality fruit, to concentrate the energy of a dozen or so plants solely upon fruit production. I use dahlia stakes, which are driven in the ground about eighteen inches at the time the plants are transplanted.

Only one central stem is allowed to develop. As it grows, it is tied securely to the stake with raffia or broad strips of cloth. Ordinary twine will cut the stems. Side shoots are pinched off as soon as they have formed two leaves. When the main stem has grown to the top of the stake, it, too, is pinched off to stop further growth. The fruit is borne on the side, or lateral, branches. Every bit of strength in the plant will go to fruit production under this system.

Where supports are used, no such intensive pruning is followed. Only the suckers are removed, the plant being raised so that the tomatoes do not touch the ground.

250. Novelty Tomatoes. Every gardener should have a spot somewhere for the novelty tomatoes. They make excellent preserves and are not at all bad for the table fresh-picked. Among these are Red Cherry, Red Pear, Yellow Pear, and Yellow Plum. Of course, one should not overlook the old favorite, Ground Cherry. It is not a true tomato; but its growing habit is similar, and its use in making preserves is not unlike that of the novelty tomatoes.

251. Diseases and Pests. Cutworms are a serious pest for the tender young plants when first transplanted. Use bran mash as a control (see Sec. 170). Or a collar of paper extending above the surface of the soil completely encircling the plant may be used.

Potato bugs sometimes infect tomato plantings. See Sec. 187.

The tomato (or tobacco) worm is a long, large, and beautifully camouflaged worm often hard to distinguish. Its presence is always denoted by the defoliated condition of the plants and the presence of its excrement underneath. Careful search will not fail to disclose it. Simply remove from the vines and crush underfoot.

252. How to Mature Late Growers in Storage. If you find that your tomato vines have a goodly portion of green tomatoes on them when a serious frost is threatened in fall, pull the plants up entire, roots and all. Carefully carry them into the basement and hang them top down, from nails driven in the studding of the ceiling. They should not be placed near the furnace, like pumpkins and squash, but in a cool spot where there is no danger of frost reaching them. The tomatoes will continue to ripen sometimes well into December. The green ones too small to ripen can be picked and used in making green pickle preserves.

253. Best Varieties. Bonny Best, Stone, and Greater Baltimore strains are probably the best. Ponderosa, also known as Beefsteak, is the largest *good* tomato. I would grow a few in any garden. I like the old Tree Tomato, and it is not the Stone, as some would have us believe. Ask an old-time market gardener in your vicinity. Earliana is also a good early variety.

Chapter XXVII

TURNIPS

> *Poverty will end; sin will die; love will triumph,*
> *and hope will plant flowers on every grave.*
>
> —David Swing.

TURNIPS

254. Varieties. If you are of the opinion that there are only one or two varieties of turnips, examine the seed catalogues! Turnips are perhaps the most widely grown root crops in the country. Purple Top Strap-Leaved is the best white-fleshed variety. Golden Ball is, to my mind, the best yellow-fleshed variety. Between these two old stand-bys you will find a wide choice!

255. Soil Preparation. Our grandfathers' practice of planting turnips as a second crop on land that had been used for early potatoes or a similar crop is suggestive of many things. One is that ground that has been heavily fertilized for such a crop does not need further fertilization to grow good turnips.

Soil preparation need not be elaborate. However, the topsoil should be well pulverized; this means that it need not be prepared deeply.

Turnips will not succeed on poor soil. They need fertility and accessible plant food. When planted to themselves, they should have generous applications of plant food.

256. When to Plant. Turnips may be planted either in the spring (for an early crop) or in mid-season for the main crop. They require from sixty to eighty days to mature, and the planting may be regulated accordingly.

257. How to Plant. Turnip seed needs to be covered very lightly. One-half ounce of seed will plant 100 feet of row or 100 square feet when sown broadcast. Work the surface up thoroughly with an iron rake; broadcast the seed when this method is followed, then re-rake. Sowing in the row, cover only one-quarter to one-half inch deep.

258. Rutabagas: Culture. To all intents and purposes, the culture of rutabagas is identical with that of turnips. The only difference is that they require approximately thirty days longer growing season.

259. Fertilizers. In well fertilized garden soil, or where the crop is to follow others that have been heavily fertilized, no additional fertilization is usually required. However, where it seems desirable to add plant food, use commercial plant foods in accordance with the manufacturer's directions. Commercial fertilizers should be of the composition nitrogen 2 per cent, phosphoric acid 8 per cent, and potash 4 per cent, and should be applied at the rate of two ounces per square yard.

260. When to Harvest. Harvest for the home table when the turnips have attained sufficient size. This means a constant thinning process, whether they were sown broadcast or in the row. The late or main crop will, of necessity, be harvested before hard frosts and stored as carrots, potatoes, or other root crops.

261. Pests and Their Control. The most common pest, doubtless, is plant lice or aphids. Underspray with a nicotine solution. Cutworms now and then are a serious problem, especially on new ground. See Sec. 170.

PART II

THE SALAD GARDEN

Chapter XXVIII

SALAD PLANTS

> *Salad, and eggs, and lighter fare,*
> *Tune the Italian spark's guitar* . . .
>
> —Matthew Prior.

CHAPTER XXVIII

SALAD PLANTS

262. Rigid Classification Impossible. It is impossible to make a rigid classification of salad vegetables for the reason that practically all vegetables are now used in salads. Ordinarily, however, when we refer to "salad plants" we refer to those green vegetables whose leaves or stalks are used in salads uncooked.

263. General Vegetables Used in Salads. Many general vegetables are now used in fresh salads. The carrot is an example. A few years ago the use of dandelions in fresh salads was unknown, at least in this country. Practically any vegetable—indeed, even fresh beets are now used—can be used in a green salad.

264. Purposes of the Salad Garden. The main purpose of the salad garden is to provide fresh green vegetables over as long a portion of the year as possible for use in salads. By a careful spacing of the plantings and a judicious use of varieties, it is possible even for the northern gardener to have a continuous supply the year around. That may seem impossible, but a reading of this section of the present volume furnishes the proof.

265. Promoting Quick, Succulent Growth. Salad vegetables, without exception, must be kept growing and brought to maturity in the quickest possible manner. This means that there must be a fertile, well tilled soil, to which oftentimes are added supplementary feedings. A plentiful supply of moisture is likewise needed; usually, in periods of drought, this can be supplied with the garden hose.

147

266. Purpose Table of Best Varieties

Name	For 100-Ft. Row	Depth (in.)	Apart (in.)	Rows (in.)	When
Celeriac . . .	$\frac{1}{4}$ oz.	$\frac{1}{4}$	6–8	15–18	Apr.
Collards . . .	$\frac{1}{8}$ oz.	$\frac{1}{2}$	2	18	May
Corn Salad . .	Packet	$\frac{1}{2}$	6	12–18	Oct. & Mar.
Cress	Packet	$\frac{1}{2}$	Drill	12–18	Mar. & Sept.
Dandelion . .	Packet	$\frac{1}{4}$	12	12	Mar.–May
Endive . . .	$\frac{1}{2}$ oz.	$\frac{1}{2}$	12	12–18	April.–July
Finochio . . .	Packet	$\frac{1}{2}$	6	12–18	Apr.
Kale	$\frac{1}{2}$ oz.	$\frac{1}{2}$	6–8	18–24	Mar. & Aug.
Lettuce . . .	$\frac{1}{2}$ oz.	$\frac{1}{2}$	4–6	12–18	Mar.–Sept.
Mustard . . .	Packet	$\frac{1}{4}$	5–6	12–18	Mar.–Apr.
Parsley . . .	$\frac{1}{4}$ oz.	$\frac{1}{8}$	3–6	12–18	Mar.–Sept.
Pe-Tsai . . .	$\frac{1}{4}$ oz.	$\frac{1}{4}$	4–6	12–18	July–Aug.
Romaine salad .	$\frac{1}{2}$ oz.	$\frac{1}{2}$	4–6	12–18	Mar.–June
Witloof . . .	1 oz.	$\frac{1}{2}$	4–5	12–16	Apr.–June
Wong Bok . .	$\frac{1}{4}$ oz.	$\frac{1}{4}$	4–6	12–18	July–Aug.

267. **Planning Year-Around Succession.** A glance at the above table will show how it is possible to maintain a continuous succession of green salad plants in the garden throughout the growing season. If witloof is grown, the roots may be taken up in the fall and stored in the cellar, where they are used during the winter for sprouting the succulent shoots which, in themselves, form an extremely edible salad plant. Thus, green vegetables from one end of the year to the other can be produced from your own garden.

268. **Salad Plants for Diabetics.** Thrice-cooked fresh vegetables are approved diet for diabetics. Salad vegetables are especially desirable.

Chapter XXIX

CELERIAC

> *Traverse therefore this little moment of time at
> peace with Nature.*
>
> —Marcus Aurelius.

Chapter XXIX

CELERIAC

269. Growing Habits. Celeriac is sometimes called turnip-rooted celery—a name which is descriptive of its appearance. Unlike common celery, it is grown for the root rather than for the tops. In growing habit and culture it is identical with celery.

270. Soil Requirements. A soil rich in humus and plant foods is essential for success with celeriac, as with ordinary celery. See Sec. 70.

271. When to Start Seed. Seed should be started at the same time celery seed is planted. See Sec. 67.

272. When to Transplant. Transplant to the open garden at the same time and in the same manner as common celery. See Sec. 69.

273. Fertilizers and Plant Foods. Celeriac requires the same sort of soil preparation and supplementary feeding as common celery. See Sec. 71.

274. Is Blanching Necessary? Inasmuch as the roots and not the tops are the main edible portions of celeriac, blanching is not necessary as in the case of common celery.

275. How to Use. Celeriac may be used in chopped salads, raw, or cooked like turnips.

Chapter XXX

CHICORY

Should we not imitate the fruitful fields, which return far more than they have received?

—CICERO.

Chapter XXX

CHICORY

276. Soil Requirements. Chicory requires a deep, rich, loamy soil free from excessive quantities of organic matter or manures. There are two or three kinds of chicory. One, witloof chicory, is often called French endive. It is valued chiefly in winter when green vegetables are at a premium. The old-fashioned large-root chicory was used chiefly as a substitute for coffee, the roots being more valuable than the tops.

Any soil condition favorable to the production of good root crops will, therefore, improve the chances of success with chicory.

277. When to Plant. Chicory is a hardy plant and not especially sensitive to cold. It can, therefore, be planted as early in the spring as the ground can be worked. Plantings may be made any time up to and including June.

278. How to Plant. Cover chicory seed one-half inch deep and drill from two to three inches apart in the row. The rows should be twelve to sixteen inches apart. Plantings may be made until June. Chicory requires from 75 to 110 days to mature properly.

279. Thinning. As the plants grow, they should be thinned out so that they stand from four to five inches apart in the row, in order to allow plenty of room for the development of good, sturdy roots.

280. Harvesting. The tender leaves may be picked during the growing season and used for cooked greens or in chopped combination salads. Some varieties when cooked are bitter and must, therefore, be cooked in two or three waters.

Witloof chicory is valued chiefly for forcing in the winter. The roots must be harvested in the fall before the ground freezes and stored away for use in forcing in the winter.

281. How to Store. Store the roots in boxes of moist soil in the cellar until ready for forcing. Sand and peatmoss are also good storing agents.

282. How to Force. The roots are arranged upright in a box and covered with moist soil or sand. About nine inches of sand or soil should cover the crowns of the roots. Keep moist and in a warm place. The tops will sprout from the crowns and will grow close together and rather compact.

283. How to Cut. If the top is cut off just above the crown several more shoots will grow out of it before the root is worthless. Cutting too deep into the crown will lose this advantage.

284. How to Use. Witloof chicory is used as a fresh salad in the same manner as Cos lettuce or endive, merely sliced open and covered with French dressing. It is a delicious and welcome addition to the menu at a time when fresh, green vegetables are unknown on many tables.

Chapter XXXI

COLLARDS

> *I have nestled lovingly in the bosom of Old Mother Earth. . . .*
>
> —John Burroughs.

CHAPTER XXXI

COLLARDS

285. Where to Grow. Grow anywhere you would grow cabbage. Collards are similar in culture and requirements to cabbage.

286. When to Plant. In the South, where collards are more extensively grown than in the North, they are sown from January to May and from August to October. In the North, they can likewise be planted in the spring and fall.

287. How to Plant. Cover the seed ½ inch deep. Sow thickly in rows, thinning out later so that the plants stand anywhere from 2 inches to 3 feet apart in the row depending upon the season and purpose for which grown. Collards are not only used on the table, but also for stock feed. When intended for the latter purpose, they may be allowed to grow closer together.

288. Best Time to Harvest. Collards do not form a head, as does cabbage, but a rosette of leaves. When these have attained sufficient size, they should be tied together loosely, gathering the whole group up and tying them tent-fashion in order to blanch the interior of the leaves. The best time to harvest is when they have reached sufficient size to make blanching possible. Allowed to go too long, they become strong and bitter to the taste.

289. How to Use. Collards may be used in the chopped combination salad, used green, or may be cooked as ordinary "greens." In either way, they are excellent.

CHAPTER XXXII

CORN SALAD

> *Nature makes no excuse for her shabby dress,
> her tears. You have but to look at her to know
> that you know nothing at all. She hears all,
> speaks nothing, but quietly holds up the mirror
> that mirrors ourselves—to ourselves!*
>
> —CHESLA C. SHERLOCK, in
> "City and Suburban Gardening."

Chapter XXXII

CORN SALAD

290. When to Plant. Corn salad is also known as lamb's-lettuce and fetticus. It is absolutely hardy and may be sown at any time that the ground can be worked. For an extra early crop in spring, sow the last thing before the autumn garden work ceases entirely before the onslaughts of Jack Frost.

291. How to Plant. Sow the seed in drills, and cover about one-half inch. Thin out later to about six inches apart in the row. The rows should be from twelve to eighteen inches apart.

292. Culture. The same culture that would be given to lettuce should be given to corn salad. See Chapter XXXIX.

293. When to Harvest. Corn salad may be used green in a mixed or combination chopped salad, or may be mixed with mustard and cooked as "greens." It may, therefore, be harvested at any time that it is large enough for these purposes or uses.

294. Winter Protection. Seed sown late in the fall should be protected in the North with a light covering of straw, marsh hay, or leaves. In the South, this is not necessary.

295. How to Use. Use in place of lettuce, when lettuce is out of season, or as a component part of a combination chopped green salad. May also be cooked with mustard as "greens."

Chapter XXXIII

CRESS

> The greatest of them all [vegetables] is Cress, a
> creation divine!
>
> —Jonathan Fitzgerald.

CRESS

296. Habit of Growth. There are two kinds of cress, upland and water. The latter is one of the few vegetables that can be grown successfully in wet surroundings, particularly in limestone regions or springs. Upland cress, as the name denotes, will succeed in the average garden situation. It is sometimes erroneously called peppergrass.

297. When to Plant. Upland cress is a thoroughly hardy plant and may be sown in the fall, if desired, in the milder sections of the country. In the North, it is commonly planted in the spring. It can be planted, as a matter of fact, any time from March to September. It requires from thirty-five to forty-five days to reach maturity, and plantings can therefore be made in succession.

298. How to Plant. Cover the seed lightly, usually from one-fourth to one-half inch deep, and plant the seed in drills. The rows should be from twelve to eighteen inches apart. When the plants are established, thin to from four to six inches apart in the row.

299. Sowing for Succession. Inasmuch as this is a quick-maturing vegetable, it should be sown for succession at intervals of not more than two weeks. Cress is, as Jonathan Fitzgerald has noted, a divine creation for all salad makers and should be on hand throughout the season. Plant in small quantities, but often!

300. How to Grow Indoors. Cress may be grown indoors during the winter in flats or shallow boxes. All that is necessary is average heat and plenty of moisture. Avoid too much.

301. How to Use. Cress is excellent in green salads; or it may also be cooked as any "greens" are.

Chapter XXXIV

DANDELIONS

> *At times, I could rise in might and wrath against those early settlers who introduced the Dandelion to this country!*
>
> —From an old farm paper.

DANDELIONS

302. Cultivated Kinds. Those who have gone afield in search of dandelions in early spring have no conception of what the lowly and despised plant will do in cultivation. Dandelion greens, as every lover of greens will testify, are quite the best of all cooked green vegetables. But the labor and bother of digging them in the lawn or along the roadsides may be largely dispensed with if a row is planted in the garden, of the cultivated varieties. The best of these are French Common and Improved Thick-Leaved.

303. When to Plant. The dandelion is absolutely hardy and may be planted as early in the spring as the soil can be worked. It may be planted in the fall, too, to provide the earliest greens in the spring.

304. How to Plant. Cover the seeds from $\frac{1}{4}$ to $\frac{1}{2}$ inch deep and drill in rows twelve inches apart. Later the plants should be thinned to twelve inches apart in the row, using those thinned out for green salads, or cooking them.

305. Culture. Cultivate and keep down all weeds, in order to conserve the moisture content of the soil. Aside from this careful cultivation, especially the first season, the dandelion requires little attention.

306. When to Cut. The sturdy plants may be cut when they have attained sufficient size to warrant it. Cut high on the crowns in order to conserve as much as possible the strength of the roots. It is better, however, to wait until large and complete whorls of leaves have been produced. Sometimes, this means waiting until the second season.

307. How to Cut. During the first season cut high on the crown. Indeed, the leaves should be snipped off without in any way injuring the crown at all. Remember that the life of dandelion plants depends upon the strength that is stored in the roots, and every effort should be made to protect them from too severe cuttings.

308. Life of Plants. The life of the dandelion plant depends entirely upon the manner in which the tops are cut. If these are ruthlessly cut the first or second season, no permanency can be expected. Indeed, many gardeners do not intend that dandelions shall ever be permanently established in any part of the garden, but prefer to treat them at best as biennials, moving to a new location every two years. If handled with care, however, there is no reason why a given planting should not last for several seasons.

309. Value of Dandelions. Dandelions are widely recommended for medicinal qualities. They contain almost as much iron as spinach, and to many people are more agreeable in the diet. In fact, dandelion greens are almost the favorite among all classes and ages. The edibility of the leaves may be enhanced by blanching them. This makes them more tasty by removing much of the bitterness found in large, green leaves.

310. How to Blanch. Cover the whorl of leaves with a wide board, or, for very large clumps, gather up and tie closely together until blanched.

311. How to Use. Dandelions, as we have suggested before, are desirable in the green, chopped salad in combination with other green vegetables, or may be used in the time-honored manner as cooked greens.

Chapter XXXV

ENDIVE

We not only work on our knees, bending our backs to accomplish something in this Divine Workshop. . . .

—Chesla C. Sherlock, in
"City and Suburban Gardening."

ENDIVE

312. Soil Requirements. Any soil which will grow lettuce will grow endive successfully. This means that it must be rich, deep, and well supplied with humus. Supplementary feedings of commercial plant foods or complete commercial fertilizer at the rate of two ounces per square yard, applied just before planting, will be very beneficial.

313. Seed Germination. Endive seed is usually of weak germinating quality. One must allow for this, and not be disappointed if it is slow to appear.

314. When to Plant. Endive, sometimes called Escarole, is largely substituted for lettuce in many sections. It has every requirement that lettuce has except that it is not susceptible to heat as lettuce is. Therefore, in the North, it is planted in spring, summer, and fall.

315. How to Plant. Cover the seed one-half inch deep and drill in rows. Eventually thin out until the plants are about twelve inches apart in the row. The rows should be from twelve to eighteen inches apart. Endive requires from 90 to 180 days to reach maturity.

316. Summer Care. Keep the weeds out of the rows and cultivate continually. Thin out so that good growth can be obtained.

317. When to Blanch. When the leaves have reached sufficient size, it is time to think of blanching. Blanching is practiced to make the plants more edible, to enhance their flavor and desirability for use in salads.

318. How to Blanch. Tie up the outer leaves compactly. A rubber band is excellent for this purpose. The outer leaves completely enclose those inside, causing them to blanch readily. It must be remembered that blanching is the first step in decay and that it must not be allowed to progress too far. Keep a close eye on what is going on and harvest your endive for the table before it is too late.

319. **Soft Rots.** Soft rots in endive are entirely the result of prolonging the blanching process too long. As noted in Sec. 318, decay sets in if this is allowed to progress too far. The remedy is not to allow the plants to remain too long before cutting and using.

320. **Types.** Endive types may be divided between the broad-leaved sorts (escarole) and the curled varieties, like Green Curled, or Large Green Curled. The old escarole is known as Broad-Leaved Bavarian, and another is Full Heart Bavarian.

CHAPTER XXXVI

FINOCHIO

Fennel is, next to Cress, the greatest of all salad vegetables.
                              —JONATHAN FITZGERALD.

Chapter XXXVI

FINOCHIO

321. When to Plant. In the North, the crop is planted in the spring, usually April. Finochio is a fennel and is grown like celery or celeriac.

322. How to Plant. Cover the seed one-half inch deep. The plants should eventually be spaced about six inches apart in the row. Rows should be twelve to eighteen inches apart. Finochio requires from sixty to seventy days in which to mature.

323. Culture. The culture is similar to that of celery or celeriac. It is the bulbous root at the base of the leaves that is used most commonly, although the large center stalks may be used also. See Sec. 73 and Sec. 71.

324. Liberal Watering Required. All the fennels require liberal watering throughout the growing season. This does not mean casual sprinklings with the garden hose; a better method is to irrigate by running trenches of water alongside the rows.

325. When to Harvest. When the leaf stalks have grown to about two inches in diameter, mound up the soil around the base of the plants in order partially to blanch them. Harvest before they become tough and stringy.

326. How to Harvest. Cut out the center stalks of the leaves and the bulbous root at the base. Either or both may be used in salads.

327. How to Use. The center stalks are often eaten like celery. The bulbous root may be sliced raw in chopped salads, or cooked like celeriac or kohlrabi.

CHAPTER XXXVII

HORSERADISH

A sweet seclusion this of sun and shade,
A calm asylum from the busy world . . .

—JOHN RUSSELL HAYES.

HORSERADISH

328. Where to Plant. Plant in a corner of the garden, as horseradish is a permanent plant, somewhat like asparagus or rhubarb. A few plants will supply the average family with all the roots necessary.

329. Size of Root to Plant. The best roots to plant are six to eight inches long and the size of a lead pencil. These may be purchased from seedsmen or may be secured from neighbors who have plants.

330. How to Plant. I quote from Farmers' Bulletin No. 1673 of the United States Department of Agriculture: "A trench four or five inches deep is opened with a hoe and the root cuttings placed at an angle with their tops near the surface of the soil. Each cutting will sprout in several places, and after they are well established the soil should be carefully removed by hand from around the cuttings. All but one good cluster of leaves near the top of each cutting should be removed. The soil should then be replaced. These plants usually make good roots the first year. As a rule the plants in the home garden are allowed to grow from year to year, and portions of the roots are removed as needed. Pieces of roots and crowns remaining in the soil are usually sufficient to reëstablish the plants."

331. Plant Foods and Fertilizers. Manure or compost should be mixed in the soil before planting; this must be thoroughly decomposed. Commercial plant foods may be used at the time of planting, and annual dressings of manure or commercial plant foods given, preferably in the spring.

332. When to Harvest. Plantings started in the spring

may be harvested in the fall, as a rule. Be sure to allow sufficient crowns or roots to remain to reëstablish the plants. Thereafter, the roots may be harvested as needed. The best practice is to cut off the tender, succulent side roots, allowing the main plant to remain intact.

333. Uses as Greens. The green, crinkly leaves are excellent for cooked greens and may be so used. Our grandfathers greatly prized them for this purpose. They are too bitter, as a rule, for use in green chopped salads.

334. Hardiness. Horseradish is absolutely hardy but is peculiar in that it does not succeed in warm climates, or in the South unless grown at relatively high altitudes. It succeeds best in the North temperate zone.

335. How to Use. Again I quote from Farmers' Bulletin No. 1673: "Horseradish is prepared by cleaning and grating the roots directly into white wine vinegar or distilled vinegar of 4½ or 5 per cent acid content. Bottled and sealed immediately, it keeps for a few weeks. Dried, ground and bottled, it keeps for some time, but this product is not as good as when the horseradish is grated fresh and mixed with vinegar. Cidar vinegar should not be used, as it causes the horseradish to turn dark."

Chapter XXXVIII

KALE

> *Nature never did betray*
> *The heart that loved her.*
>
> —WORDSWORTH.

KALE

336. When to Plant. Kale requires from 60 to 120 days to mature. It is perfectly hardy and may be planted in March, and again in September for an early spring crop.

337. How to Plant. Cover one-half inch deep. Plants should be from six to eight inches apart in the row. Rows are from eighteen to twenty-four inches apart.

338. Plant Foods and Fertilizers. The spring crop will come in early if a little nitrate of soda is spread along the rows. As a rule, good garden soil that has been properly fertilized will be sufficient for kale; and where it follows another crop that was properly fertilized, no additonal attention along this line will ordinarily be needed.

339. Hardiness. Kale is perfectly hardy in regions up to the southern part of Pennsylvania and will live through the winters in all regions having a similar climate. The crop that is intended to come on in the spring is usually sown about six weeks before frost and sown broadcast in many sections. Usually, however, the spring crop should be sown in rows in order to permit cultivation sufficient to keep down the weeds.

340. Winter Use. In regions of mild severity during winter kale is an excellent crop to have. During midsummer, especially in the South, it is not so desirable, becoming tough and stringy. Many southern growers contend that kale is at its best after the first heavy frosts.

341. How to Use in Spring. As noted before, kale will come on very early in the spring. The tender leaves or whole plants may be used. Usually at this season, however, the desire is to preserve the plants and to take off only a few leaves in order to prolong the period of production.

342. Types and Varieties. The best fall and winter kales are the Scotch Curly types, while the Siberian flat-leaved sorts are best for wintering over.

Chapter XXXIX

LETTUCE

Calm soul of all things! make it mine
To feel, amid the city's jar,
That there abides a peace of thine,
Man did not make, and cannot mar.

—Matthew Arnold.

Chapter XXXIX

LETTUCE

343. Types and Varieties. There are two main types of lettuce, head and loose-leaved. In recent years, Cos or Romaine lettuce has been treated as a distinct type. The best heading varieties are Iceberg and Big Boston, while Black-Seeded Simpson is the old favorite loose-leaved variety. Prize Head is another good one. White Paris is the best Cos or Romaine type.

344. When to Sow Seed. Lettuce culture throughout most of the gardening regions is largely limited to spring and fall culture, although in certain portions of the South it is grown right through the winter. Lettuce is a cool-weather plant, requiring from sixty to ninety days to mature, depending upon the variety. Sow seed accordingly, but remember that it will not succeed in hot weather.

345. Transplanting Head Lettuce. Head lettuce is usually transplanted to the open garden in April. You may grow your own seedlings from seed sown in flats or shallow boxes, or they may be purchased from your seedsman or dealer.

346. Soil Requirements. Lettuce requires a rich soil, well fertilized with rotted manures. Avoid fresh, strawy manures. It will not succeed on acid soils and therefore, lime is required in such situations. Use a commercial fertilizer with more phosphorus than usual for lettuce.

347. Fertilizers and Plant Foods. In addition to the recommendations made in Sec. 346, an application of nitrate of soda made after the plants have shown some growth is highly beneficial.

191

348. Sowing for Succession. Especially in the spring, lettuce should be sown for succession in order to keep a supply of tender, succulent plants on hand for the table. Usually in the fall only one planting is made.

349. Thinning. Head lettuce is either set or thinned to four to six inches apart in the row, the rows being twelve to eighteen inches apart, for garden cultivation. Distances are increased where horse cultivation is desired. Leaf lettuce is drilled in the rows and thinned as used by pulling up whole plants until those remaining have sufficient room.

350. Causes of Failure with Head Lettuce. One chief cause of failure with head lettuce in the home garden is that the seed is sown too late to produce plants before warm weather comes on. Garden slugs are another source of failure. They may be prevented by sprinkling air-slacked lime or ashes around the plants.

351. When to Plant Late Crops. Heading types should be sown in July for the late crop, and the loose-leaved types can be sown in late July, as a rule.

352. Diseases and Pests. The garden slug, an enemy that leaves a slimy trail, has already been mentioned in Sec. 350. The green aphid is another. It is a sucking insect that attacks the leaves. It is usually controlled by spraying with soap and water. Lettuce is not bothered by diseases as a rule, although young plants in the frames are sometimes attacked by rots. The remedy is to fumigate with any safe fumigant.

CHAPTER XL

PARSLEY

*Care stops at the gates, and gazes at me wist-
fully through the bars.*

—ALEXANDER SMITH.

Chapter XL

PARSLEY

353. How Much to Grow. The average family will not require much of a planting—a few feet of row should be sufficient. Parsley is used primarily for garnishing, but good cooks have discovered its uses for flavoring soups and other vegetables.

354. When to Plant. Parsley is like lettuce or kale in that it is hardy to cold, but does not like heat. It can be planted as soon as the ground can be worked, and if a fall planting is desired, it may be made in September. However, a simpler practice is to lift a few plants at the end of the season and place them in a coldframe, where they will furnish springs in early spring.

355. How to Plant. Cover the seed one-eighth inch deep. Plants should eventually be thinned to from three to six inches apart in the row. The rows should be twelve to eighteen inches apart. Parsley requires from 90 to 120 growing days, depending upon the season and variety.

356. Culture. Parsley requires a good, reasonably rich garden soil. The soil must have sufficient humus to be mellow, and worked well enough to be free from clods and stones. It is a plant of weak seed and slow, uncertain growth until established. Weeds must be kept down, and the soil in good tilth; keep the crust broken up.

357. How to Use. Use as a garnish for meats and vegetables, and in soups and cooked vegetables for flavor.

Chapter XLI

ROMAINE SALAD

> *Give me solitude—give me Nature—give me again,*
> *O Nature, your primal sanities.*
>
> —WALT WHITMAN.

ROMAINE SALAD

358. When to Sow for Early and Late Crops. Romaine salad is now generally listed by up-to-date seedsmen as a lettuce. Like lettuce is does not withstand hot weather. The early crop should be sown in March as soon as the soil can be worked. The late crop is sown in late June. It requires sixty days to mature.

359. How to Plant. Cover one-half inch deep. The plants should be thinned to stand four to six inches apart in the rows, which are from twelve to eighteen inches apart.

360. Culture. Give the same culture as for lettuce. Romaine salad is sometimes called Cos lettuce. It is in reality a coarse and larger-growing lettuce.

361. How to Use. Romaine salad is excellent as a green salad, especially when used in combination with other green vegetables and chopped fine. Use an oil or French dressing. It may also be cooked.

CHAPTER XLII

WONG BOK (PE–TSAI)

What I was thinking about was that, perhaps, when you come right down to facts, the people who don't know that they are doing it are the people who really create the beauty of this world while they are going about their regular jobs and attending strictly to their own business.

—ELLIS PARKER BUTLER.

Chapter XLII

WONG BOK (PE–TSAI)

362. When to Plant. Wong bok, popularly called Chinese cabbage, does best as a fall crop in the North. It bridges a gap in the green salad garden at this time. It should be planted in July or August, about two and one-half months before frost in your locality.

363. How to Plant. Cover one-fourth inch deep. The plants are transplanted or thinned to stand four to six inches apart in the row, and these are twelve to eighteen inches apart. Wong bok requires from forty to sixty days to mature, as a rule.

364. Soil Requirements. Wong bok demands a rich and well drained but moist soil, if it is to be grown to perfection. This means that an abundance of humus must be present in the soil.

365. Culture. Culture is similar to that of lettuce, except that it does not succeed as a spring crop.

366. When to Harvest. When the heads are well formed, they may be harvested. This is an exceedingly attractive and tasty vegetable when properly grown. The heads are self-blanching, grow in cylindrical shape, and often weigh several pounds.

367. How to Use. Use as a chopped green salad in combination with other green vegetables. The large midrib may be cooked, also. The vegetable has a distinctive and pleasing flavor.

PART III

THE FRUIT GARDEN

CHAPTER XLIII

APPLES

Every tree is known by his own fruit.
—St. Luke.

Chapter XLIII

APPLES

368. Varieties for Home Garden. Delicious is one of the favorite varieties of the present generation. It can be grown in the home garden as successfully as any other variety. Unless you have plenty of ground, your space will be limited. Therefore, grow the best and most satisfactory varieties. In the small city backyard, one apple tree will usually be all that there is room for. The variety that pleases you most, in its all-around qualities, is the one to select. Other good apple varieties are Baldwin, Northern Spy, Maiden's Blush, and Jonathan.

369. Type and Size to Buy. A three-year-old tree should be selected. It should be remembered that standards require at least twenty-five feet of space each way. Specially trained types such as pyramids, cordons, and espaliers may be purchased for the very small garden. Dwarf types may be purchased for the small backyard garden. See Sec. 377.

370. When to Transplant. Fruit trees in the dormant stage may be transplanted to the open garden as soon as the soil can be worked. This certainly means before the annual spring rains set in.

371. How to Plant. The old, old adage is that it is better to put a ten-cent plant in a fifty-cent hole than to try the reverse. To buy a good, healthy young tree and then be indifferent as to the manner in which it is planted is to court disaster.

First of all, your tree should be set a few inches deeper than it grew at the nursery. The hole should be dug deep, the subsoil thrown out or thoroughly mixed with well rotted manure or compost. In the absence of these, work in leaves, pieces of grassy sod, and bonemeal. Be sure that the roots of the tree may be spread out in a natural manner; do not wad them in a cramped ball and expect your tree to produce results.

372. **Pruning When Planting.** It is a safe rule to prune all broken roots back, at least before the point where the breaks occur. In addition, shorten all long and rangy roots, and if there is an especially heavy root development, prune back all the ends. This will cause the quick formation of many tiny rootlets or feeding hairs—a desirable thing.

Tops and side branches should also be pruned back, according to the age of the trees planted. Top branches of three-year-old trees should be pruned back about one-third of their growth, with full allowance for the size, shape, and vitality of the individual specimen. The purpose in pruning apple trees is to cause the formation of a low-headed, open-growing top. Some branches, especially those that cross one another in the center of the head, should be removed entirely.

Judgment will have to be exercised here, and unless you can procure diagrams or charts from government bulletins or similar publications, it would be best to consult the most experienced orchardist in your neighborhood.

373. **The First Season.** The first season is the most important of all. Keep in mind the future shape and contour of the tree, removing all superfluous shoots. Keep well cultivated, watered, and fertilized.

374. **The Second Season.** The main point the second season is that the first year's growth should be cut back about one-half. In cutting back, always strive to make a slanting cut *above* a bud pointed to the outside of the branch.

375. **Fertilizers and Plant Foods.** The base of the tree

Overhead irrigation for an asparagus bed on a Mid-Western estate.

The herb garden attractively laid out on a Mid-Western estate.

This tool does all sorts of things to a congenial soil!

Handy tools, kept in good condition, make garden work
a pleasure.

and a circle equal to the spread of branches overhead can be covered with manure in the fall. This will, through the action of leeching, reach the roots. The spent material can be turned under with hoe or plow in the spring. Another sure way to benefit growing trees is to make numerous holes with an iron crowbar under the spread of branches and around the root-soil. Pour a handful of commercial plant food into each hole, and fill with dirt. Give the entire area *a thorough soaking* with the garden hose, or make the application just before a general rain.

376. Diseases, Pests, and Their Control. San Jose scale is a scablike eruption of the bark of apple trees which is best treated with oil emulsion sprays specially offered on the market. A minute insect working under the scale is responsible for the damage.

The codling moth is the principal apple pest. Arsenate of lead is the best method of control. Spray as soon as possible after the blossoms fall, the mixture being made at the rate of a pound and a half of the lead arsenate to fifty gallons of water; get the spray into the calyx before it closes tight and turns downward.

Aphids or plant lice are controlled with nicotine sulphate or "Black Leaf 40," used in accordance with the manufacturer's directions.

Lime sulphur may be combined with all sprays in order to control fungous growths and diseases.

377. Dwarf Types. Practically without exception, all varieties and species of fruit trees in demand in commerce are now available in dwarf type. This means that the gardener with restricted space can grow the varieties that hitherto have been denied to him.

378. Where and How to Grow. Dwarf types are grown like the standard sorts, the chief difference being that far less space is necessary. Specially trained sorts may be grown on trellises along walks, against walls and over arches and similar supports. As a rule these forms are reserved chiefly for greenhouses of the wealthy or the especially situated amateur.

CHAPTER **XLIV**

APRICOTS

The harvest truly is plenteous, but the labourers are few.
　　　　　　　　　　　　—ST. MATTHEW.

APRICOTS

379. Bush or Tree Types. Bush types are to be preferred for the home garden, because they require practically
no pruning—only enough to keep in shape. They are lower-
growing and therefore require less room and make less
trouble in handling. Apricots are slow-growing.

380. Why Plant Two Varieties? It has been found by
long experience that the planting of two varieties of apricots
side by side will increase the percentage of pollination.

381. When to Plant. Early fall, when the plants first
become dormant, is the best time to transplant apricots.
This gives them a chance to become well established during
the winter. Apricots as a rule should not be planted in regions
where the temperature goes below 10 degrees below zero.
They closely resemble peaches in hardiness.

382. How to Plant. Apricots are transplanted in the
same manner that any shrub or tree is. Good stock should
be selected, some pruning back of both roots and tops
practiced·at time of planting, and the usual care exercised
in the actual planting. This means that a deep and wide
hole is dug, the topsoil is carefully worked around the
roots, and some humus, bonemeal, or commercial plant
food added. The soil must be settled thoroughly around
the roots. Old gardeners and orchardists recommended
tramping it down or pounding it with a spade handle. That
is likely to injure the tiny feeding rootlets. A better and
surer way is to settle the soil with copious applications of
water. A bush or tree properly transplanted *cannot be
pulled up without injury to itself!*

383. Culture. The culture of apricots is identical with that of peaches. See Chapter LII.

384. Best Varieties. The two best varieties for home garden use are Moorepark and Harris.

Chapter XLV

BLACKBERRIES

> *We are determined to be starved before we are hungry.*
> —Henry David Thoreau.

Chapter XLV

BLACKBERRIES

385. Preparation of Bed. Blackberries are not particular as to soils, but one factor is essential in any soil. There must be an abundance of moisture at the time of fruit development and ripening. The preparation of the seedbed must be such as to build up moisture-retaining qualities; this means the addition of sufficient humus to most soils to render them friable, easily worked. A soil of leafmold would be ideal.

Clays and hard soils must be broken up by the addition of straw, strawy manures, leaves, or other coarse material. Preparation should start the fall before planting, turning up the soil in large chunks in order that frost action may aid in the work. Add more humus-bearing materials in the spring, and work them thoroughly into the soil.

386. Varieties. The choice of varieties for your locality had best be left to local authorities. There are literally dozens of varieties in commerce. Consult your county agricultural agent, or write to your state college of agriculture. Perhaps a local gardener or seedsman can help you. The best general varieties for the home garden are Eldorado, Blowers, Joy, and Snyder.

387. When to Plant. The general rule is to set the plants in the spring, although in many mild regions fall planting is practiced.

388. How to Plant. A simple method to use in setting the plants, particularly where many are to be set, is to insert a garden spade in the ground at the proper spot and push it down full depth, then shove the blade to one side, opening up the soil. Then insert the plant behind the blade, withdraw the spade, and tramp the soil around the roots. Plants should be set five to six feet apart in the row. The rows are seven to eight feet apart. Eighteen plants are sufficient for 100 feet of row.

389. Supports. There are almost as many different systems of training blackberries to supports as there are systems of training grapes. Any system which will enable one to keep down the production of excessive canes, prune to improve quality of fruit, is successful. Some growers prune back severely enough to encourage short, stocky growth so that the canes are self-supporting.

A simple and inexpensive system I have followed is to set posts in the rows about eight feet apart, spaced between the plants. To these posts are nailed cross-arms eighteen inches above the ground and at the tops. To the ends of these cross-arms are tacked clothesline wire. The canes are trained to grow up between the two strands of wire, and may be tied to them for secure support.

390. Summer Pruning; Pinching Back. The quality of next season's fruit may depend upon the sort of summer pruning you practice this season. When the new, tender canes reach the top of the supports, the ends should be pinched back, or lopped off with a hand sickle. This encourages the formation of side, or lateral, branches upon which the fruit will be borne. When these get out of hand their growth may be arrested by pinching back or cutting off the tips.

391. Keeping Suckers under Control. Unless suckers, or the shoots springing up from the roots in all directions from the main plant, are kept cut off, your plantation will soon turn itself into a bramble patch. The roots of the blackberry forage in all directions and make rapid, surprising growth. Keep the suckers down!

A young orchard properly started.

So heavy was the crop, this tree had to have its branches supported.

Tomatoes and beans supported by poles.

Sweet corn getting a good start in a suburban garden.

392. When to Renew Plantings. After a few seasons the plantings should be moved to a new location. You will have to keep a sharp lookout for suckers springing up from pieces of root, but determined cultivation will kill them out of the old location.

393. Pests and Diseases. The crown borer tunnels in the larger roots and infests the crowns. There is no known remedy, save to dig out infested plants and burn them. The cane borer is a similar pest that attacks the canes above ground. Again the infested plants must be cut out and burned. The larvae of the sawfly feed upon the leaves in late June and July. Spray with lead arsenate around the middle of June. The chief disease is orange rust, a fungus which infests the entire plant and winters over in the crowns and roots. Orange-colored masses of powdery spores appear on the underside of the leaves. Dig out and destroy all infected plants, and move the plantation to a new location, using disease-free stock.

Chapter XLVI

CHERRIES

My faith is all a doubtful thing,
Wove on a doubtful loom,—
Until there comes, each showery spring,
A cherry tree in bloom.

—David Morton.

Chapter XLVI

CHERRIES

394. Varieties. May Duke is a large red, juicy cherry that ripens early in June. Governor Wood is a light yellowish red, and Black Tartarian is a large purple sort, both fruiting in June. Bigarreau ripens in July. Montmorency is an old favorite.

395. When to Plant. Cherries are usually set out in the home garden and orchard in the spring. This should be done before spring rains set in—in most localities this will mean before the middle of April.

396. How to Plant. Cherries should be transplanted in the same manner as any other tree or shrub. Follow the directions in Sec. 382.

397. Pruning. Cherries require perhaps less pruning than any other fruit tree. All the sour cherries need is the removal of all broken, crossed, or dead branches. Sweet cherries need to be pruned for low heads as they normally grow too tall.

398. Diseases, Pests, and Their Control. Robins are often a pest, especially in the case of early cherries. Where there are a number of trees, there should be enough for all, but it is exasperating to have the fruit of one or two trees eaten and maimed in this way. Mosquito netting thrown over the tree and securely fastened will solve this problem.

Aphids are a common pest. These plant lice are controlled by spraying with Black Leaf 40, or nicotine solution, just before blooming. They usually attack the tender shoots. Maggots or fruit flies infest the ripening fruit. The foliage should be dusted in early June with sweetened lead arsenate.

Slugs eat the upper surface of the leaves. Spray with lead arsenate.

In rainy seasons, brown rot is a common disease. Dust with sulphur just as the fruit begins to color and again just before picking. Leaf spot is often a serious fungous disease. It causes the leaves to turn yellow and fall prematurely. From two to four applications of sulphur or copper lime dust will usually control it, the first application to be made just after the green shucks of the young fruit have fallen.

399. Soil Requirements. Cherries have no special soil requirements, although they usually do best in a good, sandy loam.

400. Fertilizers and Plant Foods. Maintain plant food in the soil and sufficient humus to render it available at all times. Rotted manures are always good, and commercial plant foods should be applied to the roots as recommended by the specific manufacturer.

Chapter XLVII

CURRANTS

The United States Department of Agriculture recognizes the cultivated black currant as a distinct menace to the white pine timber supply of the country.

—Farmers' Bulletin No. 1398.

CURRANTS

401. Soil Requirements. Currants have no special soil requirements, succeeding on any soil of medium richness. They prefer open sunlight and a free circulation of air, but will grow even in the shade under trees.

402. Type to Select. Currants are classified according to color of fruit when ripe. We have red, white, and black currants. All are good, and all make excellent jelly, the black varieties being probably best of all. But if you live in a white-pine growing region, it would be best to forgo growing the black varieties because they are host plants for white-pine blister rust, the most serious menace we have to the future of white pine in this country.

403. When to Plant. Currant bushes may be planted in either fall or spring. Individual preference or convenience will govern in most instances.

404. How to Plant. Plant as you would any tree or shrub. See Sec. 382. Place four feet apart, the rows six feet apart.

405. How to Prune Young Shoots. Young shoots should be pruned back one-half, and most of them removed from the bush entirely. Take care to cut out all shoots springing from the base of the plant; grow as standards—that is, as small treelike plants—allowing only one main stem to remain.

406. How to Insure Large Fruit. Constant pruning, leaning to the severe side, not only will keep the bushes or plants in hand, but will insure the best quality of fruit. Currants lend themselves readily to heavy pruning, and since they are usually rank growers, it is necessary for good fruit.

407. Pests and Their Control. The currant worm is the most serious pest. It attacks the foliage almost as soon as it appears. Keep a close watch, and when the leaves are damp with dew, dust with Hellebore dust. They may be sprayed with lead arsenate; but this practice is frowned upon, especially when the fruit is near maturity, as it is difficult to get the poison off the small fruit.

Aphids, or plant lice, attack the underside of the leaves. Spray with nicotine sulphate, or Black Leaf 40. Use the same control for the four-lined leaf bug and for scurfy scale, which infests the stems.

Leaf spots are caused by a fungous disease. Dust several times with copper lime dust early in the season.

408. How to Propagate. Currants are propagated from ripened shoots placed in the soil in the fall. They usually root readily.

409. Varieties. Among the best red varieties are Cherry, Wilder, Pomona, and Fay's Prolific. A good white is Bar-le-Duc. Champion and Boskoop Giant are excellent black varieties.

Chapter XLVIII

DEWBERRIES

Two lovely berries moulded on one stem.
        —SHAKESPEARE.

CHAPTER XLVIII

DEWBERRIES

410. Habit of Growth. Dewberries are ground trailers in their natural habit of growth, making long cane growth. In cultivation, they are tied to supports, like raspberries or blackberries, to facilitate cultivation, pruning, and picking.

411. How to Place Supports. Tie the canes to wires, placed as recommended in Sec. 489.

412. When to Plant. Plant either spring or fall, with the preference upon spring planting. See Sec. 387.

413. How to Plant. Set the plants five to six feet apart, the rows seven to eight feet apart. As in the case of blackberries, 18 plants will be sufficient per 100 feet of row.

414. When to Prune; Thinning. Old canes are removed entirely immediately after fruiting. The fruit next year will be borne on this year's young shoots. Thin out the young shoots to prevent overcrowding and to improve quality of fruit. Tie to their supports as they grow, and tip back when they have reached sufficient height.

415. Culture. Dewberries require the same culture as raspberries. See Chapter LVI. While the berries resemble blackberries, they are much superior to them. Lucretia is the old favorite, and the best variety for the home garden.

Chapter XLIX

GOOSEBERRIES

Pick your bush clean before seeking another one.
—Pennsylvania Dutch proverb.

GOOSEBERRIES

416. When to Plant. For the home garden, the best time to plant gooseberries is in the spring. In milder regions, something may be said for fall planting; but for the usual gardening areas, spring planting is best.

417. How to Plant. Twenty-five bushes per 100 feet of row is sufficient. The bushes, therefore, should be four feet apart in the row, and the rows should be six feet apart. So far as the setting of the bushes is concerned, follow the directions in Sec. 382 or elsewhere. Any bush or tree must be planted so that there are no air pockets between roots and soil. The best way to settle the soil around all the tiny rootlets is to use copious applications of water.

418. How to Prune Gooseberries. Gooseberries, unlike the cane-bearing fruits, must not be severely pruned. By this is meant that fruit-bearing branches should not be pruned out as soon as fruiting is over. Gooseberries are borne on two-year-old or older canes or branches. Pruning, therefore, should be (1) to remove all branches that rest on the ground, and (2) to thin out the remaining branches so that better fruit-bearing is possible. In the case of gooseberries, remember that a sparing use of the pruning shears is the rule rather than the exception. Of course, all old wood and all dead wood should be removed; by old wood, I mean that which has ceased to bear fruit.

419. Diseases and Pests. For a complete list of diseases and pests, see Farmers' Bulletin No. 1398. For the more specific diseases, see Sec. 407. The farmers' bulletin mentioned may be obtained from the United States Department of Agriculture by writing to your Congressman.

420. How to Propagate. Gooseberries are propagated, as a rule, from cuttings. They will root naturally, if the tips are allowed to touch the soil; this is known as "layering." However, plants can be obtained from nurserymen for such low cost that it is seldom economy to propagate at home.

421. Varieties. Downing is the old favorite, the most widely grown variety in the United States, and, all things considered, the best American variety for the home garden. Industry and Red Jacket are two other good varieties.

Chapter L

GRAPES

One bunch of grapes is ripened by another bunch.

—Suidas.

GRAPES

422. Where to Plant. Grapes do best in a rich, well drained soil. They may be used for a number of purposes —for shade, for decoration, for fruit. Success for each of these purposes demands a fairly rich soil in which fertility is constant. It is a good precaution to use liberal amounts of bonemeal and well rotted manure in the bottom of each hole when planting.

423. When to Plant. Spring is the best time to set out grapevines in the North.

424. How to Plant. Grapes are prolific growers and must have plenty of room. Sixteen plants per 100 feet of row are sufficient. They should not be closer together than eight feet apart in the row, and the rows should be from eight to ten feet apart.

425. How to Prune Grapes; Training to Trellis. Grapes may be trained to any one of several systems. The Munson system is probably the best. Many writers make great mystery over grape training. To train to any system, one thing should ever be borne in mind: A strong central stem must be trained or grown up to the two principal supports. All shoots having a tendency to spring up from the crown must be ruthlessly cut out.

The Munson system is simply the training of a strong center stem and the growing of two strong lateral branches on each of two wires or supports, one above the other. Prune back these lateral branches severely. It is from the old stems that the fruit-bearing canes will grow.

The whole point about training a grapevine is to prune

back in order to thicken and strengthen the center stem. This often requires heroic treatment, pruning back again and again until strong, sturdy stems and branches are produced. The old adage that it takes five years to produce a grapevine is not at all exaggerated.

426. Fertilizers and Plant Foods. Use plenty of fertilizer in planting, and keep up annual applications of well rotted stable manures. Commercial plant foods should be applied according to the manufacturer's directions.

427. Diseases and Pests. Black rot causes green fruit to turn black and dry up. It is a more or less common disease in all parts of the country. The best preventives are spraying with Bordeaux mixture, and dusting with copper lime dust. The first application is made when the third leaf appears on a stem, the second just before the blossoms open; and two or three more applications are made later in the season.

Powdery mildew is the principal other disease. The foliage has a powdery appearance and drops prematurely. Keep the plants covered with sulphur dust, particularly during wet or damp weather.

Insects are divided into two principal classes: those that eat the foliage and those that suck the sap. The time-honored control for the former is arsenate of lead, and for the latter, the nicotine sulphate sprays like Black Leaf 40.

Japanese beetles require a "coated lead arsenate"—one that sticks to the foliage—in order to prevent defoliation.

The grape berry moth is controlled by spraying the fruit just as the fruit sets, and with two successive sprays ten days apart, as the larvae feed upon the berry itself.

428. Types of Trellises. Where fruit is the primary purpose, the amount of vine that is permitted must be carefully restricted in order to conserve all possible strength for fruit development. This means that the supports or

A young Delicious apple at the start of the second season. Raspberries at left.

A dooryard lettuce and radish plot which paid handsome dividends.

In spraying, reach every portion of the branches and foliage.

Apple trees trained in this fashion do not require much room.

trellises have to be low. Many people make the mistake of planning elaborate arbors and supports which require so much vine or cane development that quality fruit production is impossible. Where these large arbors are desired primarily for ornamental usage, the wild grape is as good as any.

Trellises may take almost any form the individual gardener desires. They may completely cover a garden walk; they may be in the form of sidewall trellises alongside a building; they may be trained against high lattice fences for screens, and they may even be trained over a summer-house.

429. Culture. Grapes in the home garden should be cultivated, at least until they are established. This means at least two seasons, and often more. Mulching is practiced in some sections, in order to conserve moisture and keep down the weeds. I prefer marsh hay as the mulching material. It is free of weed seeds, clean, and easy to handle. The mulch must be thick enough to discourage weed growth and must be renewed each year.

Grapes will respond to cultivation and fertilization twice a year. Unless the garden is so large that this is not convenient, it will repay one to follow the practice.

430. Varieties. The Concord is an old, old favorite. Moore's Early is another—a Concord-type grape that comes on earlier by two weeks at least. Worden is another good one of these so-called black types. Among the red types I prefer Catawba, Delaware, and Brighton. Dutchess, Empire, and Diamond are good white grapes for the home garden.

Chapter LI

LOGANBERRIES

> *Perfection walks slowly; she requires the hand of time.*
> —VOLTAIRE.

Chapter LI

LOGANBERRIES

431. Value of Loganberries. Loganberires were developed by a Californian, Judge Logan. They are widely grown in several sections of the country and are popular in England. They owe their popularity to the fact that they are more pleasing to the eye than their taste justifies. The berries are large, uniform, and attractive, but they are flat to the average taste. They can well, and the color is also attractive. A few plants may be grown in the average garden, if space is available.

432. Where to Plant. Loganberries may be planted along the fence, or trailed to stakes or supports along the walks or paths, or a section of the home fruit garden may be set aside for them.

433. How to Plant. Plants are set eight feet apart in the row, and the rows are six to eight feet apart. They may be planted either in the fall or in the spring.

434. Culture. The culture is similar to that for raspberries. See Chapter LVI.

CHAPTER LII

PEACHES

The ripest Peach is high on the tree.
—RILEY.

Chapter LII

PEACHES

435. Soil Requirements. Peaches do best in a light, medium soil where the drainage is good. They come into maturity and fruit-bearing much quicker than most orchard fruits, and usually are shorter-lived. See Sec. 538.

436. When to Plant. In the North, trees are usually planted in the spring. In warmer climates, fall planting is perhaps best.

437. How to Plant. In commercial practice, peach trees are planted twenty feet apart each way, in order to admit of complete cultivation, good circulation of air, and plenty of feeding area for the roots. The home garden may not be able to spare this much room, but they will not suceed if overcrowded.

Never plant a peach tree more than one year old. Select strong, sturdy stock. See Sec. 540.

438. Where Peaches Will Succeed. Peaches are a warm-climate fruit and will not succeed in our more severe northern winters. If the temperature in your locality gets down to 10 degrees below zero in the winter, the fruit buds will be killed, and no fruit can be expected.

Trees should preferably be planted on a northern slope in order to retard as much as possible early growth in spring. If warm exposures induce growth and heavy frosts subsequently occur, the crop will again be lost. Peaches, furthermore, must be protected from high, drying winds and should have a sheltered location.

439. Northern Varieties. There are literally dozens of peach varieties, not all of which are on the market. The old, safe rule to follow is to select those varieties which experience has demonstrated to be successful in your neighborhood. Your nurseryman will be glad to give you the benefit of his experience. Hale's Early, Champion, and Elberta are all good varieties that have succeeded in widely separated portions of the country. All are freestone types, the only sort that should be planted in the home garden.

440. Pruning. Peach trees require drastic pruning right from the start, in order to head them low and induce the formation of sturdy fruit-bearing wood. Cut the stem back to six inches above the ground. Prune back the roots before planting. All fine side branches should be removed.

Several sprouts will spring up from this stem. Retain not fewer than three or more than six, and cut them back two-thirds of their growth. The second and third years, treat the side branches that develop from these prunings in the same manner. The point is that a low-headed, sturdy tree is to be encouraged. As soon as this has been accomplished, the chief pruning necessary is to cut out branches that cross each other in order to keep the head open. The peach bears its fruit on the wood of the previous season's growth, and some of this wood must always be retained; therefore, *some* pruning will be necessary every year. It is best not to permit the trees to bear before the fourth year.

441. Dwarf Types; Where to Plant. Dwarf trees of standard varieties may be obtained from many dealers, and are especially valuable in the small home garden. Standard trees may be trained, however, against a wall or fence under the cordon and espalier systems of training. In a sheltered location they will be more likely to produce a crop season after season.

Dwarf trees should be planted where other trees would be planted, the only difference being that they can be set much

A dozen strawberry plants produced several fine breakfasts for this city gardener.

A small fruit corner in a Pennsylvania home garden. Temporary grape arbor at right.

Summer-pruning a young apple tree.

Grapes cut short do not require supports. Taken at the home of John Muir in California.

closer together—sometimes as close as eight feet apart each way.

442. Pests and Their Control. The plum curculio is usually the worst pest of the peach or similar fruiting trees. It is a native insect, the adult beetle of which lives over the winter in any crevice or protection it can find. The old-time method of control is to spread sheets on the ground under the trees and shake these fellows off about the time the fruit blossom petals fall. Dump the beetles in a can of oil, or burn. Repeated efforts of this sort will destroy most of them, and this is perhaps the simplest control for the small gardener who has only a few trees to worry about. However, applications of lead arsenate made at the same time will generally catch them, the first application to be made when the leaves first begin to develop.

Another serious pest in some localities is San Jose scale, a minute insect that burrows in the bark of branches and trunk, under a scalelike protection. Repeated sprayings with lime sulphur or some of the oil sprays especially prepared by manufacturers are recommended. These applications are usually most effective in the dormant stages.

Other insects readily divide themselves into the sucking types and the chewing types. As noted in other chapters, the control for the former is nicotine sulphate or Black Leaf 40, and for the latter, lead arsenate.

Leaf curl is one of the most serious of the peach diseases. It causes the young leaves to curl and fall prematurely. It is controlled by spraying with lime sulphur before the buds begin to swell in spring.

Brown rot is identical with the disease of the same name that affects cherries. See Sec. 398.

443. Best Varieties. In addition to the varieties mentioned in Sec. 439, the following are generally grown: Crawford, Alton, Fitzgerald, Heath Cling, and Niagara.

CHAPTER LIII

PEARS

> *Indeed, what is there that does not appear marvelous when it comes to our attention for the first time?*
>
> —PLINY THE ELDER.

Chapter LIII

PEARS

444. Soil Requirements. Pears demand a heavy soil,
because they do not succeed unless wood is freely developed.
They bloom early and therefore must have a sheltered position such as would be afforded by a windbreak, a group of
buildings, or a north slope, to retard blooming until settled
weather is more likely.

445. Type of Stock to Buy. Buy grafted stock from
your nurseryman. It will save time and is cheaper than any
other.

446. When to Plant. Plant either spring or fall, whichever succeeds best in your locality.

447. How to Plant. Because of their natural upright
habit of growth, pears can be planted closer together than
most orchard fruits. They come into bearing earlier than
apples and are often planted between the rows of apple
trees. When the apples mature and begin to bear, the
pears must be cut out. In the home garden, where closer
attention and pruning is possible and will be practiced,
they may be planted as close as twelve to fourteen feet
apart.

448. Culture. Pears should be well cultivated, and the
soil kept well supplied with fertilizers—especially where the
space is restricted. They require more pruning than apples
because of the normally heavy formation of wood and their
habit of growing tall and upright. Prune back to encourage
an open head and low-growing habit. Keep the head open.
Pears normally form a great many fruit spurs, and this
must be noted in pruning. Dwarf types may be grown,

255

too, or the standard sorts trained in pyramids and espaliers.

449. Pests and Their Control. Fungous diseases, chiefly
rust, are the worst pests. Spraying with lime sulphur, the
first application to be made just after the blossoms fall, followed by three more applications at intervals of three weeks,
will generally keep these in control and permit the formation of attractive fruit. The same treatment will generally
control scab, a fungous disease similar to that found in
apples, although some people prefer to dust with copper
lime.

Among the insects, San Jose scale is serious in many sections. See Sec. 442.

The fall webworm hides in nests on terminal branches and
feeds on the leaves. Burn the nests with torches and spray
the foliage with lead arsenate.

Pear thrips are very minute insects that feed on the small
fruits. Spray with nicotine sulphate just as buds open and
again after the petals fall.

Aphids, or plant lice, are controlled with nicotine sulphate, and the leaf eaters with lead arsenate.

450. Best Varieties. Kieffer and Bartlett are, of course,
the old standard favorites. The latter ripens in September,
while the former is seldom ready before October and November. Among other varieties are Sheldon, Seckel, and
Clapp's Favorite. Seckel is a small pear of excellent flavor
and is preferred by many home canners.

Chapter LIV

PLUMS

Plums abound everywhere in the thickets and the cultivated ones are prized by every householder. Thus all, even the savages, know its tempting qualities.

—Letter of early traveler (1741).

PLUMS

451. Types to Select. Japanese varieties are widely grown in many sections, but they do not reach their greatest perfection in the Middle West or South. In those regions, native varieties grafted on wild plum stock do the best. Japanese plums are too often grafted on peach roots, and this makes them heir to the short-lived tendencies of this fruit.

452. Soil Requirements. Plums will succeed in almost any soil reasonably rich and well drained. In habit of growth they differ from apples and pears in that the roots grow closer to the surface.

453. When to Plant. Early fall planting is best. Since plums have a wide-growing root habit, a large hole must be dug and well prepared, and the roots spread out naturally.

454. How to Plant. Plums normally are planted twenty feet apart each way, although the dwarf types may be planted closer together. Select a sheltered location in order to retard growth in spring until danger of frost is past, as plums are the first fruit to bloom.

455. Pruning. Plums require very little pruning, especially the Japanese sorts. Pruning should largely be confined to maintaining the shape of the tree. Japanese sorts make a strong growth the first year, and the temptation is to thin them out. Do *not* "obey that impulse," because fruit spurs will thickly set along these strong growths and tend to equalize things.

Unlike many fruits, several varieties of plums (particularly the Japanese) set fruit so thickly that the fruit must be thinned out to prevent rotting in the clusters.

Where they insist on making a strong, rank growth, the best method of control is root pruning. Small trees may be lifted, and the strongest-growing roots pruned back.

456. Culture. To all intents and purposes, the culture of plums is like that recommended for cherries. Cultivation is very beneficial, reasonable fertility must be maintained, especially on light soils.

457. Pests and Their Control. Aphids are a common pest on plums. Spray with nicotine sulphur or Black Leaf 40 whenever they appear.

Plum curculio is the most serious pest. Follow directions in Sec. 442. In addition, gather all fruits that may be infected and burn them, in order to trap the larvae before they emerge as adult beetles and go into hiding.

458. Best Varieties. There are literally thousands of varieties of plums grown in the country today. Many of these are identical, because of the old practice of nurserymen giving their own names to a general variety. For instance, Burbank's Golden is the same plum as Stark's Gold.

The best varieties for table use are the gages, so far as country-wide planting is concerned. These are: Greengage, Transparent Gage and Cullin's Golden Gage. Victoria is another good one for the table.

The best for cooking and canning are Burbank and Abundance.

Chapter LV

QUINCES

All our wants, beyond those which a very moderate income will supply, are purely imaginary.

—Henry St. George (1719).

Chapter LV

QUINCES

459. Uses of Quinces. Quinces are not edible as a raw fruit, but are highly prized for canning and the making of jellies. No other fruit has its flavor. A bush or two will be sufficient to supply the average family.

460. Tree or Bush Types? Quinces do best in the home garden when grown in bush form.

461. When to Plant. They may be planted either spring or fall, according to the locality. Most gardeners start in the spring, however.

462. How to Plant. Since quinces eventually attain considerable size when grown in bush form, resembling a fully matured common lilac, they should be allowed plenty of room. They require no special location or soil.

463. Varieties. The two commonly grown varieties are Champion and Orange.

CHAPTER LVI

RASPBERRIES

I come to pluck your berries. . . .
— MILTON.

CHAPTER LVI

RASPBERRIES

464. Soil Requirements. While raspberries are not particular as to the soil, they undoubtedly do best in a rich, well worked garden soil where drainage is good. In preparing soil for a raspberry bed, work in plenty of humus which may be supplied through liberal applications of animal manures, decayed straw, leaves, or compost. Have the soil in the best possible condition before planting.

465. When to Plant. Fewer losses will be incurred if the planting is made in the spring, in most localities.

466. How to Plant. Plants are propagated from root divisions or cuttings taken from young shoots that have been rooted in the fall. Red varieties will not propagate from new canes taking root where they touch the ground; they are propagated like blackberries.

Raspberries are set two feet apart in the row, and the rows should be at least four feet apart.

467. Best Types of Supports. For the home garden, the best type of support is a double strand of wire supported by cross-arms attached to ordinary fence posts placed eight to ten feet apart in the row. At least two strands of wire on each side should be used, and three are better. Do not allow the canes to grow more than five and one-half feet high, as a rule.

468. Field Culture. In field culture, in order to make them stocky and capable of self-support, raspberries are usually allowed to grow only about three feet in height. Rows are placed farther apart in order to admit of easy horse or machine cultivation and spraying. In other respects, it is similar to the best home garden culture.

469. Summer Pruning. When the new shoots have reached the desired height, pinch off the tips or cut them off with a hand sickle. This will encourage the growth of lateral branches upon which the fruit will be formed. These, in turn, may be tipped back if they have a tendency to make too long a growth, although such pruning is usually deferred until the following spring before growth starts.

After fruiting is past, all old canes should immediately be cut back to the ground in order to give the new tender shoots a better chance. They will not bear fruit again; next year's fruit will be borne on the new tender canes of this year's growth.

470. Cultivation; Mulches. In the large plantation, or in field culture, cultivation should be constantly practiced not only to keep down the weeds and suckers, but to conserve all the moisture content of the soil that is possible. Keep the plantation in good tilth at all times, and you will be greatly repaid when fruiting season comes again.

In the small home garden planting, mulching probably will be most satisfactory, at least from early spring until the canes have ceased to fruit. The mulch will assist in retaining moisture. Remember that an enormous quantity of moisture is essential for a good fruit production. Marsh hay is preferred for mulching material, and it should be put on thick enough to keep down the weeds—at least twelve inches deep.

471. Controlling Suckers. Established raspberry plants will sucker in all directions the roots penetrate, and unless the suckers are ruthlessly cut out on sight they will soon turn your neat raspberry bed into a hopeless bramble patch. They are readily identified as they spring up from the roots. As soon as they appear through the mulch, chop them out,

Beans growing on poles along the garden path.

Onions drying after digging, before being sacked for
storage.

Pole beans trained to supports.

Navy beans as grown on a suburban lot.

going deep enough to cut the root. Constant cultivation will tend to keep them in check, if deep enough.

472. Propagation. Red varieties are propagated by root division, or the digging up of well rooted suckers and transplanting them. Black varieties will readily self-propagate if the tips are allowed to touch ground and root. As soon as roots have formed, cut the old cane and transplant the new rooted growth.

473. Types and Varieties. As already indicated there are two commonly grown raspberries, the red and the black. In recent years, however, a yellow raspberry has been listed by many nurserymen. They may also be divided as to habit of fruiting—the main crop sorts, either red or black, and the so-called ever-bearing sorts, which produce a second crop in the fall.

The most commonly grown varieties are Cuthbert (red) and Cumberland (black). Other good ones are Latham (red), Brandywine (red), St. Regis (red), and Golden Queen (amber).

Chapter LVII

STRAWBERRIES

> . . . *the forest abounding in game, the streams bursting with fish, the prairies covered with tall grass concealing the wild strawberries!*
>
> Israel Putnam.

STRAWBERRIES

474. Soil Requirements. Since strawberries are heavy feeders, they require a rich soil abounding in humus and plant food. It must be capable of retaining a high moisture content, but, contrary to general opinion, should not be shaded. Open exposure to sunlight is essential.

475. Preparation of Beds. Thorough and painstaking preparation of the strawberry bed will repay the work entailed. Remember that it must support the plants and their myriad of offspring for three years; the more manure and fertilizer that can be incorporated into the soil in the very beginning, the better the crops that will be harvested. Spread your manures on the surface of the soil—they should be well rotted—and spade under. If manure is not obtainable, compost, leafmold, or straw may be used. Hard clay soils must be broken up with this addition of humus to encourage moisture retention, so important at fruit-bearing time and in the production of strong new plants.

476. When to Plant. The best time to start a new strawberry bed is in August or September, as soon as the young plants can be obtained. For small garden planting, potted plants are to be preferred. If you already have a strawberry bed, you can select strong runner plants and transplant them whenever they are ready. Plants started at this time will, in a normal year, save an entire year in reaching full fruiting capacity.

477. How to Plant; Different Systems. Strawberries may be planted in hills, in the single row system, or in the double row system. When planted in hills, only one plant is allowed in the rows, runners being constantly cut off. The single row system permits runner plants to form between the original plants set out. The double row system is similar except that two rows of plants are set out originally and runner plants permitted to form between them, all runners branching out to the sides of the row being cut off.

There are variations of these systems, of course, and each has its uses. For the hobby rider, the hill system is good; the single row system is the least trouble in restricted areas, and the double row system is preferred for field culture.

In the home garden, strawberry plants are set one foot apart in the row, and the rows are three feet apart. If double rows are to be planted, stagger the plants so that the double rows are one foot apart, and allow four to six feet between the double rows—whatever is a convenient width for easy cultivation.

478. Culture. After the first frost the plants should be protected with a light covering of straw or hay. Its principal purposes are protection from the winter sun, which is far more injurious than the freezing, and reduction to a minimum of losses from "heaving"—that is, alternate freezing and thawing which heaves the plants out of the soil, exposes the roots to the air, and results in the death of the plant.

Do not remove the covering until danger of killing frosts is past in spring. All plants that show evidence of "heaving" should be immediately pressed firmly back into the soil.

Give a good cultivation as soon as possible to catch all weeds developing, taking care not to injure the feeding roots of the berries. Then give a liberal application of commercial plant food in accordance with the manufacturer's directions. Some bonemeal will also be beneficial.

The plants should then be mulched carefully with clean straw or marsh hay, and the area between the rows also

An apple tree in the first season.

This half-acre of raspberries earned a high-school boy his education.

Pear trees grow upright.

String beans and corn in a family garden.

covered with it. This will conserve the moisture in the soil, keep the fruit clean, and tend to make it easy to identify and control runner plants.

With the exception of ever-bearing sorts, strawberry plants should not be allowed to bear fruit the first year. Pinch off all blossom stems that form, in order to encourage a good root development for the heavy duty ahead the next two seasons.

479. Supplementary Feeding of Plant Foods. I have pointed out that the strawberry is a rank feeder. It must, therefore, have an abundance of plant food available at all times. In properly prepared beds, the humus necessary has already been supplied before planting. After the bed has been established, the simplest and easiest way in which to continue to furnish plant food is through the application of commercial fertilizers and plant foods.

Barnyard manure may be applied between the rows during the winter and turned under at the first spring cultivation. Poultry manure, if available, is also good. It should be applied at the rate of one pound per square yard of surface. Commercial plant foods are applied at the times and in the amounts recommended by their manufacturers.

480. Cultivation _vs_. Mulches. In the home garden mulching is to be preferred; but it must be remembered that at least one thorough cultivation should be given in the spring after removing the winter covering and before applying the mulch. In large field plantings mulching is, of course, too expensive in labor. Cultivation constantly throughout the season will be necessary.

481. Controlling Runners. Runners are new plants that appear on long thin stems from the main plants. They will readily take root, if they come in contact with the soil. Unless the formation of these runner plants is discouraged, the strength of the parent plant will go into them instead of into the production of quality fruit. They must be constantly snipped off with scissors or a sharp pocketknife. Where new plants for the development of a new bed are desired, the strongest of these runners may be permitted to root and develop, later to be transplanted to their new location.

482. Propagation. This question has already been partly answered in Sec. 481. Where sturdy plants are to be developed, allow the runners to root in small pots of good soil. They can then be cut loose from the parent plant, to develop on their own until they are ready to be transplanted.

483. Renewing Beds. It is not profitable to maintain a strawberry bed more than three years. The first year is given over to the development of sturdy plants, and fruit-bearing is discouraged. This means that two years of heavy fruit-bearing remains. After that, even though the plants may appear to be strong, the fertility of the soil will be so thoroughly exhausted that a poor crop is almost certain to result. Dig up the old bed and set about restoring plant food to it. While this is being done, a good crop to grow on the spot is muskmelons.

In the meantime, a new strawberry bed should be ready to come into full bearing. This means that runner or new plants have been set out a year in advance.

484. Best Varieties. There are literally hundreds of strawberries available for the gardener, of which only the better ones are listed by nurserymen or specialists. Consult your local growers or neighboring nurseryman.

Progressive remains the most widely grown ever-bearing sort. The "ever-bearing" tag is a misnomer in that it is chiefly an autumn fruiting variety and must not be allowed to fruit all during the season if a crop is to be realized. The fruits are small but tasty. Americus is another strawberry of this type.

Senator Dunlap is an old, old favorite of the main-crop sort. When at its best, it is hard to beat. Brandywine is a good late variety. Mastodon is a widely heralded sort of huge proportions.

APPENDIX

APPENDIX

485. How to Spade the Garden; Trenching. Dr. W. A.
Orton, writing an article in 1924 at my instance for *Better
Homes & Gardens,* declared that few gardeners knew the proper
art of spading the garden, and described the English method of
"trenching" as being proper. I can testify, after having seen
Dr. Orton's vegetable garden, that it certainly produced results.
I quote Dr. Orton's method:

"How, then, should you spade a garden? Provide yourself with
a strong fine-tined spading fork, a short-handled, sharp spade, and
a steel garden rake. Begin at one side of the garden and mark off
across it a strip six feet or more in width. At right angles sub-
divide this, in your mind at least, into 'spits' twenty inches wide.
Begin by removing the soil from the first spit to a full spade's
depth, casting the dirt into near-by depressions if any exist, or in
more perfect technique wheeling it to the end of the garden where
the work is to be finished.

"Break up and loosen the subsoil in the bottom of this trench
without removing it. Fill it then with any waste vegetation
available—sods, cornstalks, leaves, or strawy manure—clearing in
this way the surface of the next spit or twenty-inch strip. Dig
back thus far, turning the earth over and forward to cover the
rubbish you have just trodden down, creating in this way another
trench to be filled in turn with garden débris and covered with six
inches of soil.

"So one goes across the garden, until the last trench at the
edge is filled with the first spit of another strip of equal width and
adjoining the first. Having thus reversed your direction, work
back to the starting point, and so on until the garden is done."

486. Herbs. There should be a spot in every home garden
for herbs, so prized by our grandmothers in the days when flavors

and condiments were not so easily obtained in bottles and cans. A small bed will supply the average family with all the herbs necessary to add *spice* and interest to the garden.

Most herbs may readily be grown from seed, or from plants purchased from the seedsman or nurseryman. Practically all of them require winter protection in the form of a covering of clean straw or marsh hay, at least until thoroughly established. The annual sorts will have to be replanted, of course, each year, and these should be moved to different ground.

Among the herbs you may want to grow are: anise (annual), for garnishing and flavoring; balm (annual), for balm tea and wine; sweet basil (annual), for flavoring; burnet (perennial), for salads and soups; caraway (annual), seed used in pastry, bread, and flavoring; chives (annual), for flavoring sausages and salads; dill (annual), for flavoring vinegar; fennel (perennial), seeds for flavoring, boiled leaves in sauces; horehound (perennial), for colds and dyspepsia; mint (perennial), for flavoring; peppermint (perennial), for intestinal disorders; mustard (annual), for salads; parsley (annual), for flavoring and garnishing; pennyroyal (annual), for stimulant and also to keep away mosquitoes; rosemary (perennial), tea used as headache remedy; sage (perennial), for seasoning meats, poultry, and tea as a tonic; savory (annual), for flavoring; tansy (perennial), for bitters; thyme (perennial), for seasoning, and wormwood (perennial), used medicinally as bitters.

487. Home Storage Methods. Unless adequate storage facilities are provided to carry the surplus of the crop through the winter, there is little point in gardening. Of course, the thrifty housewife will can and preserve and even dry many vegetables and fruits, but there is still a need for storage facilities for root crops and the like.

The main considerations to bear in mind for a storage place are that the vegetables and fruit must be protected from freezing, there must be adequate ventilation to prevent rapid destruction from fungus diseases, and sufficient humidity to keep the things stored in good condition. A storage place too wet will promote rapid losses; a place too dry will likewise seriously impair the quality of the vegetables and fruits by causing them to shrivel. Frost is, of course, fatal.

Where large quantities are to be stored it will pay the gardener to build an outside storage shed or cave. Information on how to build these may be obtained from the United States Department of Agriculture at Washington, D. C., or from your state agricultural college.

Small quantities of vegetables may be stored in outdoor pits. These take various forms, some merely being barrels that are filled with potatoes, carrots, turnips, cabbage, and the like, and covered with straw and dirt. Celery may be stored outdoors by standing the heads close together inside twelve-inch board frames. The tops are covered with cornstalks, straw, or hay to a sufficient depth to prevent freezing.

In storing root crops like cabbage, pull up the entire plant and store roots down in dirt. Poles are set around them to support boards over the tops, projecting about two feet above the surface, the whole then being covered with an adequate mound of dirt.

The most satisfactory method of storage for the small home garden is to provide a storage room in the home cellar, as described in Sec. 488, below.

488. How to Convert a Cellar into a Storage Place. The method herein described is one that I used for several years with gratifying success. It can be followed by any householder, and it solves the problem of how to store fruit and vegetables successfully in the average modern warm basement. The expense need be only that for materials, as the average man is handy enough with saw and hammer to do the work himself.

In a corner of the basement, build double walls of ship-lap, or tongue-and-grooved lumber, insulated with double thicknesses of building paper. The dead air space thus created will keep out furnace heat. Provide for a door, which should also be double-walled. The corner selected for this storage room must have at least one outside window, and two would be better.

Bins are built at convenient height around the inside walls. These should not be too large or deep, in order to insure constant ventilation around the stuff stored. The bins are made of slatted stock spaced half an inch apart, and preferably should not be over eighteen inches deep and two feet wide.

Humidity is maintained, especially on cement floors, by spreading two inches of sand over the floor. This sand is kept moist, not wet, by sprinkling water over it whenever necessary. On the other hand do not allow the sand to become dry, or it will absorb the moisture of the vegetables stored in the room, causing them to shrivel.

Ventilation is provided by removing one of the small window panes. In its place insert a piece of galvanized iron in the center of which has been cut a round hole identical in size with a piece of joined galvanized pipe which is soldered to it. This pipe is about two inches in diameter and extends downward along the wall within six inches of the floor. At the lower edge a damper is placed to regulate the flow of cold air into the room. Cold air seeks the lowest level and therefore will come down the pipe to the floor.

Warm air, on the other hand, rises and leaves the room through a fine wire mesh inserted either in a top pane or at the top of the same galvanized iron section to which the pipe is soldered.

This sort of ventilator can be made by any neighboring tinsmith and at low cost. It provides perfect ventilation, needing only to have the damper regulated when the weather changes suddenly. In my own case, the only trouble I had was when the thermometer unexpectedly went down to 22 degrees below zero one night and I had failed to close the damper tightly. Some of the potatoes in a low bin were frosted.

Fruit, root crops, and canned fruit may be stored in this room. Pumpkins, sweet potatoes and squash must not be kept here. Just lay them on a shelf near the furnace.

489. General Fertilizer Chart

Vegetables	Fruit	Fertilizer	Quantity per Sq. Yd.	When
All	All	Manure	12 pounds	Before plowing
All	All	Poultry manure	1 pound	After plowing
All	All	Commercial plant foods	Mfr.'s directions	Before planting

490. Home Pruning Chart

What	How	When
Apple	Prune annually. Keep head low and open by cutting back and removing branches that cross. Remove dead branches.	February or early March
Blackberries	Remove old canes after fruiting. Tip young canes when they reach top of supports or to 5 feet. In spring cut back lateral branches one-half or more of growth.	July and March
Cherry, Sour	Remove only dead branches, crossed branches.	February or early March
Cherry, Sweet	Prune merely to head low.	February or early March
Currents	Remove a few of oldest canes each year, retaining a few as they fruit about three times.	February or early March
Gooseberries	Remove only the oldest canes each year. Branches may be tipped slightly to encourage more fruit buds to form.	Midsummer
Grapes	See Sec. 525.	
Peach	Never head back as fruit is borne on previous year's growth. Tip back only injured branches.	February or early March
Pear	Keep heads as low and open as possible. Remove water sprouts.	February or early March
Plum	Remove only dead branches.	February or early March
Quinces	Tip back branches and head low.	February or March
Raspberries, Black	Remove old canes after fruiting and pinch back tips of young canes when at top of supports.	After fruiting
Raspberries, Red	Remove old canes after fruiting and tip back young growth following spring.	July and March

491. HOME SPRAYING CHART

What	What for	When	What and How to Use
Apple and Pear	San Jose scale	Dormant, as buds swell	2 qts. lime sulphur to 5 gals. water. Cover thoroughly
	Scab, curculio, green fruit worm, cankerworms	When fruit buds have spread apart	Bordeaux and lead arsenate combination spray
	Codling moth and above	When petals drop	1 pt. lime sulphur, 1½ ozs. lead arsenate, 5 gals. water
	Codling moth and scab	Two weeks after above	1 pt. Bordeaux, 1½ ozs. lead arsenate, 5 gals. water
	Second brood codling moth, scab, fungous diseases	Late July	Same as above
	Aphids (plant lice)	At once	1 teaspoonful 40% nicotine sulphate to 1 gal. water, or regular spraying material
Cherry	San Jose scale	Same as for apples	Same as for apples
	Rot, leaf spot, curculio	1. Before blossoms open; 2. after petals fall; 3. 10 days later	1 pt. lime sulphur, 2½ ozs. lead arsenate, 5 gals. water
Grapes	Black rot, mildews, curculio, rose chafers	When leaves are one-third grown; 2. before blossoms open; 3. just after fruit sets; 4. 15 days later; 5. 15 days later	Bordeaux and lead arsenate, according to manufacturer's directions for combining, or Pyrox
Currants and Gooseberries	Mildews and worms	As leaves appear and at 2-week intervals	1 qt. lime sulphur, 2½ ozs. lead arsenate, 5 gals water
Peach	Leaf curl and brown rot	Before buds open	2 qts. lime sulphur, 5 gals. water.
	Curculio	Just after blooming, and 2 weeks later	1½ ozs. lead arsenate, 1½ ozs. lime, 5 gals. water
Plum	Curculio, brown rot	Before blossoms open	1 qt. lime sulphur, 2½ ozs. lead arsenate, 5 gals. water
	Above	After blossoms fall, again 2 weeks later, again mid-June	1 pt. lime sulphur, 1½ oz. lead arsenate, 5 gals. water

'Each story's hook is keenly sharpened, pulling you into the center of a tortured psyche... Revelations come through a steady drip of plot tinged with unease, with each story wholly delivered and wholly strange.'

The Stake

'A rare book — it's political without drowning in politics, it's innovative without languishing in theatrics, and it also blends the historically accurate with the personal. It's part satire, part social commentary, and 100% a good story with rich, compelling characters.'

Kirkus

'Cárdenas brilliantly transforms his "book of ideas" into an unraveling interrogation into Antonio's past, employing unorthodox paragraph structures that slip seamlessly between long passages of fast-paced stream-of-consciousness, unexpected song lyrics, and sudden dialogue.'

Booklist

'Cárdenas is conjuring a modish and streamlined maximalism that soaks postmodernism and hyperrealism in multicultural and social media colloquialism. *The Revolutionaries Try Again* could be spun as the *The Recognitions* of our age, with Otto reborn as Antonio. In any case, it's revolutionary.'

Culture Trip

'Like its cast of characters, the novel is colorful and disarming, bristling with idealism and disillusionment and profoundly embattled intelligence; like the country it brings to life without ever fully inhabiting, it's noisy and claustrophobic and a dizzying thrill to get lost in.'

Electric Literature

'What begins as an Ecuadorian political farce in Mauro Javier Cárdenas's *The Revolutionaries Try Again* quickly becomes the most exciting experimental novel in years — a vision so uncompromising in form and sensation that readers will leave sighing, swearing, and returning to page one.'

Tony Tulathimutte, author of *Private Citizens*

MAURO JAVIER CÁRDENAS

ONEWORLD

A Oneworld Book

First published in Great Britain, the Republic of Ireland and Australia
by Oneworld Publications, 2021

Copyright © Mauro Javier Cárdenas, 2020

The moral right of Mauro Javier Cárdenas to be identified as the
Author of this work has been asserted by him in accordance with
the Copyright, Designs and Patents Act 1988

ISBN 978-0-86154-009-9
ISBN 978-0-86154-010-5 (eBook)

Printed and bound in Great Britain by Clays Ltd, Elcograf S.p.A

Oneworld Publications
10 Bloomsbury Street
London WC1B 3SR
England

MIX
Paper from
responsible sources
FSC
www.fsc.org   FSC® C018072

CONTENTS

S 8

WHEN ANTONIO WAS ARTURO

Once again his daughters and his former wife packed their lives and left him to summer in Czechia with Babička and Děda, and unlike the previous seven summers, Antonio wasn't anxious for them to leave already so he could sleep with former girlfriends or new girlfriends or whomever he happened to meet at bookstores or nightclubs or on the internet, on the contrary, he was anxious that they were leaving him because on the one hand he didn't want to be without them (Ada, his eight-year-old, was becoming an ace on the soccer field, and Eva, his five-year-old, was already tinkering with the upright piano he'd abandoned years ago), and on the other hand he'd resigned himself to a so-called stable family life in Los Angeles alongside his former wife due to his daughters, so he didn't want to be alone and risk chancing upon any more women like Dora (philosophy major, S3) or Silvina (science fiction writer, S7) who might remind him of the other lives he could have lived if he'd left his former wife when he was planning to, three weeks before conceiving Ada and three months before he was asked by her parents to marry her, and although one never really knows why one does what one does — at least I like to believe I don't always know, Antonio writes, so as to feel less programmed by the catastrophes of my childhood — it is likely that his desire to avoid chancing upon any more women like Dora or Silvina who might rattle the family arrangement that was allowing his daughters to bloom beautifully was what led him, on summer #8, to join a website called Your Sugar Arrangements for $69.99 a month.

—

An internet executive overdoses on heroin and his companion doesn't phone the paramedics but instead leaves him to die on his yacht, the internet reports, a companion with a history of not phoning the paramedics in similar circumstances and whom the internet executive met through a website called Your Sugar Arrangements, which is how Antonio first heard of Your Sugar Arrangements: what in the world is this website, Antonio remembers thinking, and since he doesn't inject himself with heroin and can't isolate himself dangerously inside a yacht — I have no interest in yachts, Antonio writes, or people who frequent yachts — on one of his first evenings alone on summer #8, as he was waiting for a stool at Salt Air, he angled his phone so no one could see him browsing a site called Your Sugar Arrangements (YSA), typing Arturo Ventanas as his username and joining this website out of curiosity, he told himself, not expecting to become a Sugar Daddy (SD) to any Sugar Baby (SB), as advertised on the website, nor expecting to become another successful male looking to fuel mutually beneficial, no-strings-attached (NSA) relationships with beautiful young women, as also advertised on the website, although financially he'd done okay enough to maybe belong to the Practical designation in the SB allowance section called Expectation / Budget ($1,000 to $3,000 monthly), as opposed to the High (more than $10,000 monthly), although he selected Negotiable (openly negotiable to any amount) because in the past he'd experienced bouts of nihilist spending (mostly on clothes from Saint Laurent) so he didn't want to rule out the possibility of throwing away his database analyst salary on these new types of arrangements.

—

One day you're at Saint Ignatius Catholic Church marrying someone because she's expecting your child, one day you're at the same church listening to Schubert's Piano Trio No. 2 in E-Flat during your lunch hour, one day the young pianist who performed in that Schubert Trio is unbuttoning your jeans at the Pelican Yacht Harbor in Sausalito: her YSA name is Jasmine and she claimed to be a classical pianist who was studying at the Curtis Institute of Music, a claim that, unlike the many other claims on the many other profiles he has been encountering on Your Sugar Arrangements, turned out to be true, and perhaps because she already knew about the excess of falsehoods on Your Sugar Arrangements, she messaged him that she was performing at Saint Ignatius Catholic Church, so there he was in the audience during his lunch hour, two days before he was to meet her in person for the first time, sitting in the pews amidst the Catholic paraphernalia of his youth and at least a hundred retirees who seemed to believe they were entitled to free classical music during their lunch hour and at the same time seemed to be performing the joyousness of being alive, isn't this incredible, Gertrude, at last we have time to listen to this beautiful music, the nineteenth-century music Antonio used to fumble when he was twenty-one and learning to play the piano, the tempestuous music of Chopin and Rachmaninoff that he later rejected as tonal kitsch, the Schubert Piano Trio No. 2 in E-Flat that he is listening to now as he runs SQL queries at Prudential Investments, remembering that afternoon a few weeks ago at Saint Ignatius Catholic Church, sitting in the pews and feeling like he'd been invited to participate in a public game of foreplay, yes, Arturo, you will watch me rousing the retirees with my pianistic vitality, and you will not talk to me after my performance, not yet, you will just watch me bow to the audience of the elderly, I won't even know if you're in the audience, but please don't imagine you're at one of those peep shows your hairdresser told you about, the kind where you insert a handful of coins to see me behind a glass pane because we're in church, for god's sake, and a decrepit priest just announced the afternoon program, and a beautiful woman in the balcony is about to film me from the wrong angle, yes, Arturo, that's my mother and she has at least two rich boyfriends right now and she's about your age, although you will never tell me your real age is thirty-nine, just as you will never tell me that one day you were at Saint Ignatius Catholic Church about to marry someone because she was expecting your child, or that nine years later, when you showed up to see me at Saint Ignatius, you didn't feel any longing or regret or any of the strong emotions associated with returning to the church where you married someone because she was expecting your child, no, you were simply listening to my rendition of the Schubert Piano Trio No. 2 in E-Flat, enjoying the wonders of being alive just like the one hundred and one retirees around you, isn't this incredible, Arturo, and that evening you will message me and tell me you were in the audience and praise me and tell me you recognized the cellist I was playing with from a performance of Steve Reich's Cello Counterpoint at Carnegie Hall, and two days later I will cancel on you minutes before our dinner at Salt Air because I panicked about you knowing my real identity—I didn't want to mix up my life in YSA with my real life, Arturo, Jasmine messaged him later—and despite your messages reassuring me that you also had an incentive to be discreet—I deleted your voicemails, Jasmine said a few days later, I was scared to listen to them—I didn't change my mind until later that night, after you sent me a link to your publications, although I had already done a search on you to verify you weren't a criminal, and three days after Jasmine canceled their first dinner at Salt Air, the game of public foreplay continued in the Bay

Area, during dinner at Sushi Ran in Sausalito, where Arturo and Jasmine engaged in a heated conversation about John Cage, Chopin, etc., trying to impress each other without touching each other just yet—I don't know why I canceled on you or why I later changed my mind, Jasmine messaged him later, I don't think we make decisions like these logically, I had a gut feeling that something terrible was going to happen during dinner, that's all, I just didn't think you could possibly know so much about classical music, everyone in YSA exaggerates themselves 150 percent, everyone is tall and handsome and then they turn out to be bald businessmen or scrawny tech people—I just remembered another reason I originally didn't want to meet you, Jasmine messaged him later, you told me you were a novelist, so I immediately assumed you'd be one of those cynical emo pretentious types who would tell me how depressing the world was, I don't know why I remembered that just now as I was practicing my scales—and after dinner at Sushi Ran, Jasmine said let's stroll to the pier, so they strolled arm in arm to the dark pier and stepped down to the empty Pelican Yacht Harbor, joking that in movies something terrible always happens in these kinds of harbors, and when they reached the end of the harbor she approached him and kissed him, and he unzipped her white jeans and discovered she was not faking her arousal, and she unbuttoned his black jeans and discovered he was not faking his arousal, and he wondered whether the knees of her white jeans would be soiled by the damp floorboards such that later her mother would be able to guess what her nineteen-year-old daughter had been up to, and he looked around at the dark sea and the vacant yachts and thought life is unbelievable and beautiful, there's even a discarded bench cushion Jasmine can repurpose to lie down, and then it was over and she didn't ask him for an allowance and he walked her back to her mother's 1980s BMW and she was gone.

WHEN ANTONIO WAS NICOLA

To be Nicola, Antonio thinks, to ride his Shadow VLX, far, to the Nuart Theatre, toward the traffic of 405, to be Nicola instead of Antonio just as Nicola's brother, Matteo, had wanted to be Nicola, to tell his former wife, when she was eight and a half months pregnant with Ada, and his mother, who was visiting for Christmas, that he had to leave them for six hours to watch The Best of Youth at the Nuart Theatre, three hours of Nicola Carati and his family on Saturday afternoon, three more hours on Sunday evening—if you're feeling strong enough, Nicola says to his daughter, drive to your mother—to ride to the Nuart Theatre on a motorcycle that rattles him if he crosses the sixty-miles-per-hour mark, to answer dismissively when his former wife and his mother ask him why he needs to watch such a long movie now, can't you wait, his mother said, any minute now your daughter will be born, to not know why he felt the urge to see Best of Youth, no, Antonio thinks, even then he must have known he was riding to the Nuart Theatre to see Best of Youth because Dr. Adler had told him to (because Dr. Adler knew he wanted to become a writer, knew his misgivings about being a father, his dread about being a husband, even knew his dreams because she encouraged him to write them down and share them with her—I knew a woman who knew my dreams, Antonio writes—and when small birds sighed, Theodore Roethke says, she would sigh back at them—did you agree to become a father to please Dr. Adler?—does it matter now?—dear Dr. Adler, Antonio writes, thank you for the new family you've given me—an Italian movie like a Tolstoy novel, Dr. Adler said—), to know why he felt the urge to see Best of Youth but to not know how to explain this urge to his former wife or his mother, but perhaps Dr. Adler, who used to believe and perhaps still believes that only the interaction between doctor and patient changes the patient, in other words only in the warmth of Dr. Adler's office could Antonio rehearse how to be other than what he was, told him to watch Best of Youth not for literary reasons but because she wanted him to learn how to be Nicola, as he has indeed tried to do, watching Best of Youth so many times over the years that he has come to believe he can speak Italian like Nicola—voltate!—to learn how to be a father from a movie might sound ridiculous, Antonio writes, but how else do men learn to be fathers different from their own monstrous fathers?—holotropic breathwork?—tried it once already—constellation therapy?—twice—okay you're excused, be Nicola—to be Nicola, who plays limbo with his young daughter late into the night, who playacts at being Charlie Chaplin to amuse his young daughter, who, after his wife leaves him to join the Red Brigades, rearranges his life so he can spend most of his time with his young daughter and never remarries just as Antonio's mother never remarried while Antonio and his sister lived with her—your daughter has softened you, Nicola's sister says—yes, Antonio writes, that's what daughters do—and one day Nicola's daughter, who despite being abandoned by her mother has become a lighthearted adult—children are more resilient than we think, Nicola says—receives a letter from her mother, who's finally out of jail, and Nicola's daughter asks Nicola what she should do, and Nicola says if you're feeling strong enough, drive to your mother, and so she does, waiting for her mother with a bouquet of flowers outside the library where her parents met—Mama—embracing her mother—you tried to overthrow the government and now you have to ask permission to play music for me, Nicola's daughter says to her mother inside a church in Florence—to be Nicola's daughter listening to her mother performing Bach on the church organ for her for the first time—Bach's Invention No. 2 in C-Minor, Antonio writes, which I have played for my daughters, too—contemplating the vast universe of those years without her mother—everyone in your dreams is you, Dr. Adler said—Mama—but no, unlike Nicola's daughter, Antonio hadn't been feeling strong enough to board a plane to Baltimore to help his mother handle his sister, who couldn't discern what was / wasn't imaginary anymore, or yes, perhaps he thought he could pretend he was as strong as Nicola's daughter because he had a steady database analyst job at Prudential Investments, two daughters and a former wife who tolerated his erratic attempts to remain with them, so about twelve months ago, a few days after Antonio's mother called him and told him his sister had accused her plus Obama of conspiring against her and had thrown her out of the house she owned in Baltimore (for years Antonio didn't care about houses or cars or whatever else people purchase to pass the time before they die—the pitiful concerns of philistines, I probably thought back then, Antonio writes—and so for years Antonio ignored his sister whenever she asked him to please bring his daughters to her new house in Baltimore, a house his mother often talked about not because it was a luxurious home that stood as a symbol of his sister's success in life, but because she knew that house was a comfort to his sister, who had rejected almost everyone in the family as retribution for what she perceived as their rejection of her—a house was a comfort to her, Antonio's mother said, a place of her own—but unfortunately one evening one of his sister's neighbors had parked her car in front of her house, waiting to pick up her kids at the bus stop, and his sister, thinking her neighbor was conspiring against her, had allegedly threatened to shoot her neighbor and the other families at the bus stop if they didn't get off her property, for which she was arrested and charged with multiple

counts of assault and cruelty to children—Ms. Marta Terranova
stated that Estela Jiménez came to her car and started beating on
the window with a knife, the police report says, to the point that
one of her children begged Terranova to drive away because she
didn't want to die—and so Antonio's mother was concerned that
his sister, alone and unsupervised, would aggravate her unfortunate legal situation as she awaited her trial proceedings), Antonio
surprised himself by boarding a plane to Baltimore, renting a
compact economy car, and driving from the airport to his sister's
house, unannounced, of course, armed with the disastrous resolve of the reasonable, no, Antonio thinks, he doesn't want to
think about his sister ranting at him about radial frequencies
from satellites with lasers, or about his sister throwing him out of
her house, or about him and his mother in a government agency
filling out forms to commit his sister to a mental institute, so
much of that trip to Baltimore he has already forgotten anyway
and if he were to think about it too much his mind would be
less likely to erase it—I don't intend to write about my sister here,
Antonio writes, among my so-called sugar arrangements—nor
do I want to give you the impression my so-called sugar arrangements are a diversion from thinking about my sister's misfortunes, Antonio writes, because of course my so-called sugar
arrangements are a diversion, but so are all other activities that
allow me to pass the time without thinking of the misfortunes
that have happened and are still happening to my sister—and
although of course Antonio's ashamed of his avoidance, no one
needs to know, he won't tell anyone, and thankfully he no longer
believes in a god that can strike him for avoiding his sister's misfortunes, so yes, Antonio will rather think about Jasmine from
Your Sugar Arrangements, or he'll rather rereread A Lexicon of
Terror & Other Stories by his last former girlfriend, the science
fiction writer he still likes to call Silvina (S7), or transcribe the

conversation he recently had with Dora (S3), another former girl-friend, whom Antonio hadn't seen in almost five years, since around the time his second daughter was born (Dora had demanded that he stop sending her sporadic messages, however seemingly innocuous they might be, resorting to the hackneyed language of breakups to do so—it is disrespectful of you to continue doing so not only to me but to my boyfriend, Dora wrote, and since we're living together he is well aware of any and all efforts you've made—so he hadn't had any contact with her through any medium in those five years, until recently, when he discovered through casual Facebook research that her new relationship had ended since she'd posted a public picture of Bailey, her dog, along with a comment about how her new former boy-friend had stolen her dog and could someone please talk some sense into him—I was not surprised their relationship had ended, Antonio writes, I knew their day would come because it comes to all of us—and so after exchanging seemingly innocuous Face-book messages during the spring, Dora agreed to meet him on a Sunday afternoon outside of Menotti's Coffee Stop in Venice Beach toward the beginning of summer #8), or he'll rather think about his upcoming arrangements this week and the next, or about anything other than his sister's unreason, or her misfortunes due to her unreason, or the accretion of misfortunes that culminated in her unreason, or her whereabouts since she ran away from her trial proceedings in Baltimore a few weeks ago.

DORA & HER DOG BY ANTONIO JOSE JIMÉNEZ

What would you endure jail for, Dora said, I would endure jail
for my daughters, Antonio said, I'm not telling you this so you
think I'm a good person, father, etc., this is simply the first answer that comes to mind, and because Dora withheld her response for too long, and because he knew she might not offer
him another audience, Antonio continued, speaking to her of
I've Loved You So Long, a French movie they'd seen together
in which a mother endures jail for killing her son (the revelation toward the end of the movie that the mother knew that her
son was dying, and that she had injected her boy to spare him
because she was a doctor and knew how painful his terminal
illness would be, had been so unbearable to Antonio that he
had to rush to the bathroom of the Nuart Theatre to conceal
his sobbing from Dora—in my own so-called fiction I skirt
the verb to sob because of its melodramatic acoustics, Antonio
writes, nevertheless to weep aloud with convulsive gasping was
what I did at the Nuart Theatre—), I think jail in that movie
is the mother's equivalent of killing herself, Antonio said, the
question has been on my mind because I did go to jail, Dora
said, because apparently her new former boyfriend had gifted
her a dog, a dachshund she was carrying with her that Sunday
outside of Menotti's Coffee Stop on one of those BabyBjörn
carriers that are popular in Abbot Kinney among fathers who
want to showcase to the world that they, unlike their own fathers,
are good fathers, keeping their newborns close to their chests,
after I ended the relationship we enrolled in couples therapy to
mediate custody of our dog, Dora said, I'm going to need most
of your cigarettes to hear this story about you and your dog,

Antonio said, last winter he traveled to Miami with Bailey and did not return him, Dora said, so she filed charges in small-claims court, won, but apparently the judge didn't have the jurisdiction to issue an injunction for her new former boyfriend to return her dog, I called the police anyway, Dora said, but the police informed her they couldn't enter his house without a court order so she put up flyers with pictures of her dog and of her new former boyfriend in the neighborhood in Manhattan Beach where she used to live with him and her dog, did you tape or hammer your flyers to the telephone poles there, Antonio said, why are you asking me these questions are you going to write about this, Dora said, the story of you and your dog is compelling to me because it externalizes what during breakups often remains, against one's will, internalized, Antonio said, elaborating his point by recounting a story by Charles D'Ambrosio in which a screenwriter at an insane asylum asks a ballerina at the same insane asylum why she burns herself with cigarettes, because it externalizes her pain, the ballerina says, I actually handed out most of the flyers, Dora said.

—

The expectation of unconditional love should be reserved for the relationship between parents and children, Antonio said, because it's unreasonable to expect adults to burden one another with unconditional love, and since Dora did not reply Antonio continued, telling her that after he was surprised by the news that he was going to be what he never wanted to be, a father, his former therapist said that one of the most wonderful aspects of being a parent was that you could love someone without worrying about them leaving you, that is absolutely not true, Dora said, children do leave their parents—I knew what she meant, Antonio writes, so I didn't attempt to amuse her with insouciant counterarguments—and perhaps because Dora used to complain he purposefully excluded his life as a father from their relationship, which lasted almost a year, he softened his tone and told her how in his life now he pined after Saturday afternoons, when Ada has her soccer matches, and that to watch Ada score three or four goals per game was beautiful to him, as if he was watching an apparition of himself as a boy playing soccer in Bogotá but much better, although he didn't connect Ada and himself across time until his mother visited and said she's just like you, Antonio, running furiously after the ball — Ada, Antonio writes, my sensitive eight-year-old who paints I'm Sorry canvases for her mother when she splashes too much bathtub water — I am still seeking that kind of unconditional love, Dora said, admitting this probably made her a romantic, it does, Antonio said, but there's nothing right or wrong about being a romantic.

—

Someone called me about my dog, Dora said, was it a man or a woman, Antonio said, guessing it had to be a woman because only a woman would understand the plight of another woman in search of her dog, or at least that's what Antonio thought at the time, sitting next to Dora and her dog outside Menotti's Coffee Stop, a woman, Dora said, a store owner who had seen her dog with a blond woman who happened to be the new girlfriend of Dora's new former boyfriend, that just proves how benighted he is because white girls are the worst and they age horribly, Antonio said, I drove by the store owned by the woman who had called me about my dog, Dora said, what kind of store was it, Antonio said, I'm not telling, Dora said, but I found my dog nearby and snatched it from her, how did you manage to snatch your dog away from the blond woman, Antonio said, for legal reasons I can't tell you too many details, Dora said, did the blond woman chase after you, Antonio said, no, Dora said, the blond woman did not—Dora didn't tell me if the blond woman was already pregnant when she snatched her dog from her, Antonio writes, but the blond woman was pregnant—I'm glad I didn't have children with him, Dora said, obviously the blond woman didn't love your dog enough to chase you and therefore did not deserve to keep your dog, Antonio said, he filed charges against me, Dora said, assault and theft, she didn't think the charges would go through, months passed and nothing happened, but then they did go through and she had to hire a criminal attorney and place her dog in a witness protection program, I've heard of dog therapists and dog dentists so I guess a dog witness protection program isn't too far-fetched, Antonio said, that's just what I called me hiding Bailey outside of California, Dora said.

—

One night at the apartment Dora was sharing with her sister and her brother, a night Antonio would prefer not to forget, Dora shared with him the video her soon-to-be-new father had recorded of her, her two siblings, her soon-to-be-former mother, and her soon-to-be-new mother, all of them in what looked like a train station in Beijing at the moment the adoption transaction was taking place, her brother pretending to be delighted, her older sister as enraged as she was when Antonio met her years later, little Dora smiling in confusion about what was happening to her, her new father recording a video that years later he was to share at a family gathering as a tribute for Dora's former mother, whom he was to bring back from Beijing to marry soon after leaving Dora's new mother—Dora's family history is more complicated than I or anyone can even attempt to reconcile, Antonio writes, and to this day I would not wish it on anyone—enough, Antonio thinks, closing the file entitled Dora & Her Dog and scanning the messages that have been arriving since he began writing about Dora two hours ago, at 7:00 a.m., messages that contain words like autoregressive forecasting, intraday transaction posting, we are now accepting submissions for our Nature issue, the principal assumption of the geometric distributed lag model (GDL) is that the maximum impact of marketing occurs in the period in which it takes place and that its influence declines geometrically to zero thereafter, your suboptimal SQL query is slowing down the Teradata box, pursuant to the terms of the Bail Bond contract and promissory note you agreed to indemnify Any Day Bail Bonding Inc. against any and all claims incurred due to Estela Jiménez's failure to appear in Baltimore's Superior Court you are hereby given ten days to pay $110,000 for failure to appear, attorney fees, interest, and recovery expenses, and as Antonio removes his headphones, which have been transmitting Eight Lines by Steve Reich on repeat, he hears his work phone ringing inside his cubicle at Prudential Investments, Ron Graebel here, Ron Graebel says, I'm the owner of Any Day Bail Bonding I just sent you an email how are you today, you shouldn't call this phone I need to, give me a minute I'll call you from a conference room, Antonio says as he hurries toward Bermuda, the conference room without windows so that no one in the office can see him, okay, Antonio says, I hate making these calls, Ron Graebel says, you have a business to run I understand, Antonio says, do you know your sister's whereabouts, Ron Graebel says, no I, Antonio says, no, you and your mother are responsible for her I know you know that, Ron Graebel says, my mother and I, Antonio says, my sister isn't well she hasn't talked to us in a year, as owner and the one directly responsible to pay the court I would feel a lot better about this case if you would submit the full bond amount to be held in our security deposit account to cover the liability or at a minimum proof of funds, Ron Graebel says, we reserved Bermuda for 9:00 are you almost done, Antonio's coworker says, I'm done I'll call you back, Antonio says, I do expect you will, Ron Graebel says.

—

Aside from finishing law school I'm acting now, Dora said—Dora, Antonio writes, the least expressive woman I've met—she had discovered acting was her calling and acting is about portraying our reactions to dramatic circumstances, life and death, just like in fiction, and Antonio disagreed and said that he subscribed to António Lobo Antunes's belief that we should remove the dramatic charge from fiction because nothing's really that dramatic, someone is always leaving us or dying or going to the insane asylum, these miseries just happen to us and will continue to happen to us, to which she replied by speaking of metaphorical icebergs, the surface of things, etc., but Antonio did not refute these handed-down notions of narrative because he wanted to be amenable so she would agree to a handful of Fridays with him during summer #8, I've changed, Dora said, explaining that her former therapist had encouraged her not to be so black-and-white, to be more comfortable with the gray aspects of life, which included seeing Antonio again, and Antonio said I am Dora's gray area, but Dora didn't laugh, I have begun to see myself again as I was as a three-year-old, Dora said, so open and cheerful, ambling with her new father to the neighborhood ice cream shop, it's remarkable to see oneself as a three-year-old again, Antonio said, across twenty-seven years of life, I would do things differently now, Dora said, and Antonio interpreted this as a reference to her cruelty after she ended their relationship, a topic Antonio had no interest in pursuing (what good would it do now?—besides, Antonio writes, cruelty is embedded in the structure of endings—the day after Dora ended their relationship, Antonio revealed to her, despite his distaste for the hackneyed language of so-called love, that he loved her—I did not conceal my sobbing from her, Antonio writes, and she was taken aback because while we were together she hadn't known—I love you too, she said, but it's too late, she was already seeing the older man who was to steal her dog—just last summer I heard the same response to my untimely revelation of so-called love from Silvina, Antonio writes, the other former girlfriend I wish I could have kept—), if I have learned anything about breakups, Antonio said, and I haven't really learned anything about breakups, and here she interrupted him and said why do you always qualify yourself like that, and he said because I believe this business of learning is a mirage we impose on ourselves to feel better about our fated lives, does that include what I just said about changing, Dora said, that wasn't my intention but yes, Antonio said, reaching across the table to rest his hand on her forearm, wanting her to believe he could believe she could change, why shouldn't we nurse our delusions, Antonio said, if we find consolation in them?

—

I thought it through, Dora said, all the possible angles, whether I was in the wrong and should let Bailey go, or whether I was willing to abide by my principles and endure jail for what truly matters to me, and since Antonio remained quiet she continued, telling him a friend of her new former boyfriend had contacted her and told her that her new former boyfriend was enjoying himself with this business of the dog, getting even with her through her dog, how did his friend know about her dog, Antonio said, I emailed his friends and coworkers, she said, pleading with them about her dog, and as Dora removed her baseball cap to rearrange her hair, Antonio could see what looked like scabs on her forehead and the excessive makeup she had applied to cover them—in my own so-called fiction I don't provide descriptions of people because I don't remember what people look like, Antonio writes, but I remember Dora's forehead because I became concerned Dora wasn't well—she must have intuited that he was considering whether she'd derailed aspects of her mind as a consequence of spending a year plotting the recovery of her dog because she changed the topic and asked him about his relationship status—no way I'm risking a summer affair with Dora, being what I was thinking, Antonio writes—and so Antonio spoke to her about his child custody proceedings and how he had to attend a mandatory orientation where a man described how he had to enter a special building from one door, and how the mother of his child had to enter the same special building through another door, on the other side of the building, and how the man was only allowed to see his son in a special room inside that special building for a limited number of hours—I dream of that building often, Antonio writes, or perhaps I no longer dream of that building and it has simply become one of the images I have to contend with, in other words it is my building now, a building shaped like the Pentagon or the doomed fortresses of Jacques Austerlitz—he spoke to Dora about resignation and how his daughters need a lot of attention, and how he has come to define happiness collectively, and that it was ridiculous, given that most adult relationships end anyway, to pursue a relationship with another adult at the expense of his daughters, who were so little still—I thought I knew the effect my monologue would have on Dora, Antonio writes, the narrative of self-sacrifice, etc., but we were both wearing sunglasses, so I couldn't tell how she was feeling, although even if she hadn't been wearing sunglasses I wouldn't have known how she was feeling—I think your mother giving you away for adoption so you wouldn't die of hunger after your father died in a motorcycle accident is your mother's equivalent of killing herself, Antonio didn't say.

—

I had to turn myself in, Dora said, trying to lighten up her anecdote about jail by saying that she had tried to turn herself in on a day the computer registration systems were down, so she decided to come back another day because if the systems were down she wouldn't know when she was getting out, now would she, I was in jail for one night, Dora said, what was jail like, Antonio said, apparently where you first sit gives away whether or not you've been in jail before, Dora said, and because Antonio didn't want to think about or share with Dora how a year ago his sister had also been in jail after threatening to shoot her neighbors, he asked Dora if walking her dog had become stressful to her, in other words was she worried about running into her new former boyfriend or his future former girlfriend, no, Dora said, showing him her dog's new, difficult-to-snatch harness, I knew I would have to live with this new burden of worry before deciding to snatch my dog from that woman, Dora said, plus she also knew her new former boyfriend was still in Miami, and as Dora and Antonio watched the sun come down outside of Menotti's Coffee Stop—in my so-called fiction I never describe landscapes or weather, suns coming up or going down, Antonio writes, what's the point? everything's searchable online and metaphorical weathers are a bore, but that Sunday the sun was coming down and I didn't know how I was feeling about seeing Dora again—Antonio said this is my favorite time of day, things coming to an end, and since Antonio didn't want her to think he was being metaphorical about endings, he mentioned that these particular colors of sundown reminded him of sundown at Burning Man, a weeklong party in the desert he used to attend when he was in his twenties, speaking to her of people standing atop RVs, the sense of anticipation, the biggest party of their lives about to begin, the fluorescent lights on art cars and the wonderland castles about to be animated by portable generators, and because Dora wasn't smiling he said next time I will add puppetry to my Burning Man story to amuse you better, and Dora said what makes you think I'm not amused?

—

In retrospect I have assumed she didn't want me to leave just yet because she had suggested we walk her dog along the beach toward Santa Monica, Antonio writes, but unfortunately I had to go because my oldest daughter Ada had taken money from her mother without asking and upon being caught had cried for almost two hours, afraid of what I would say to her, I don't want to make Ada wait any longer, I said, I'm also worried about handing out a fair punishment, a lesson about consequences, I explained to Dora, without getting too upset at Ada, and yet Dora seemed upset that I was done with her and her dog, hugging me politely, sideways because of the dog on her chest, our torsos barely touching, kissing each other's cheeks too quickly, letting her dog lick me and playacting at licking him back, neither of us saying let's meet again soon, awakening, later that night, at least three or four times, worried that the excessive smoking I'd done with Dora might have corroded my new tooth implant, ambling, the next morning, from the extra-small studio apartment my daughters call The Other Home, across the laundry room that connects my building with their building, to the apartment where I used to live with my former wife and my two daughters, who were almost done packing for their annual summer trip to Czechia — my former wife and I have nothing in common besides our daughters and perhaps a proclivity for buffoonery, Antonio writes, so our relationship should have ended before we conceived Ada and it has, many times, including a divorce proceeding that led me to write to an acquaintance dear John, thank you for your invitation to join your book club but my life has been reduced to four-way settlement meetings in which a family attorney lectures me about the deleterious impact of pizza on my daughter so he can assign an additional $25 to my former wife's spousal support, but stay tuned, even Moses Herzog recovered — my former wife has tried to date others and I have tried to date others but we both want to see Ada and Eva every day, Antonio writes, so we're not dating anybody anymore — last week my former wife bought me a bookshelf so I wouldn't have to lug my books between Home and The Other Home but didn't tell me it was for me so she was upset I hadn't remarked on it, Antonio writes — I bought you a beautiful bookshelf and you don't say anything, Ida said — perhaps that's the only way adult relationships can last, Antonio writes, by exhaustion, although I wouldn't take relationship advice from me.

WHEN ANTONIO WAS A DATABASE ANALYST

Or perhaps nature no longer exists for me because of my job, Antonio thinks, all these years at Prudential Investments running SQL queries and at the same time not at Prudential Investments running SQL queries, pretending I am not running SQL queries eight hours a day inside a cubicle in the financial district of Los Angeles, I am not here, no, I am at my Jesuit high school in Bogotá praying to our Madre Dolorosa and sprinting after a soccer ball across a barren field that will never see grass (for the last twelve years he has been writing about his Jesuit school years in Bogotá inside a cubicle in the early morning, before beginning his eight hours of SQL queries at 9:00 a.m., and because on the other side of his cubicle wall a product manager has been spending her early morning hours arguing about financial health features on conferences calls with technology managers in multiple time zones, he has had to train himself to write about his Jesuit school years in Bogotá with music set to the highest volume, the same Arvo Pärt / Olivier Messiaen playlist on repeat every day for the last twelve years, which has been transmitted to his ears through oversized circumaural Sennheiser headphones whose headband cracks in the middle after a year or two such that the file cabinet inside his cubicle has become a junkyard of cracked oversized circumaural Sennheiser headphones as well as of obsolete electronics like PalmPilots, Nokias, BlackBerries encrypted by Prudential Investments, all of them stashed inside their sturdy laminated boxes containing limited warranties printed in microscript by Robert Walser, and in that junkyard of a file cabinet you can also find a decade of Antonio's 1040 tax returns, birth certificates for both of his daughters, a bail bond contract assuming obligation for his sister, who due to an accretion of misfortunes he'd rather not think about has been hearing conspirative voices incognizant of the spatiotemporal regulations in the USA, signed documents committing most of his database analyst income to his former wife according to rules set by a mean-spirited divorce attorney), such that, in the early morning, before beginning his eight hours of SQL queries, he has been simultaneously existing in Bogotá, in the alien musical landscapes of Arvo Pärt / Olivier Messiaen, and (not) inside a cubicle in the financial district of Los Angeles, and perhaps this accretion of pretending he isn't where he is has disrupted too many of the pathways inside his brain accountable for his relationship to nature, window after window into nature shuttered by a decision-management hub inside his brain that he hasn't imagined in terms of pathways or operational linkages or tentacles connecting and disconnecting themselves to artifacts from nature like palm trees or cordilleras or panoramas abloom with inspiriting vegetation but in vaguer terms than that, thinking instead of the garbological assemblages he'd seen years ago at an exhibit called The Alternative Guide to the Universe, which, because he barely remembers the details of that exhibit, he has to search online as he considers writing about his (non) relationship to nature inside his cubicle in the financial district of Los Angeles instead of thinking about his sister, yes, there it is, The Alternative Guide to the Universe at the Hayward Gallery in London (he'd actually purchased The Alternative Guide to the Universe catalogue that came with that exhibit, a catalogue that contains essays about fringe physics, symbolic devices, the symbiosis between magic and technology, and one about counternarrative by Antonio's former fiction-writing teacher, who almost ten years ago at the New York State Summer Writers Institute had wondered why Antonio didn't write in Spanish instead of in English, advising him against writing sentences that seemed to contain two or more sentences from two or more narratives at once—pues ya ve que no he cambiado en nada, profe—), and later that evening, after concluding his eight hours of SQL queries, he searches through his The Alternative Guide to the Universe catalogue and finds that the artist responsible for the vague garbological assemblages Antonio has been associating with the decision-management hub that has shuttered his windows into nature is called Richard Greaves, who apparently studied theology and hotel management and quit his job to dedicate himself to assembling his own asymmetrical visions of the world out of abandoned barns, coffeemakers, nicked shovels, computer keyboards, old razors, twine, rope—a nail stops the evolution, Richard Greaves says, but a rope is patient—parsing discarded objects in the forests of Quebec based on his nebulous linkages to them, Antonio writes—and as Antonio marvels at how what seemed like an incondite associative thread turned out to be quite pertinent to his reflections about his (non) relationship to nature, he imagines Richard Greaves spreading his cargo of trash on a kitchen table, trying to find linkages between gnarled tricycles, giant tacks, newsletters about toolboxes, recognizing that this image of Richard Greaves has its origins in Vertigo by W. G. Sebald (and here Antonio searches online inside Vertigo for the word table and finds the passage that according to him describes his own method of composition—I sat at a table near the open terrace door, W. G. Sebald writes, my papers and notes spread out around me, drawing connections between events that lay far apart but which seemed to me to be of the same order—), and yet unfortunately for Antonio the catalogue for The Alternative Guide to the Universe only contains five photographs of Richard Greaves's houses or huts or installations or anarchitectural visions or whatever one wishes to call them—buildings on the verge of disintegration, Valérie Rousseau calls them in The Alternative Guide to the Universe catalogue—and so Antonio orders a book called Richard Greaves Anarchitecte, thinking that if he can spend a few hours contemplating more photographs of Richard Greaves's installations he would be able to construct more compelling visions of the decision-management hub that has shuttered his windows into nature, meanwhile, as he waits for Richard Greaves Anarchitecte to arrive, he tries to imagine Richard Greaves's garbological assemblages in terms of whatever comes to mind, no, he doesn't have enough of an imagination to construct compelling visions out of Richard Greaves's installations without the aid of additional photographs of his installations, in other words (1) his imagination seems to subsist on the hope that a vague juxtaposition of data signals from disparate sources might yield an associative thread of interest, (2) it is likely the decision-management hub that has shuttered his windows into nature is also responsible for shuttering his windows into visual art, such that the only piece from all the modern art museums he has visited in the last twelve years that has stayed with him is an erased movie at the MoMA in New York (and here Antonio searches online for MoMA + movie + erased + free jazz and doesn't find what he's looking for so he searches his old journals for the name of the piece, hoping this search will yield an associative thread of interest (his journal pages during his first trip to New York in October 2010 are empty so he browses through the video catalogue of the MoMA online and eventually finds it, The Death of Tom by Glenn Ligon—after footage of his reenactment of the last scene of a silent-film adaptation of Uncle Tom's Cabin was processed, the gallery label text says, Ligon discovered that the film was blurred and the imagery had disappeared and yet the artist recognized an affinity between this spectral footage and his own earlier work—no, Antonio thinks, nothing of interest for him here except the memory of him watching Ligon's spectral footage in a dark room for an hour or two—perhaps memories in which we see ourselves from a dubious omniscient vantage are uncanny not because of their content, Antonio writes, but because of the vantage from which we see ourselves—there I am in the dark in New York watching an erased movie and that person who's me cannot see the observer behind me who's also me—)), and then Antonio wonders if perhaps it isn't just his windows into nature or visual art that had been shuttered by the inordinate amount of time he has spent pretending he isn't where he is but all his windows into the outside world, including the ones that look out into what is happening to his sister, in other words Antonio receives a call from the private investigator hired by Ron the Bail Bondsman in Baltimore to interrogate him about his sister's whereabouts and Antonio tells him no one in our family knows where she is because my sister believes our family + the Pentagon + Obama are conspiring against her, and after the call with the private investigator ends the windows into what has been happening to his sister (losing her job as a Senior Actuarial Associate, losing her house, fleeing Baltimore before a judge would deem her mentally incapable to stand trial for allegedly threatening to shoot her neighbors) shut and he goes on living inside his Richard Greaves assemblage without his sister's misfortunes, without calls from private investigators, without visual art, without nature, without descriptions of landscapes or nature anywhere in his recollections of his Jesuit school years in Bogotá, and although at first he'd thought he was against descriptions of nature in his fiction due to his affinity with the aesthetics of Doing Without, he has come to believe that all these years pretending he hasn't been running SQL queries eight hours a day inside a cubicle in the financial district of Los Angeles not only have given birth to this decision-management hub that has erased nature for him but have also atrophied this decision-management hub such that it has begun to erase everything at random, yes, so much of his life in the last twelve years has consisted of erasures that have included nature, visual art, his sister, hundreds of passages about avant-garde music that he'd tried to commingle with passages about his Jesuit school days in Bogotá, and while he waits for Richard Greaves Anarchitecte to arrive he wonders if searching for all the other passages he has erased in the last twelve years might yield an associative thread of interest, and it occurs to Antonio that as the erasures have accumulated throughout the years his imagination has had to subsist on a pool of material that's now a puny fraction of his original material, in other words perhaps all he has left is his Jesuit school in Bogotá and the music of Arvo Pärt / Olivier Messiaen he has been listening to while writing about his life at his Jesuit school in Bogotá, and yet if he were to write about nature for the Nature issue of Conjunctions perhaps he would be better off skipping any mention of decision-management hubs born out of pretending he isn't where he is or any mention of windows or erasures and focus instead on what still remains for him of nature: there was once a barren soccer field at San Luis Gonzaga High School in Bogotá where I would play soccer every day with friends I haven't seen since I moved to the United States twenty-one years ago, and my friend Rafael would kick the ball so out-of-bounds, toward the giant palm trees surrounding the soccer field, that we used to call him Monkey Shooter, and whenever we needed a quick rest we would sit on rocks like prehistoric eggs next to Don Jacinto's cafeteria and prattle about the future of Colombia, that is all that comes to mind when I think about nature, Antonio would write in his essay about nature, I am not a nostalgic but that is all that nature means to me, thank you for asking (and then a week later the bail bondsman calls his work phone again and says the ten days are up and if his private investigators can't find his sister Antonio and his mother will have to pay the $110,000 as per the bail bond contract they signed, and then Richard Greaves Anarchitecte arrives in the mail and Antonio contemplates photographs of his installations, hoping to find an associative thread of interest (no, Antonio thinks, nothing except Greaves's spiderwebs of twine, perhaps Antonio prefers these assemblages to exist for him as they have existed for him before, as vague hubs of vague associations — I make the shape of the house with the twine, Richard Greaves says, then I build — such that if a wind came and swept it all only these skeletons of twine would remain)).

F 8

WHEN ESTELA WAS ANTONIO

Your sister wrote beautiful letters, Antonio's mother says, when she was nine or ten your grandfather called me from Chapel Hill and said Estela is going to be a writer, Leonora, she has written us a fantastic letter that reads like an adventure story in which Estela's stranded at the Miami airport with her mother who doesn't speak English and her baby brother who drools, because due to a mishap by the travel agency in Bogotá, Antonio's sister wrote, my Mom was told at the counter in Miami that she had to pay extra to fly back to Bogotá but she didn't have extra to fly back to Bogotá, grandpa, imagine that, my Mom only had a few dollars in her pocket and no credit cards even though you told her to apply for a credit card for emergencies, so there we were, grandpa, stranded at the Miami airport without money, without food, sharing our sad tale with a Cuban waitress so she would bring us free orange juice and crackers, and at this juncture in the recording Antonio's mother repeats the words historia jocosa, which Antonio will try not to translate as jocular story, his mother repeating that his sister's letter was a jocular adventure story as if unconvinced by her dramatization of the jocular aspects of his sister's letter, and years later your grandfather shared that letter with me, Antonio's mother says, and I asked him if I could keep it and he said no, Leonora, you've already read it, this letter was meant for us, plus whenever I'm upset or worried I read it again and laugh, didn't my sister study literature in high school, Antonio says, she was fascinated by books, Antonio's mother says, she would read all the time and write wonderful book summaries, whereas for math she would cry that she didn't want to learn math do you remember she would read the books that had been assigned to you and she would summarize them for you, no I don't remember, Antonio says, remember when you won that book contest even though you hadn't read the book, Antonio's mother says, The Metamorphosis, Antonio says, your sister was the one who summarized that book for you, Antonio's mother says, and you didn't want to win that contest but you did and you had to present it in front of the whole school so you would say to your sister help me, please, no Toñio now you have to read the book, she was such a quick reader and I would say to her Estelita what's that book about, and she would summarize it for me, but read it Mom, she would say, I don't have time please summarize it for me, I would say, and she would tell me, but after she graduated from high school she didn't read anymore, when I grow up I am going to have my own money so that no man will mistreat me, your sister would say, and so after high school she stopped reading and focused on studying finance, numbers, which she was never very good at, studying and working with numbers overextended her, Antonio, but she had this need to feel financially secure so she sacrificed what she was good at, don't you remember you used to write, I would say to her, no Mom I don't remember, don't you remember you used to write to your grandparents, no Mom I don't remember, that humorous letter like an adventure story you sent to your grandparents, no Mom, that jocular letter that I didn't find after your grandfather passed away, Antonio's mother says, although I did find many of the other letters you and your sister sent to your grandparents but not that one—dear grandparents I want to thank you for the pistol, Antonio wrote, I also want to inform my uncle Luis that if I visit this summer I am not going to break his airplanes because I build airplanes too and know how hard it is to assemble them—dear grandparents I'm in second place at school, Antonio's sister wrote, but if I get twenty over twenty in music and the boy who is in first place gets sixteen over twenty then I will be the best student—my sister stopped reading completely and never wanted to talk about books, Antonio says, because it reminded her of how much she used to enjoy it, Antonio's mother says, and look how your lives turned out, Antonio, the one who became a writer is you.

THE REVISIONIST BY HELEN SCHULMAN

Why not not do something as inevitable as being home on time for dinner, Antonio reads, not remembering having read this or any other thought from Hershleder, the protagonist of The Revisionist, which Antonio has been rereading for almost a decade, and although he doesn't ever remember too many specifics from The Revisionist, he does remember this short fiction as (1) a performance of delay, (2) too dependent on its reversal at the end, (3) paradoxical because despite knowing about (2) he always cries in the end, and of course once he rereads The Revisionist, as he's doing now, Hershleder's delay becomes less about (1)(2)(3) and more about Hershleder's desire to delay his trajectory back home, Hershleder's desire being Antonio's desire, of course, though less so over the years, yes, why not watch a movie during the day instead of going home, Hershleder thinks, why not enter the Silver Horse, as Antonio had done many years ago as he waited for an acquaintance to let him into a nightclub nearby (how ridiculous the word nightclub sounds to him now—just as ridiculous as all those years I wanted the freedom to exhaust myself at nightclubs, Antonio writes—), and so as he waited for his nightclub acquaintance, Antonio hesitated about entering the Silver Horse because he liked to believe he wasn't the type to enter the Silver Horse or any other so-called gentleman's club due to a faulty youthful logic of why pay for women to dance for me if I can just pick them up at nightclubs— completely different pleasures, Antonio writes—the fading wise man of the flesh, eh?—go away—and yet to pass the time that night almost a decade ago he did enter the Silver Horse, where he discovered a glass room like an aquarium that the manage-

ment had named the Smoking Room, and because this room
had been built by the management in the back, facing the stage,
and because this room had been sealed by the management
such that inside the music sounded muffled—ahora ya soy un
Axolotl—Antonio could watch the dancers on the stage and the
men interacting with the dancers working the floor as if he were
watching a television show with the sound off, with the added benefit that he didn't feel as guilty about staring at the dancers from
inside the aquarium, plus every now and then the dancers
would step out of the television and into the aquarium and ask
him for his name, a smoke, a dance, and so every Friday or
Thursday, soon after marrying his future former wife, who was
already four or five months pregnant with Ada, he wouldn't do
something as inevitable as being home for his future former
wife, but instead he would switch on the television at the Silver
Horse for an hour or two—a show without consequences, Antonio writes, unlike pursuing women at nightclubs—and one evening, during summer #1, while his (not yet) former wife and his
newborn were in Czechia with Babička and Děda, he switched
on the television to find the most beautiful woman he'd ever
seen in his life—call me Hari—and she stepped out of the television and into the aquarium, lit a Camel Light, and then (and
he will never forget this moment—I will never forget this moment, Antonio writes—a moment he hasn't shared with anyone because who wants to hear about a thirty-year-old South
American flummoxed by a beautiful hippie at a strip club?—the
moment when he said to himself dear god—dear god who
doesn't exist, Antonio writes—dear god, please, just this once,
inhaling and summoning all the available knowledge he'd accumulated over his thirty years of life and then) he said this,
that, everything, anything she might care about, Che Guevara,
she said, his biography by Jon Lee Anderson, he said, which

he'd happened to have been reading, recent graduate of Evergreen State College, she said, Grateful Dead concerts with my parents when I was a child, she said, and so they exchanged phone numbers and a week later they drove together to Burning Man, a party in the desert marketed as a transcendental utopia that is just an excuse for Americans to consume psychedelic drugs—welcome home!—what's your playa name?—Cosmic Harenina at your service—Berthe Trépat at your service— joven!—and perhaps years from now, when he's old and alone and banished from his loved ones, he will no longer remember that their safeword was elephant, or that Hari, the most beautiful woman he'd ever encountered, would politely request that he slap her legs, face, thighs, that he tie her to chairs, drag her by a dog collar to a water bowl on his kitchen floor—I didn't know I could be into this, Antonio writes—and perhaps years from now he will no longer remember the night he'd shown up at the Silver Horse at 1:45 a.m. and she'd told him to wait for her outside but on the corner nearby because she wasn't allowed to leave with customers, and so he waited for her on the corner nearby and she swung open the door of a taxi still in motion and said quick, jump in, and so he jumped into the taxi as if into a toboggan—wheeeee—and inside the taxi she provoked him on purpose so he would slap her in the face, and he did comply and slap her in the face—don't mind us we're role-playing—and when they arrived at her rundown hotel near Venice Beach and she said quick I am not allowed to bring anyone with me and there's cameras everywhere—the closet-sized room in a sliver of hotel inserted between buildings as an afterthought where she was living in complete squalor, Antonio writes, the floor and bed and desk covered in vintage summer dresses, glitter, handmade leg warmers, which were banned from the Silver Horse soon after—no hippies allowed, buddy—but what

Antonio will never forget, even when he's old and alone and banished from his loved ones, is that moment he said dear god, please, just this once—dear god, Antonio said when he saw Dora for the first time, please don't let me approach her I have a three-year-old daughter at home—dear god, Antonio said when he saw his former wife for the first time at a ski cabin in Tahoe, her face as red as a lobster because she'd snowboarded without sunblock, dear god please end her relationship with that retrograde investment banker soon—a lobster is an excellent choice—and god said goddamn it, Drool, fine, just this once—will you forget Hari's voice, too?—I used to ask Hari to leave messages on my voicemail just so I could hear her voice, Antonio writes, a voice I can't describe without thinking of preschool, mantel, nurse—Hari did volunteer at Casa Linda, a preschool in Santa Monica, Antonio writes, the same preschool my daughters would attend years later—sana sana / culito de rana—and when you are old and alone and banished from your loved ones, you will dial the deathbed number assigned to you and Hari's voice will tell you again no se que decirte pero, how do you say it, me gustas mucho?—commuters, Hershleder thinks, men who travel to and from their wives, their children, the office, men with secret lives in foreign lands, Hershleder thinks, who delay going home by having yet another round of drinks, and although Hershleder doesn't delay his trajectory back home by entering a so-called gentleman's club or attending Burning Man with a dancer from the Silver Horse—while in his heart he lusted after irresponsibility, Hershleder thinks, he was never bad enough—pues fíjate que yo sí—and here Antonio, proud of his former irresponsibility, decides not to search for the divorce papers his former wife filed five years ago, as soon as Eva was born, which document the consequences of his irresponsibility (but of course Antonio does search for them and does reread

them—Antonio goes out partying several times a week, his former wife wrote, usually around 7:00 p.m. and doesn't return until three or four in the morning—I am frightened of him and
frightened for the welfare of my daughters, his former wife
wrote—), Hershleder does encounter someone in the subway
who sells him a Thai stick, which he does smoke, and so the
ghosts that lived inside him, Hershleder thinks, spiraled around
in concentric circles—I ask the court to order a random full-
panel alcohol and drug test, his former wife wrote—and so
Hershleder decides to walk a mile and a half to Itty and the kids,
a mile and a half from his home and future heart failures, Hershleder thinks, and as Antonio rereads The Revisionist, he wonders
if he should start adding a date next to the passages he has underlined and will underline as a way to track what has mattered
to him about Hershleder's trajectory over the years, or perhaps
he should add a date next to the passages he should have underlined but didn't—there was a locker room of vile language in the
homeless woman's head, Antonio doesn't underline, but her face
seemed apologetic—he made a mental note to give in to Itty,
Antonio underlines, she'd been begging him to agree to get a
pup for the kids, 9 12-15-22-5 25-15-21, Antonio underlines,
stopping to decode what Hershleder's son had once said to
Hershleder at bedtime, bringing tears to Hershleder's eyes, and
just as Antonio can never remember too many specifics from
The Revisionist after he's done rereading it, he can't remember if
in his previous readings he'd also stopped at this juncture in The
Revisionist, three pages away from the end, once Hershleder has
reached the front porch of his house, hesitating, thinking of his
wife, Itty, the potter, hungry for connection, attention, stopping
at this juncture of The Revisionist and thinking why go on, I
know how it ends and I don't feel like reading three more pages
of short sentences in English, and so he stops reading and goes

to sleep—good night Hershleder, good night Hari—and weeks later his former wife says your daughters want a dog and he says no, we don't need a dog, what difference would a dog make in our lives, a dog won't exist for me just as the outside world doesn't exist for me, just as his sister doesn't exist for him unless he receives calls from the owner of Any Day Bail Bonding asking for his money, as Antonio does the next morning on his work phone at Prudential Investments, you and your mother signed her bail, Ron Graebel says, you are responsible for her, my sister's disappearance is a tragedy for our family, Antonio says, especially for my mother, who can't endure the thought that her daughter might be living in a homeless shelter somewhere in the United States, this shows a welcome sincerity, Ron Graebel says, it is disheartening to us to have your private investigators threatening us over the phone, Antonio says, I'm not aware of any specifics as to dealings you have had with the investigators they are financially motivated to find her, Ron Graebel says, it is unnecessarily callous to call my uncle Lucho to make accusations that my mother is hiding my sister in Colombia, Antonio says, I did hear from my office manager that you have been uncooperative with them, Ron Graebel says, I understand you have a business to run but can we avoid adding more suffering to the already unbearable suffering my mother is going through, Antonio says, the investigators deal with all sorts in our business and at times it's hard to know who is sincere and who is lying, Ron Graebel says, this is not some theoretical suffering I am talking about, Antonio says, I am sure they are as frustrated as you are, Ron Graebel says, my mother is physically ill from everything that has been transpiring with my sister, Antonio says, keep in mind they are trying to save you from paying the full bail amount, Ron Graebel says, but I will speak to them and convey your thoughts, and weeks later Antonio returns to that sentence he'd underlined in The Revisionist about giving in to Itty about getting a pup, and once again Hershleder's reaching the front porch of his house, and a young jogger is entering Hershleder's house, and Hershleder is wondering what's the meaning of this, and Hershleder's jamming his key at a lock that doesn't fit, and Hershleder's ringing the bell and waking everyone up and Hershleder and the jogger are shouting at each other, please, sweetheart, Hershleder's wife says to the jogger (to the jogger!), and she's sitting on the slate steps and explaining to him, Dr. David Hershleder, M.D., patiently and for the thousandth time, that this is no longer his home, that he has to stop coming around here, upsetting her, upsetting the children, that it's time, Dave, to take a good look at himself, when all Hershleder is capable of looking at is her, his wife, sitting with him on the stoop of his house in his neighborhood while his children cower inside.

I was an accident, Katerina said, and because both of my parents were still in graduate school, they shipped me to Seoul to live with my grandmother, what were they studying, Antonio said, physics, Katerina said, pausing because their waiter was approaching with an ice bucket for their bottle of Cava, and then or later Katerina didn't comment on the solemn Arvo Pärt concert they had heard at Disney Hall, which looks like a Marriott hotel inside, incidentally, but she did seem delighted to answer all of Antonio's questions about her upbringing even though she'd just met him via Your Sugar Arrangements, and perhaps because of the bottle of Cava or the exaggerated height of her heels, or because of her asymmetrical purple hair or her boredom with the admiring stares around her, or because neither Antonio nor Katerina had any expectations of courtship, loveship, marriage, Antonio was delighted, too—it was all so wonderful and forbidden that I wanted nothing more in this world, Bohumil Hrabal writes, and I resolved to save eight hundred and more a week selling hot frankfurters because at last I'd found a beautiful and noble aim—as carefree as Antonio had been when, in an identical so-called upscale setting but in different restaurants, he'd met with Fiona, Akira, Valerie, Charlotte, Yoko, all of them invented names attached to YSA usernames like Little Birdie, Evil Evie, Lolita in Venice, Uzi Kitten, Giggle Girl, and one of them was a student at Columbia whose thesis was about fog and chaos theory, and Melanie played for a Chinese ensemble and wanted an adventure before returning to Stanford, and Hana from UC Riverside wanted someone to take her out to a nice dinner every now and then, and Lulu had metal braces on her teeth and did research on algebraic topology and had always fantasized about being a call girl, and Silvina II, his favorite, whose body was covered in cut marks, lived with her parents in Santa Monica and wanted an occasional allowance for tattoos, and so far most of them had no qualms about sharing their earliest memories with him, which he tries to write down the morning after meeting them—how else will I remember any of them?—I remember riding inside the front basket of my mother's bicycle on our way to school, Fiona said—I remember my mother unbuckling her baby carrier from her shoulders and putting me down on a chair at the airport, Charlotte said, soon after she'd adopted me, and I became so desperate that I fell to the floor as I tried to reach her—and if his so-called sugar arrangements happen to ask him why he has joined what in public he likes to call our beloved website, he tells them the heroin + internet executive + yacht + black widow backstory, and they both laugh and Antonio toasts to not being dead, and sometimes, in his extra-small studio apartment, also known as The Other Home, which consists of one platform bed without legs and seven bookshelves with hundreds of novels in English and Spanish—have you read them all, Arturo?—no but all of them have bookmarks on the last page I read of them—he has to cover their mouths so as to not wake up his neighbors (Antonio would rather not think about that now—are you embarrassed to think about sex while at your place of employment, Drool?—yes so what?—the selectively prudish database analyst ha ha—shut up—), and if any of his so-called sugar arrangements falls asleep (after doing what Antonio would rather not think about now), as Antonio often does since he has been scheduling two new sugar arrangements per week and still has to wake up early for his database analyst job, he lets them sleep because why would he wake up a beautiful college student and ask her to leave, although if they stay past

4:00 a.m. he's barely able to sleep, sliding between apparitions
of his former wife banging on his front door and the sounds of
his wall heater, of his neighbors opening and closing drawers in
search of teacups or spoons, of the 6:00 a.m. garbageman drag-
ging recycling bins down the steep flight of stairs underneath
his apartment, and if they happen to say what about you, Arturo, what is your earliest memory of childhood, Antonio says
(in a cheerful tone that avoids hints of submerged disturbances)
unfortunately I don't remember anything about my childhood,
which is true, and of course none of them press him as to why he
doesn't remember anything about his childhood, just as none of
them press him about why he can only meet them after 9:30 p.m.
during the week, not that he's going to tell them the truth if they
do press him — I have to draw numbers on my daughters' backs
at 8:45 p.m. before bedtime — and sometimes, on his way to meet
his so-called sugar arrangements, the driver of the car he has
ordered at 9:15 p.m. mistakenly parks in front of the apartment
where his daughters have just fallen asleep, three doors down
from him, and he has to call the driver and say can you please
back up I will explain in a second — ugh — and because he always
meets them after 9:30 p.m. he doesn't have to worry about receiving calls or messages from Ron the Bail Bondsman demanding
his money or from his sister's attorney in Baltimore informing
Antonio that his sister has faxed a medical form from an ambulatory community health center in Milwaukee — dear Thomas,
his sister wrote, I have followed the court requirement to see a
doctor but I can't go back to Maryland due to lack of appropri-
ate shelter and employment — and Lina from Mills College has
been dating older men since high school but joined YSA for a
week so she could buy her best friend a bicycle, and Silvina III
from UCLA had never been to a nice restaurant before and she
was so surprised she was enjoying herself that she said you're

doing such a good job seducing me, Arturo—who will ever want to hear about how much I loved her long bowed legs, Antonio writes, which I will never see again?—when my mother was mad she would use metaphors that made no sense, Anna said, the house is messy like a calendar, she would say—my mother was a set designer for movies, a freshman at the Rhode Island School of Design said, and she would take me with her to the prop stores, did you have a favorite movie set, Antonio said, Elektra in New York because its set had a strange shop that required my mother and I to shop for doll heads though the movie was never finished—high school teachers should be required to draw a diagram of life on the board and explain that one day everyone will age horribly, Antonio said to Katerina, and that in the finite number of years before they become ambulatory carcasses, they should enjoy their bodies without worrying about ridiculous concepts like monogamy and marriage, which were probably invented by ancient carcasses trying to constrain their spirited young wives, and don't listen to anyone who tells you an excess of sex will result in an excess of punishment because no punishment will come for enjoying yourself if you are careful about concealing your excesses — I like learning, sex, and spending money, Gloria said—and when years later my mother was finally done with her graduate program in physics she came to visit me in Seoul, Katerina said, and I remember thinking who is this pretty lady, pausing because their waiter was approaching with their tray of oysters, although when my mother told me not to eat candy before dinner I rushed to the kitchen and said grandma, Katerina said, grandma, you need to beat up that woman.

A LEXICON OF TERROR & OTHER STORIES BY SNÆBORG OCAMPO

Borges concealed his fondness for mirrors by affirming the opposite, the narrator of Mirrors Aren't Terrifying says, a narrator called Jules Jakobsdóttir who's lecturing her bathroom mirror about how she isn't amused by her reflection across multiple dimensions because (a) multiple dimensions are a cliché and (b) they are probably a sign she needs medication, which is strange because she's already on medication ha ha, and in some dimensions a benevolent professor version of herself lectures the bathroom mirror version of herself about the ontology of clichés—if you no longer speak your native language on a daily basis, Professor Jakobsdóttir says, nostalgia will exalt the clichés of your native language—and in other dimensions a dentist version of herself offers the bathroom mirror version of herself LSD instead of Novocain for reasons that will only become apparent to readers of The God of the Labyrinth, and in this dimension, the one where Antonio is rereading Mirrors Aren't Terrifying, the first story in A Lexicon of Terror & Other Stories by Silvina, he can't recall if he'd told Silvina that the concept of a reflection across multiple dimensions reminded him of something Peter Ström, a New Age therapist, had told him during one of the two constellation therapies Antonio underwent with him, back when Antonio and his former wife were still trying to separate without rupturing their daughters' lives—but before I tell you what Peter Ström told me, Antonio writes, I would like to explain that, in constellation therapy, facilitators like Peter Ström operate under the assumption that present difficulties are influenced by traumas suffered in previous generations of the family, even if those affected now are unaware of the original events in the past, and these systemic entanglements, as Hellinger calls them, or invisible loyalties, as Iván Böszörményi-Nagy calls them, or quantum quackery, as cynics like me call them, or los tentáculos invisibles, as my mother, a facilitator like Peter Ström, probably doesn't call them, are said to occur when unresolved trauma has afflicted a family through an event such as murder, suicide, incest, death of a mother in childbirth, war, emigration, abuse, in other words an event so traumatic that it causes a rift in the family system—there is a deep need for justice and retribution within family systems, Hellinger says—in other words even if you luck out and your father isn't as horrifying as mine, Antonio writes, you're still probably doomed by a suicidal uncle you and your parents didn't even know—and now that I've explained constellation therapy, Antonio writes, I would like to explain the mechanics of the therapy itself—although here Antonio stops writing and tries to remember the steep stairs to Peter Ström's subterranean home in Hollywood Hills, which at the time didn't bring to mind his psychotherapy sessions with Dr. Adler in a subterranean office in Santa Monica almost ten years prior to his first constellation therapy—my objective is to peel myself like an artichoke and become who I am in a year, he'd said to Dr. Adler during his first session with her, and five years later they would sometimes joke about what he'd said to her in that first session—I am exhausted by this ceaseless examining of myself, he'd said to Dr. Adler during his final session with her, I can't keep battling these inherited undercurrents—and after descending toward an audience of ten or twelve people in Peter Ström's pleasant living room in Hollywood Hills, Antonio's former wife says to Peter Ström my husband and I want to work on our relationship, so Peter Ström draws family charts on a chalkboard for both him and his former wife and asks her to pick representatives from the audience so that one of these representatives will become her father, one of them will become her grandmother (he doesn't remember what any of these representatives looked like, except Peter Ström, who looked like J. M. Coetzee, at ease in his humorlessness), and these representatives aren't told what his former wife's parents were like, but they are told by Peter Ström to behave whichever way they feel in the moment, in other words you're vessels of complex energetic forces, Peter Ström says, and because Antonio's former wife was raised by her grandmother in Czechia, a grandmother who protected his former wife from her older, abusive sister, a grandmother he can easily imagine because his former wife has told him about her and there's a picture on the fridge of this grandmother holding his former wife when she was a baby, and since this grandmother died when his former wife was thirteen, when the representative for her grandmother says to his former wife I want to hold on to you forever, please don't let me go, his former wife cries inconsolably, and Peter Ström says you can't start your own family if you don't let your grandmother go, do let her go, tell her you love her and say goodbye, but his former wife refuses, she cries inconsolably and refuses, and then he's in a different constellation therapy session months later and the representative for his mother says I am scared of you, or perhaps he is the one saying to the representative for his mother I think you are scared of me, and then Antonio and the representative for his mother jostle each other because Peter Ström has asked Antonio to hold hands with his mother but instead of holding hands they're clasping their hands as if trying to push each other off a ring, and at some point, before or after the jostling with his mother, Peter Ström picks a sturdy man from the audience and tells him to stand behind Antonio and place his arms on Antonio's shoulders, a sturdy man who isn't a representative of any family member of yours, Peter Ström says, but a representative of all men across multiple generations, which is what Silvina's concept of a reflection across multiple dimensions brought to mind as he read Mirrors Aren't Terrifying for the first time, soon after Silvina & Antonio started sneaking into each other's life during summer #7.

—

Ulrica Thrale (the protagonist of Ramifications of Scholarships) boosts her college application by playacting on the cello, the harpsichord, the viola—show me the version where I play the triangle, Ulrica Thrale says—jokes do pass the time, Ulrica Thrale's best friend says—by performing a panoply of extracurricular activities that might impress the college admissions officials, but unfortunately every extracurricular activity ramifies into other extracurricular activities—the cello ramified into learning Italian → volunteering at The Cinematheque → handmaking kaleidoscopes, Ulrica Thrale says—and because her parents aren't around to advise her against submitting her complete ramifications, she submits a college application the size of an encyclopedia, which clearly (according to the admissions letter that Ulrica Thrale never receives) is a sign of the applicant's brilliance, and although Silvina didn't submit a college application the size of an encyclopedia, she did try to impress the admissions officials with a panoply of extracurricular activities to be admitted to Princeton, which is also what Antonio had done to be admitted to Yale, after he graduated from high school in Bogotá and arrived in Chapel Hill, North Carolina, starting a newspaper at his community college and volunteering at Big Brothers Big Sisters so he could be considered as a transfer student to Yale or Harvard or Stanford—I attended a Jesuit high school in Bogotá, Antonio writes, and although my grades were almost perfect, I was often suspended from school for misconduct—please don't expel Antonio this time he did have an altercation with his father, Father Ignacio—such that when the time came for me to apply to Yale and Harvard and Stanford I had to write a long letter to the principal of San Luis Gonzaga begging him to please answer no to the question in the college application asking if this student ever had any behavioral problems at school—and yet according to Antonio he'd wanted to be admitted to Yale or Harvard or Stanford not because he wanted to change his miserable life, as Ulrica Thrale was trying to do—when I arrived at Princeton I thought at last I have ceased to be what I have been, Silvina said—all of your priors will be expunged and none of your priors will be expunged do you understand, Ulrica Thrale's math teacher says—but because he needed to prepare himself for the great task of returning to Colombia and running for office so he could save the poor and so on, and yes, he did possess this impulse to return to Colombia to run for office, but one of the many aspects of Ramifications of Scholarships that disrupted his attempts at writing fiction was Silvina's openness in writing about her own shame about having less money than others, an openness Antonio didn't possess back then because there was no way he was going to acknowledge to anyone, even to himself, that part of the reason he'd never returned to Colombia to run for office had to do with finally having a job in Los Angeles that allowed him to have enough money to spend on expensive clothes—my mother glued acrylic nails inside our garage, Antonio writes, which she had converted into a nail salon where she also sold difficult to find imports like Toblerones, and since we didn't have a car I always had to beg my classmates for a ride, such that I had to drop out of tennis lessons after school when I was in elementary school because no one could give me a ride back home—your son has tremendous potential in tennis please find a way for him to continue lessons, Doña Leonora—and perhaps because during summer #7 Silvina was living in such precarious conditions (she had just graduated with a masters in neuroscience, her boyfriend had broken up with her so she had to move out of his apartment to a temporary sublet above Gratitude Cafe, didn't have a job yet and didn't have the kind of parents who could provide financial assistance—dear financial aid office at Yale I misled you when I wrote down that my mother's annual income was $700, Antonio writes, I was too embarrassed to ask my mother how much she accumulated per year from her acrylic nails garage business—dear financial aid office at Yale the summer before flying to you I sold Hawaiian shirts at the mall so I could afford the plane ticket from Chapel Hill to New Haven, Antonio writes—dear financial aid office at Yale I will always love you—), Antonio had felt a kinship with Silvina, although he didn't think about her in terms of kinship back then, when he would drive her home whenever they ran into each other at the literature in translation series at Skylight Books and she would answer his questions awkwardly and he would try not to flirt with her because he was sure she was waiting for him to flirt with her just so that she could say to her friends see, these Latin American men are all alike, sure she was worried he was going to reach across and grab her leg any minute now as he drove her to her sublet above Gratitude Cafe, and yet one night, out of despair or boredom or because here was this beautiful science fiction writer on his passenger seat, Antonio said to her I don't feel like going home yet would you like to stop for a drink somewhere, and Silvina said sure, and Antonio said great (and not much else so as to not risk blurting out anything that could change her mind), driving to Tabula Rasa on Hollywood Boulevard, where their knees almost touched as they

half swiveled on the barstools not out of coquetry but because
they were both anxiously fishing for statements in each other's
monologues that could feed their own monologues so as to cast
a loop of compatibilities, in other words they were trying to
create the illusion of fluidity because according to the mating
culture of the United States fluidity amounted to chemistry,
and this so-called chemistry was supposed to be a good sign
and not just one accretion of traumas called Antonio at birth
sniffing another accretion of traumas called Silvina at birth and
saying, like the song in that movie where Philip Seymour Hoff-
man listens to an ersatz god on an earpiece before he dies
alone, I know you, you're the one I've waited for—my father
lives in a homeless shelter, Antonio—soon my sister will live
in a homeless shelter too, Silvina—and after they finished their
drinks at Tabula Rasa they danced to dancehall in a corner
of the bar and he asked her if it was okay if he flirted with
her and she said yes, and so he kissed her, and so they exited
the bar and they entered her temporary bedroom above Gratitude Cafe, where he discovered Silvina's predilections weren't
too dissimilar from Hari's—elephant?—no, Antonio writes,
Silvina picked László Krasznahorkai as her safeword to amuse
me—and where, the next morning, he awoke to discover he
was still there—dinosaur jokes straight to the left, sir, Au-
gusto Monterroso says—and although he doesn't remember
everything they said to each other the next morning, he likes
to believe he will always remember her box set of the complete
works of Silvina Ocampo, which he encountered in her temporary kitchen and which he carried to her temporary bedroom,
where he said are you trying to change your name to Silvina
so you can say you wrote these, and Silvina said my Venezue-
lan father wanted to call me Silvina but my Icelandic mother
hated my father so much that she picked a name he couldn't

pronounce, and because Silvina frowned at Antonio every time he called her Silvina, twisting her mouth in disapproval, he continued to call her Silvina, exaggerating his fake Italian accent so that it sounded like Silvína.

—

Parallel Longings, the most experimental of Silvina's stories, is written in the form of a Q&A with the chatbot of a detective agency called Parallel Longings, which clients hire to investigate what happens in their parallel lives—our detectives have special access to subspace corridors, the chatbot replies to the question how do your detectives travel between parallel lives—and as Antonio rereads Parallel Longings, imagining its subspace corridors as those apocryphal tunnels connecting monasteries to convents in the Dark Ages or the Renaissance or whenever, he tries not to populate these subspace corridors with his sister, with images of his sister pacing back and forth along the subspace corridor linking her to him and deciding to fly from Baltimore to Los Angeles to spend one day with him, months before her mind was overlaid with too many errors of comprehension—does the white noise of airplanes soothe you as much as it soothes me?—who is this?—topo number two—my answer is your answer, Toñito—on long airplane rides to Czechia the white noise of the plane would blank my ability to read and all I could manage to do was watch saccharine movies featuring charming reversals, Silvina—and what I wanted to tell you, Antonio writes, no, I don't want to tell you anything— plus you already know that, before the onset of the misfortunes that await all of you, Antonio thinks, you won't become something other than what you are, in other words if your sister spends six hours each way inside a plane to see you for a day no red alert will force you to notice her desperation, no red alert will alter the intractable passageways that constitute your so-called stable family life in Los Angeles to warn you that no one boards a plane from Baltimore to Los Angeles to see anyone for a day unless that someone is desperate to reconstitute the passageways that might reestablish who she has been before an accretion of misfortunes began to disrupt her perceptions — let's play topos, Toñito — how do you play topos? — easy just repeat after me topo / topo / topo — desperate to untrace the passageways already overtaken by conspirative voices incognizant of the spatiotemporal regulations in the USA — my little brother thinks he's better than me because he spent two years at Yale what a sham — no red alert will warn you and your former wife that if your sister spends six hours each way inside a plane to visit you for a day you probably shouldn't reprimand your sister for eating all the baby carrots in the fridge — that is so rude, Estela — just as no red alert warned Antonio that, as summer #7 was coming to an end, as his daughters and former wife were boarding a plane from Czechia to Los Angeles, he was beginning to relegate Silvina to where the rest of his former companions were already fading and not fading from him, even though he didn't want to relegate Silvina anywhere — but before I tell you about The End of Silvina I want to tell you about Thomas Bernhard, Antonio writes, about that one afternoon inside a food court sushi place in the financial district of Los Angeles where Silvina, knowing I was organizing a marathon reading of Correction by Thomas Bernhard, one sentence per person, one shot of Cava per appearance of the word Cone, surprised me by gifting me a hardcover first edition of Correction by Thomas Bernhard — she didn't have enough money for food why would she spend $35 on me? — don't be a moron, Toñio — the hardcover first edition of Correction by Thomas Bernhard with two statues on the cover that reminded him of the human figures on Easter Island, the best gift anyone had ever given him, Antonio realized as she handed him the beautiful hardcover first edition of Correction by Thomas Bernhard, displacing in seconds all the wrongheaded gifts he'd received from former girlfriends throughout the years like thin belts, boxer shorts, franchise coffee, a pillow shaped like a pair of breasts, a snowboard, and either because Correction by Thomas Bernhard was the best gift anyone had ever given him or because he already knew that Silvina would be gone from him soon after the end of summer #7, even if he didn't want to acknowledge it to himself just yet — I have come to define happiness collectively, Antonio writes, and it's ridiculous, given that most adult relationships end anyway, Antonio reassures himself, to pursue a relationship with another adult at the expense of my daughters, who are so little still — his face, trying to suppress his impulse to cry, adopted a pained look that he tried to soften by repeating thank you so much, Silvina, thank you so much — find me Silvina's hands at that precise moment please — anything you say, boss — and, a week later, at the marathon reading of Correction by Thomas Bernhard, he bunched next to Silvina at a booth in Gratitude Cafe and pretended he wasn't spending every other evening with her (why did he encourage her to keep their relationship secret? so as to not upset Silvina's friends whose advances she'd turned down in college? so that there would be less explaining to do once it was over?), and, many months later, after the relegation had been completed and Silvina's apparitions had shifted from being painful reminders of what could have been to being forms of consolation for him — where are you taking me now, Antonio? — everywhere I go you go, Silvina — he boarded a plane to Baltimore to check on his sister, who, as she became less suspicious about the purpose of his unannounced visit, ranted at him with the same fervent repetitions, the same manic delivery of Thomas

Bernhard—I don't understand why Bernhard's always so pissed, Silvina—read his autobiography?—an autobiography that chronicles Bernhard's terrible upbringing and repeatedly acknowledges how this terrible upbringing has irreversibly marked him—by means of the cruel words my mother shouted at me she achieved peace and quiet, Thomas Bernhard says, but every time they plunged me into the most terrible pit of suffering, from which I have never escaped as long as I have lived—and as Antonio rereads Thomas Bernhard's autobiography he finds in the back of it some notes he'd written years ago about a coworker of his who reminded Antonio of Doc Brown in Back to the Future, a jovial man in his seventies who'd lent him a VHS tape on Borges and had told Antonio about growing up with his eccentric parents, both of them railroad workers, Doc Brown said, and sometimes my father would appear before my mother in one of his military costumes and recite poetry to her, and my mother, not to be outdone, would unearth her toga from the closet and refute my father by reciting from her side of the poetry stack, I knew a woman, Doc Brown recited, lovely in her bones, and last year, Doc Brown said, after I awoke from a coma, the heart surgeon asked me if I understood where I was, what had happened to me, and I wanted to tell him I was fine but didn't know how, couldn't articulate a simple statement to confirm I understood him so I panicked and began to declaim from Julius Caesar, friends, I said, Romans, countrymen, lend me your ears, I come to bury Caesar, not to praise him, and so the heart surgeon called his nurses, Doc Brown said, alarmed that perhaps I'd become deranged because I was talking nonsense and crying as I remembered my parents reciting poetry to each other in our living room, my parents, both dead, whom I miss every day—I wish I had parents I could miss, Silvina—my father's medication has shriveled the tentacles that tie him to his outer galaxies, Silvina said, but he has gained so much weight that he looks as if three versions of him have been crammed into one—and perhaps this image of Doc Brown's parents reciting poetry to each other has become an essential element in Antonio's narrative of how adult relationships should unfold, Antonio thinks, or at least the kind of adult relationships he would have liked to have for himself, and yes, during summer #7 Antonio did ask Silvina to read to him, although he doesn't remember what exactly he'd asked Silvina to read to him (later he will find in his phone's iTalk app (1) a 6:17 recording of Silvina reading from War & War by László Krasznahorkai, (2) a 1:46:43 recording of his mother telling him about her childhood, soon after losing track of his sister for the first time, (3) a 37:59 recording of his sister ranting at him, which he'd secretly recorded in Baltimore in case he needed to present evidence she was not well in order to commit her to a mental institute), and yet he does remember the story Dora read to him during summer #3 on the BART train on their way to see a Chekhov play in Orinda during their weekend trip to San Francisco, a story called Gooseberries by Anton Chekhov, a bafflingly slow story centered around a stern monologue warning you about the perils of happiness—there ought to be behind the door of every happy, contented man, Chekhov says, someone standing with a hammer continually reminding him with a tap that there are unhappy people, that however happy he may be, life will show him her laws sooner or later, trouble will come for him, disease, poverty, losses, and no one will see or hear, just as now he neither sees nor hears others—an inadequate story for the occasion because Antonio & Dora were still young and light in each other's presence and they were on the BART train on their way to see a play in an outdoor theater and they were carrying a picnic basket with sparkling wine, prosciutto, baguette—but there is no man with a hammer, Chekhov says — a quiet story they brushed off, Antonio thinks, just as they brushed off the homeless man who boarded the BART train and handed out miniature sign language instructions with a plea to please help him, a man that offended Antonio because Antonio was sure the man was pretending to be a mute, and neither Antonio nor Dora nor anyone else on the train handed the man who was pretending to be a mute any change, and so the man sat there, defeated, waiting for the next train stop so he could escape his embarrassing predicament, and a UC Berkeley student who looked as if she'd just come back from a Peace Corps assignment began to speak to him in sign language, and he replied to her in sign language, and she replied to him in sign language, and he replied to her in sign language, and Dora & Antonio could hear the man who wasn't pretending to be a mute emitting guttural sounds as he spoke to her in sign language desperately, and as Antonio rereads Gooseberries by Anton Chekhov, he no longer finds the story bafflingly slow, or he does but finds the slowness reassuring, likely because he no longer feels like a carefree young man with a picnic basket, yes, (1) he has so many white hairs now that Ada has given up on plucking them, (2) after his evening soccer games his shins are so banged up that he has to submerge his legs in Epsom salt baths to feign recovery, (3) let us avoid an inventory of ailments, please, recalling instead, as he rereads Gooseberries by Anton Chekhov, that on the same BART train ride but in the other direction during an offsite in Concord for his database analyst job, months before his sister began to misperceive the inconcrete as concrete, months after he had relegated Dora to where the rest of his former companions were already fading and not fading from him, he'd listened to Mary Gaitskill reading Symbols and Signs by Nabokov on his oversized circumaural Sennheiser headphones and had thought about Dora and Chekhov and their picnic basket—so wonderful to see us again on this train, Dora—you have quite an imagination, Antonio—no, he won't relisten to Symbols and Signs by Nabokov because he knows this time Dora and Chekhov will be the background and his sister will be the foreground, but of course he does relisten to Symbols and Signs by Nabokov, in which an old Russian couple visit their son at his sanatorium on his birthday, but unfortunately they can't see him, the nurse informs them, he has tried to take his life and seeing you might disturb him—the boy, aged six, Mary Gaitskill reads, that was when he drew wonderful birds with human hands and feet—yes, Antonio thinks, no one is near his cubicle at Prudential Investments so he can listen to Symbols and Signs by Nabokov without needing to suppress tears as the old defeated Russian father says, lying to himself, that they will get their boy out of the sanatorium the next day—all this, and much more, the mother had accepted, Mary Gaitskill reads, for, after all, living does mean accepting the loss of one joy after another, not even joys in her case, mere possibilities of improvement—she thought of the recurrent waves of pain that for some reason or other she and her husband had had to endure, Mary Gaitskill reads, of the invisible giants hurting her boy in some unimaginable fashion, of the incalculable amount of tenderness contained in the world, of the fate of this tenderness, which is either crushed or wasted, or transformed into madness.

—

Jules Jakobsdóttir's daughter reads Mirrors Aren't Terrifying and concludes she can improve her mother's story with speech-to-text software, so she (i) records herself reading her mother's story, (ii) runs the speech-to-text software, (i.ii) records herself reading the speech-to-text version of her mother's story, (ii.ii) runs the speech-to-text software, (i.iii) records herself reading the speech-to-text version of the speech-to-text version of her mother's story, repeating herself until her process transforms her mother's story into Garbled Mother Generator, a story by Jules Jakobsdóttir's daughter (who also happens to be called Jules Jakobsdóttir), and just as the casual reader is about to conclude that Garbled Mother Generator by Silvina Snæborg Ocampo is a straightforward process story about teenagers and their damn electronic devices, Jules Jakobsdóttir begins to receive transmissions from the Garbled Mother Generator, which instructs her to visit her mother at her homeless shelter—apparently my sister has driven from Baltimore to Milwaukee because she'd heard the homeless shelters there were better for women, Silvina—your sister's storage, Antonio's mother said over the phone, we have to find the name of your sister's storage company in Baltimore—but by the time his mother discovered the name of the storage company in Baltimore where his sister deposited her belongings after she lost her house, all of his sister's belongings had already been auctioned off—now folks today we're going to auction off Missus Pimber's things, Israbestis Tott says, I think you all knew Missus Pimber and you know she had some pretty nice things—why worry about her things Mom don't we have enough to worry about already?—not her things Antonio her personal things that can't be replaced, Antonio's mother said—which Antonio does not want to imagine—the last time your sister came to visit me she removed all your childhood pictures from my albums to scan them and she never returned them to me, Antonio.

—

If someone would have shared with Antonio the amusing anecdote of a woman who, having had enough, drives to Washington, D.C., enters the Pentagon, asks the receptionist if she could please speak to a supervisor because her life has become unbearable due to the satellites orbiting her, please stop spying on me, Antonio would have chuckled, or perhaps Antonio would have chuckled later, once the amusing anecdote reaches the part where the receptionist at the Pentagon calls the woman's mother, and the woman's mother has to explain her daughter's unfortunate circumstances and assure her she's harmless, don't worry, the receptionist says, thousands like her arrive here every year, I'll tell her to go on home, except of course Antonio didn't chuckle when his mother called him and told him she'd received a call from the receptionist at the Pentagon — how did she manage to drive from Baltimore to Washington in her condition, Antonio? — just as Antonio doesn't chuckle now when he sees homeless people talking to themselves in downtown Los Angeles, homeless people screaming at the air or the Pentagon, for weeks Antonio could hear the screams of a homeless woman from his sixth-floor cubicle on South Flower Street, all those years prior to his sister's illness he didn't chuckle when he walked past homeless people talking to themselves because he just didn't see them, homeless people not existing for him like those thousands of inconvenient memories of childhood his mind has managed to wipe from him, hundreds of insensate people on the streets who, some would argue, would stop malfunctioning if they simply swallowed their medication — I tell you it's selfish not to take the pills because I know, Graham Caldwell says, because I take them too you understand, Dad? — except what if your acute powers of discernibility betray you without you noticing so you're suspicious of anyone who tries to convince you that you need medication, Antonio thinks, believing instead that your family is conspiring against you by asking you to please see a doctor who could prescribe the right medication for you, listen, you can't force someone into a mental institution, you can't force someone, once she's in a mental institution, to talk to you over the phone, moreover, once she's in a mental institution, she can prohibit anyone in the mental institution to talk to you or even acknowledge to you that she is there, in other words if you're suddenly afflicted by a perceptual disorder there is no way to unwind your disorder unless you agree to take your medication, in other words if you suddenly believe the inconcrete is concrete you could lose your job, as my sister did, you could threaten to shoot your neighbors and end up in jail, as my sister did, you could lose your house, as my sister did, you could decide to run away to Milwaukee after the judge finds you incompetent to stand trial, as my sister did, and yet in Baltimore there is one way to institutionalize someone without their consent: if someone fills out a form attesting that the person in question is a danger to herself, as Antonio and his mother did, the police can capture the person in question, as the Baltimore police did, and the person in question can then be institutionalized for no more than two weeks, but if during those two weeks the person in question refuses to take any medication, as Antonio's sister did, if, moreover, during those two weeks the mental institution refuses to communicate with you so you can explain the particulars of her unfortunate situation, as the New Horizons Hospital did, then after two weeks she is free to go, as Antonio's sister had been, refusing to talk to Antonio and his mother ever again because see, my mother and my brother were conspiring against me (and here Antonio tries not to think about the message he sent to the private investigator this morning informing him that his sister's probably at some homeless shelter in Milwaukee), in other words if you suddenly controvert what others agree isn't there there's no rapid process of retroversion unless you agree to swallow your medication.

—

All this, of course, Silvina reads, indeed his whole history, originated in the distant past, said Korin, and here Antonio rewinds
the recording of Silvina reading from War & War by László
Krasznahorkai, trying to remember where he'd recorded her, all
this, of course, Silvina reads, indeed his whole history, originated
in the distant past, said Korin, no, Antonio thinks, he can't remember where he'd recorded her so he rewinds the recording to
the beginning again, listening to Silvina's voice again and thinking of Krapp's Last Tape, which he'd seen once by himself when
he was still twenty-five or twenty-two and once years later with
Dora—we lay there without moving, Krapp hears himself say,
but under us all moved, and moved us, gently, up and down, and
from side to side [pause]—rewinding to the same part of the recording where Krapp talks about a woman lying stretched on the
floorboards with her hands under her head, her eyes closed, the
whole world moving under them, all this, of course, Silvina reads,
indeed his whole history, originated in the distant past, said Korin, yes, Antonio thinks, he'd seen Krapp's Last Tape twice: the
first time he'd been twenty-five or twenty-two, his sister still a
Senior Actuarial Associate in Baltimore, Dora and his former
wife and Silvina still many years in the future, and because he
was still trying to understand whether he could become a writer
he was reading everything and attending so many performances
for the first time, Waiting for Godot, for instance, Krapp's Last
Tape, both of them on the same weekend by the same theater
troupe, and what he remembers of that first performance by the
Gate Theatre from Dublin, almost fifteen years ago, aside from the
audience laughing during the banana jokes, is the feeling that
this rewinding business was as amazing a literary device as
the letter writing in Herzog by Saul Bellow, and what he remembers of that second performance by the Cutting Ball Theater,

eight or nine years later, is Dora reading his copy of Krapp's Last
Tape while smoking outside the theater before the performance,
and Dora's impassive presence in the audience next to him, and
old Krapp so alone on the stage, passing the time before he dies
by listening to tapes of himself as a young man talking about
a woman whom he wishes to remember, again and again, we
lay there without moving, Antonio can recite from memory, but
under us all moved, which is how it had once been with Dora,
with his former wife, with Silvina, although he can remember
so few specifics about his time with Silvina, Silvina reading a
1,178-word sentence from War & War by László Krasznahorkai
and laughing when she reached word 439 because the sentence
was still going, pausing at word 839 to ask if he wanted her to
keep going, of course I do, Antonio says, keep going, going on,
call that going, call that on, listening to the recording of Silvina
reading a sentence from War & War by László Krasznahorkai
and hearing in the background the white noise of cars speeding
by, which meant he'd recorded her on her temporary bed, in
her second sublet apartment, near the off-ramp highway traffic,
the windows in her room open because it was summer #7 still,
Silvina outstretched on her bed in her cutoff jean shorts and a
Motörhead T-shirt that was falling apart, her feet on my hands,
Silvina & Antonio floating above the earth like Hari & Kris in
Solaris, but unfortunately this is all that he can scrape out of
this 6:17 recording of Silvina so he checks again to see if there's
any more recordings of Silvina in his iTalk app, yes, yes there is,
a fifty-five-second unlabeled recording of him testing where to
place the phone in his car because he was interviewing László
Krasznahorkai that week while driving him around Los Angeles:
this should work, he says, [turns down music from Messiaen's
Saint Francis of Assisi], can you talk a little bit while the car is
running, hmmk so I, hmmk, she says, [in a Muppet voice], this is

not really helpful, hmmk, he says, [in a Muppet voice, both laugh], let's try again let me ask you a question when was the last time you were really fucked, he says, [he laughs], all right, she says, [in a tone of resignation], just kidding what's your favorite book, he says, that's a nice question, she says, I think you might have been there for it heeey, [both laugh], so I am seeing that girl I think on Sunday, she says, what are you talking about Sunday is my day, he says, you are just going to have to, you're going to take a few hours off, she says, I am not sharing you with some girl who doesn't want to hang out with us, he says, [she laughs], you just said you couldn't blame her before you went on your death-wish spiral, and that's it, Antonio thinks, fifty-five more seconds of Silvina on top of the 6:17 of her reading War & War by László Krasznahorkai—perhaps my best years are gone, Krapp hears himself say, when there was a chance of happiness, but I wouldn't want them back, not with the fire in me now—Krapp should have recorded her instead of himself talking about her, Silvina—you think Krapp could withstand hearing her voice directly, Antonio?—all this, of course, Silvina reads, indeed his whole history [final time], originated in the distant past, said Korin, as far back as the time he first announced the fact that though an utterly mad world had made a madman of him, pure and simple, it didn't mean that that is entirely what he was, for while it would have been stupid to deny that sooner or later, nat-urally enough, that was how he'd finish up, or rather, sooner or later, reach a state resembling madness, it was obvious that whatever might in fact happen, madness was not a particularly unfortunate condition that one should fear as being oppressive or threatening, a condition one should be frightened of, no, not in the least, or at least he personally was not scared of it, not for a moment, for it was simply a matter of fact, as he later explained, that one day the straw actually did break the camel's back.

—

Ulrica Thrale's granddaughter (the protagonist of A Lexicon of
Terror who's of course also called Ulrica Thrale) arrives at her
father's sanatorium to inform him she's a management consul-
tant now so she will be going away to Kansas City, and the next
day she arrives to inform him she's an investment banker now
so she will be going away to Salt Lake City—we plant cauli-
flowers and groundhogs in the garden here, one of the nurses
says—and the next day and the next she continues to arrive
at her father's sanatorium with a brand-new profession and
her father always says permutations, connectives, infinitary
annotations, scalars, and what Ulrica's father says to Ulrica
next made Antonio cry the first time he read A Lexicon of
Terror—good one, Snivel—back at the beginning of summer
#7, when he'd asked Silvina to please share with him a copy of A
Lexicon of Terror & Other Stories, no I don't even have a copy a
Gloom Hulk who isn't me wrote those stories, she'd said, hmmk,
he'd said, in that case we're going to Skylight Books to purchase
a copy of A Lexicon of Terror & Other Stories, installing himself
afterward at Gratitude Cafe to read Silvina's stories and Silvina
saying I'm not sitting here while you compose eldritch thoughts
about those stories I wrote in high school so she escapes up-
stairs, and although Antonio doesn't believe in so-called epiph-
anies he does like to believe that, as he was reading Silvina's
stories for the first time, imagining Silvina's footsteps above him,
he produced an actual epiphany for himself: if Silvina can write
about her miserable childhood—her father covering all the mirrors in the house when he still lived with Silvina and her mother,
her father recording his jumbled pronouncements that he would
then send to the local radio station—so can I, and so Antonio
rewrote large swaths of his first novel set in Bogotá, sharing with
Silvina some of the worst episodes of his childhood in Bogotá

in frantic monologues over dinner that he then assigned to his characters the next morning, and as he remembers those frantic monologues over dinner he thinks of that time during summer #7 when Silvina's sublease above Gratitude Cafe expired and she didn't know what to do with her ragged mattress, why don't you leave it on the sidewalk, Antonio said, I'm not sure I can do that, Silvina said, of course you can everyone else does, Antonio said, so he helped her haul her ragged mattress to the sidewalk in front of Gratitude Cafe, and Silvina became quiet, looked nervous, as if someone was eyeing her as the two of us carried her ragged mattress downstairs, what's the matter, Antonio said, I feel extremely uneasy about breaking any laws, she said, I think I'm afraid I'll make one mistake and be deported or end up in a homeless shelter—I don't think my mother will ever recover from knowing my sister ended up in a homeless shelter, Silvina—what about you how do you go on, Antonio?—it takes tremendous energy to keep functioning while carrying the memory of terror, Dr. Van Der Kolk says—and at Ulrica's father's sanatorium he says to her transmissions, emissions, subspace corridors, sensors, difficult job, I will write to your boss, Ulrica's father says, I will come with you.

WHEN ANTONIO WAS TOÑIO

You would spend hours playing soccer with your sister, Antonio's mother says, or you would combine your toys so that your helicopters would fly over her dollhouse and her Barbies would sunbathe inside your Star Wars station, and you would do earthquake, remember?, no, Antonio says, I don't remember, when you were done playing with Barbies, Antonio's mother says, because your sister would dress them, pick hats and purses for them, parade them, allow them to ride in your helicopters, the two of you would spend hours playing with your toys, and all of a sudden, perhaps because you were tired, you would do earthquake and the dollhouse would fly out in pieces and your sister would run out and say Mom my brother did earthquake on my house, so that would be the end of your games for the day, but other than that the two of you got along very well, playing soccer or hide-and-seek in our patio since we couldn't leave that house in Mirandela because your father would lock it before going to work, eventually he handed me a key after I protested so much, although I couldn't leave the house just the same because he would call every fifteen minutes, and if I didn't answer the phone, he would imagine I wasn't home and that would turn into a terrible altercation, so you would arrive home from school and we would spend our time playing together, and because you wanted to play soccer we spent a lot of time in the patio, and you would climb on the fence, standing on the ledge of the cement wall below and attaching yourself to the wire mesh above, and from up there you would chat with Don Jorge, the elderly man next door who would always say to me Leonora, if anything happens, because he would hear your father screaming and threatening us, if he lays a finger on you or something happens, you shout for us and I'll come out immediately, Don Jorge would say, and I have a gun, and one day he said to your father we're here, next door to you, and we've been listening to your screaming, you know I am armed and all I have to do is jump over the fence and bring my sons with me, who were huge, by the way, you want to act macho with your wife, you're going to have to act macho with us, in any case you would tread along the fence and call out Don Jorge, Don Jorge, and that dear old man would trudge toward our fence, because he was quite old already, approaching you with chocolates in hand, Don Jorge don't give him chocolate or he won't eat his dinner, I would say, ay Leonora just one piece of chocolate, or he would bring you candy, the chewy kind, toffees, I think, and because he was so nice I would say fine, Toñio, eat the candy, those were the days when it occurred to you to sell water for dogs you probably don't remember that, no, Antonio says, I remember I would put leaves in empty cologne bottles, and you would say water for dogs, Antonio's mother says, here the water for dogs, and so the neighbors would stroll by and ask what's in that water, ah, it's a special, magical water to cure street dogs from their sickness, you would say, because there was a lot of street dogs in that neighborhood I don't know if you remember they were all over the streets, dirty and beaten up, we had La Pelusa and La Cuca, I mean La Perla, our unruly street dog, and so it was so funny to see you selling water for dogs, trying to because you never sold a bottle so you would give them away at the end, and so people would tell you okay, can you give me one bottle for the street dogs over there, if you're going to give it to them yes, otherwise you have to pay me, yes, it's for the street dogs over there who are thirsty, and so I would bring out a bowl and we would fill it out with your water for dogs, and so it was this great

adventure for you to climb on the fence and hand them the bowl
with water for dogs, yes, you and your sister got along very well,
playing soccer or hide-and-seek in the patio in that house in
Mirandela, that long stretch of patio that culminated in a dilapidated house next to ours, which had a window with what
looked like prison bars from where a boy with Down syndrome
would watch the two of you play, a boy who must have been
eighteen whereas you two were around six or seven at the time,
and because I was worried he might say something improper, I
was always nearby when he was by his window, shouting out of
excitement as he watched the two of you play, and sometimes
you would get scared and ask me why does he shout, Mom, and
I would say because he's stirred by your games, because he can't
play, because he's trapped in that house by himself, why does
he have those eyes, Mom, that face, because he was born with
a problem and he's always going to be like that, oh so he's sick,
you would say, no he isn't sick he just doesn't have a long life
ahead of him, but after the three of us finally escaped from that
house in Mirandela, Antonio's mother says, I never heard what
happened to that boy again.

NOTES TO MY BIOGRAPHER BY ADAM HASLETT

Bureaucracies have trouble thinking clearly, Franklin Caldwell
Singer says, I, on the other hand, am perfectly lucid, I, Antonio
thinks, am perfectly lucid, too—Franklin Caldwell Singer isn't
lucid, Antonio writes, although most of his faculties seem
intact—is he also suffused with light?—I am perfectly lucid, too,
Antonio's lamp says—and yes, Franklin Caldwell Singer, on his
journey to see his son, the only person who meant anything to
him—unfortunately some of my children bored me, Franklin
Caldwell Singer says, but Graham never did—on his last journey
to see his son in a borrowed Saab before he dies, does seem perfectly lucid at first, just as almost twelve months ago Antonio's
sister had seemed perfectly lucid when Antonio first appeared
unannounced at her house in Baltimore, suspicious he was
there, sure, but who wouldn't be if he'd never visited her before,
welcoming him to her house and offering him leftover ceviche,
her favorite dish with heaps of red onions on top, which he de-
clined because he didn't know how long it had been sitting out
on her counter, I already ate, he said, thank you so much—do
you remember us eating too many green mangoes in Bogotá,
Toñio?—our soured teeth, yes—the bowls of ciruelas and
grosellas—and after Antonio settled his bags in his sister's guest
room and sat on her couch in her dark living room, his sister,
while four split screens on her television tracked the perimeter
of her house, as she paced around the subspaces of her living
room, approaching the one small window in the kitchen that
hadn't been shuttered to yell at her neighbors to leave her alone,
told Antonio everything, an everything he likes to believe he
doesn't remember anymore just as he likes to believe he doesn't

remember the rest of it (when his sister came to see him in Los Angeles one last time, months before she was arrested for allegedly threatening to shoot her neighbors, she brought along photocopies of a military article explaining advanced techniques in mind control, handing them to him and asking for his help—I promised her I would read them, Antonio writes, but I never did, although I remember the diagrams of spy aircraft like geometry assignments—but instead of helping her (what could he have possibly done to help her?) he sobbed in front of her, which didn't help because she stopped telling him anything—I don't want to make you cry, Toñito, Antonio's sister said—), and in her dark living room in Baltimore, as she grew more comfortable with the possibility he was in fact her brother, her everything became a rant that, because of its length and recursiveness, reminded him of Correction by Thomas Bernhard, I know how to appear sane, she said, even if you call the police I know how to appear sane and calm and reasonable, yes, officer, no, officer, that doesn't sound like an adequate explanation of quantum mechanics, officer, laugh, Toñio, that was a joke, when two policemen questioned me yesterday they were impressed at how sane I appeared why would anyone call to report me they can't take me away against my will I haven't done anything, restraining herself from sharing with those two policemen the conspiracies she was sharing with Antonio as she grew more comfortable with the concept of her brother as her audience, Iron Man, she said, radial frequencies from satellites with lasers, covert psychological training, swatting the imaginary insects around her head, are you recording me don't record me let me see your phone, Antonio's sister said, of course I am not recording you, Antonio said, although moments before he had begun recording her in case he needed the evidence as part of the process to commit his sister to a mental institute against her will, and as Antonio rereads

Notes to my Biographer by Adam Haslett, he tries to think about gradations of incoherence in fiction instead of his sister's incoherence in Baltimore, about how in the works of, say, Miquel Bauçà, the lack of linkage between contiguous statements complicates the text—the buttonholes on his shirt more and more match the color of his trousers, Miquel Bauçà says, no doubt this is why his wife has finally been able to sing at the opera house—whereas in Notes to my Biographer the linkage between most contiguous statements contains no complications—the nude dancing incident in the Louvre in a room full of Rubenses was of a piece with other end-of-the-war celebrations at the time, Franklin Caldwell Singer says—in other words Franklin Caldwell Singer, like Antonio's sister, is lucid enough to know you might think his statements might be interpreted as incoherent so he tries to convince you his statements are not incoherent by strengthening the logic of his linkages, and Franklin Caldwell Singer does succeed in planting seeds of doubt about what's sane and what isn't, for instance Antonio could believe in one spy dressed as a reindeer trying to obtain Franklin Caldwell Singer's industrial secrets, but not two spies dressed as reindeers on two separate occasions (Antonio's mother, determined to believe her daughter did not have the disturbance with the horrendous name, would explain to Antonio over the phone why she thought his sister was telling the truth about her coworkers spying on her at home—they've bugged her house, Antonio's mother said, because they knew things we had just talked about at her house—and so his sister started storing all her phones in the freezer, as she'd asked him to do when he arrived at her house in Baltimore), and yes, Antonio did record his sister twice, when he'd first arrived and later that day, after she'd tired of her own rant and he drove with her to dinner at Sí Señor, but no, he will not listen to his recording of her threatening to throw

herself out of his compact rental car or her accusing him of thinking he's better than her because he spent two years at Yale (what
would be the point of transcribing her incoherence in Baltimore?
unlike Adam Haslett, who lightens Franklin Caldwell Singer's incoherence with humor, Antonio cannot yet see the humor in his
sister's fate—why don't you delete the recording then?—listening
to it would be the equivalent of staring at a naked person asleep
on the sidewalk—delete it then—), please, Graham Caldwell
says to his father just as Antonio had said to his sister at Sí Señor,
settle down, no one in this restaurant is spying on us, and while
on the one hand Franklin Caldwell Singer remembers his son
Graham as a child—he used to bring me presents in my study
on the days I was leaving for a trip, Franklin Caldwell Singer
says, and he'd ask me not to go—on the other hand Graham
says to his father I thought my own father was dead, you didn't
call for four years but I couldn't bear to find out, couldn't bear to
go on and find you dead, and so it was like I was a child again,
and here Antonio stops reading, as he always does when he
reaches this passage, unable to continue (of course Antonio
knows why this passage always makes him cry—of course I
know so what?—cry you son of a bitch—Antonio has been pretending his father's dead since Antonio left Bogotá, twenty-four
years ago (Antonio would rather not think about that individual
right now (playing basketball with that individual in his grandmother's patio in preparation for his intramural matches at San
Luis Gonzaga (playing chess with that individual at a second-
rate tennis club while American music played in the background—sailing / takes me away—cry you piece of shit—by a
pool with the tallest diving board he'd ever seen—here are these
memories of that individual what am I supposed to do with
them?—his mother calling him almost a year ago and telling
him that that individual had remarried and his new wife was

accusing him of abusing her teenage daughter from a previous marriage and he was therefore in hiding—I think this is connected to what's happening to your sister, Antonio's mother said, but your sister doesn't want to hear anything to do with him—Antonio finding a way to call that individual who was in hiding to check if he was okay how do you explain that?—children are programmed to be fundamentally loyal to their caregivers, Bessel van der Kolk says, even if children were wronged by them—it's not far down to paradise / at least it's not for me—)))), I can't sleep, Tata, Eva says, let's count bunnies, Antonio says, I tried but they ran away, Eva says, it happens come let's try again together, Antonio says, and after Antonio tucks in Eva he returns to the living room and to Franklin Caldwell Singer and his last journey to see his son before he dies (although Franklin Caldwell Singer never says this is my last journey before I die, if you read Notes to My Biographer as many times as Antonio has, you might also conclude it is the narrator's last journey due to the fact that (1) Franklin Caldwell Singer is seventy-three years old, (2) his road trip includes trying to say goodbye to other family members, who refuse to see him, (3) he has driven from a place where he has nothing left—the eviction notices in Baltimore, he says, the collection agencies—), and after Franklin Caldwell Singer's done exhausting his son with his incoherence just as in Baltimore Antonio's sister had exhausted Antonio with hers, Franklin Caldwell Singer says my son looks so young as he weeps, as he did in the driveway of the old house on the afternoon I taught him to ride a bicycle, the dust from the drive settling on his wetted cheek and damp eyelashes, later to be rinsed in the warm water of the bath as dusk settled over the field and we listened together to the sound of his mother in the kitchen running water, the murmur of the radio, the stillness of evening in the country.

WHEN ARTURO WAS ESTELA

My mother was tired of me biting my sister, Ismene said, and perhaps because she thought I didn't understand biting hurts other people, she bit me in the face, leaving a mark that was embarrassing to explain at school—I like not being seen, Ophelia said, that's why I volunteer at Lighthouse for the Blind—my parents escaped from Laos and spent ten years in a refugee camp in Thailand, Joanna said, and you could tell which members of our family had been born into the camp because they were much shorter due to the food rationing (Joanna told Antonio her grandmother still helps North Koreans escape to Thailand by guiding them through the same trails her parents used to escape, so he asked her to please describe those trails to him, but she had been too little to remember them so he has come to imagine them as the insides of anthills or the dark subterranean passages for birds in the Seuss books he reads to his daughters—Joanna grew up in Kansas, Antonio writes, where she learned about the Flying Spaghetti Monster—dear Flying Spaghetti Monster who definitely exists—Joanna is a marine biologist, Antonio writes, and because of her autoimmune disease she approached our arrangement with abandon, as if sleeping with an unpublished older novelist had been on her do-before-death list—), and as Antonio rereads the few fragments he has managed to jot down from his arrangements so far (most mornings like this morning he's too depleted from his arrangements or from soccer to thoroughly document his arrangements so most memories of them have already vanished from him), he receives a YSA message from Goth Raver, who wants to know if he would like to meet her tonight, and although she does look like a goth raver into psychedelics and bondage, and although it's probably a bad sign that she's not college verified and she has contacted him first even though he has no public photos and she hasn't requested access to his private photos (Antonio likes to believe he has become an expert at filtering arrangements by their photos (if photo = too naked, delete indicator = 1) and by their messages (if first message = I know what I'm worth my exact compensation requirements are $$$, delete indicator = 1)), but of course his filtering system doesn't always perform as coded, or it does but he makes concessions if that week he has no new arrangements in the queue (an arrangement who'd failed both the photo and message filters but was too striking to skip told him she'd been arrested by a policeman who'd posed as an SD so before entering Antonio's apartment complex she asked him if he was with law enforcement because according to her if you are with law enforcement you can't say you aren't), or he'll make concessions if on the same morning he receives a message from both Goth Raver asking him if he would like to be her SD and Ron the Bail Bondsman informing him the private investigator has found his sister in a jail in Milwaukee, and although Antonio would rather exhaust himself at the soccer field tonight, Goth Raver looks so striking in her photos that Antonio agrees to meet her tonight at 9:30 p.m. at Salt Air, and fortunately she looks as striking in person as she does in her photos (unlike his arrangement the previous week who'd claimed to be a poet and a model and turned out to be a tedious tech writer with a cake blog), and so Antonio orders the usual bottle of Cava and the usual tray of oysters and does the usual toast—for not being dead—thinking life is unbelievable and beautiful, unconcerned about the photos with blood coming out of what looks like a knife wound on her chest that she's sharing with him, unconcerned about her

telling him how she'd been approached by a wealthy tech entre-
preneur at the San Francisco airport and how he hired her to be
his secretary on the spot and of course she knew why he hired
her but she was not going to give him what he wanted, and as
usual a black car transports them to The Other Home, where she
undoes the white ankle straps of her stilettos and places them on
his windowsill, which surprises him because most arrangements
who come with stilettos know to leave them on, not that he
minds how on the windowsill the stilettos are facing each other
like spectators who are too shy to look toward his bed, where he's
pecking her feet with his lips, suppressing an impulse to bite her
calves because he's too drunk for the right calculus of teeth, rub-
bing his cheek on her black leather miniskirt as if putting himself to sleep—goodnight cow under the moon—osculating her
thighs that even in the dark he can see have glitter and bruises
on them (he will have to make sure there's no glitter on his face
tomorrow morning—why is your face sparkly, Tata—no it isn't
did you see that platypus over there?—), but as they entangle
each other further, outstretched on his bed, his hands on her
legs, her breath on his neck—the sea / the sea—she jumps up
and informs him she needs to use the bathroom, where she
stays for too long, and when at last she's done he hears her opening his file cabinets in the kitchen but he doesn't rush to ask her
what does she think she's doing because that might sour their
arrangement, and when she returns to the living room she's
holding the card that says I am sorry you hurt your foot Tata
and the photo of his daughters and his former wife that he keeps
hidden on top of his fridge, a card and a photo she drops on the
floor because her hands are jittery, although she doesn't seem to
mind them and of course he's not going to ask her if she injected
herself in his bathroom, motherfucker, she says, as if he's slighted
her somehow, as if someone had pressed a button requesting a

pantomime of horror but she didn't understand the complete instructions, please, Antonio says, calm down, terrified about waking up his neighbors because it's past midnight and she's almost screaming that she needs to leave, don't come near me, motherfucker, she says, even though he's nowhere near her or making any attempt to come near her, order me a car now, she says, and so he, dumbfounded, orders her a car, and she, dredging up more bile, curses at him and conducts an uneven performance of storming out, returning to pick up her stilettos from the windowsill and concluding her uneven performance of storming out, but it isn't over yet because she's still downstairs, screaming so much that Antonio, three floors up, can hear her, so he rushes downstairs and she screams where is my car, motherfucker, please, Antonio says, it's coming, showing her the screen of his phone, which he's holding with both hands in case she tries to snatch it from him, and the trajectory of the Prius on the screen culminates with the Prius picking up this barefoot pantomime of horror, and fortunately there are no neighbors carping at him from their windows, or at least he can't see any of them, but unfortunately it isn't over yet because at 5:30 a.m. she sends him a YSA message saying unless you bring me five thousand dollars by noon I am contacting your wife, who I'm sure will be thrilled to receive screenshots of your YSA profile and photos of me in your foul bathroom, so here it is then, Antonio thinks, at last my turn has come—I don't want to listen to your family constellations conjectures right now—if a family member is ejected from the family system—I'm not your intergenerational if / then puppet—I've always despised plot, Grace Paley says, the absolute line between two points, not for literary reasons but because it takes all hope away—unfortunately my son is not giving himself the opportunity and prefers to follow the path of his father—but I've done nothing wrong, Antonio thinks, unwilling to give in, moreover, I could press charges for extortion, and yet despite having done nothing wrong, if Goth Raver contacts his former wife, his so-called stable family life will be upended, for how will he explain to her the existence of Goth Raver from Your Sugar Arrangements, and so Antonio calls Nicolas, his one college friend, a wealthy Chilean who's also a member of Your Sugar Arrangements but in New York, explaining the Goth Raver backstory and asking him for the name of an attorney, verga, Nicolas says, that's heavy, but how would she even contact Ida did you like lend that raver your phone or tell her your real name, she was going through my stuff and maybe she found my name on one of my utility bills in the kitchen or maybe she did a reverse photo search online, Antonio says, mira, Nicolas says, my friend is an immigration attorney but what you need is a criminal attorney let me ask my friend for a referral but text me a photo of Goth Raver or no deal ha ha, and while Antonio waits for a referral from Nicolas, Antonio tries to contain his panic because it's 9:30 a.m. already — breathe, motherfucker — no, he will not wait for Nicolas, who has always been unreliable in any case, he will search online for a criminal attorney with good reviews, and once he finds one that can see him at 10:30 a.m., he cancels his meetings at Prudential Investments and rushes to meet this random criminal attorney he found on the internet, are you sure you didn't do anything to her, the criminal attorney says, you have to trust me and tell me the truth or I can't help you, nothing, Antonio says, showing the criminal attorney her photos and her messages, Goth Raver, the criminal attorney says, examining her photos as if they were assignments from a class on American pornography, I know, Antonio says, has she contacted you again, the criminal attorney says, yes she texted me at 9:45 a.m., Antonio says, showing him a message that says I know you read my message on the site if you don't deliver the money by noon expect to see me and my boyfriend at your doorstep, and so what I want to know, Antonio says, is whether I should press charges for extortion before she contacts Ida or wait to see if she's bluffing, and clearly the random criminal attorney from the internet doesn't know the answer because he says let me check with my colleagues, calling one colleague, two colleagues, okay, the criminal attorney says, we don't want to alert the police since she might be bluffing, so don't press charges, stay put, print her photos and messages, place them in a folder with a note I will write for you and carry this folder with you at all times, pay me two thousand now and two thousand later, that way you're protected if she contacts your family or if the police have to get involved, but Antonio decides to wait before signing any contracts because Nicolas has finally messaged him a referral, and so he leaves the office of the random criminal attorney from the internet and calls Nicolas's referral, explains the extortion backstory, and the referral says she's too busy for his case so she refers him to another criminal attorney, who has time to meet him in two days, meanwhile, the random criminal attorney from the internet messages him to say on second thought I need the full four thousand now, which confirms Antonio's suspicions that the random criminal attorney from the internet is trying to scam him, meanwhile, back at his desk at Prudential Investments, it's 12:00 already, 12:05, 12:10, but his phone doesn't ring, 1:30, 1:45, but he receives no YSA messages from Goth Raver, no texts, but what if Goth Raver and her boyfriend are already waiting outside my apartment, Antonio thinks, so that night he decides to sleep at the apartment where his daughters live, as he's allowed to do three times a week at most, standing by the window of his former wife's bedroom to check if there's any strange cars outside his apartment, three doors down, why are you standing by the window, Tata, Ada says, I am waiting for the Flying Spaghetti Monster, Antonio says, let's play Monster, Ada says, who can tell me which Dr. Seuss book contains underground tunnels for birds, Antonio says, oh I know, Ada says, running to the living room and returning with I Had Trouble in Getting to Solla Sollew, which he has read to Ada and Eva many times before, read it, Tata, Eva says, I Had Trouble in Getting to Solla Sollew by Sandra Boynton, Antonio says, come on, Tata, I Had Trouble in Getting to Solla Sollew by Dr. Seuss, I was real happy and carefree and young and I lived in a place called the Valley of Vung, Antonio reads, and nothing, not anything ever went wrong, is he a cat, Tata, Eva says, an invented Seuss creature I think, Antonio says, he looks like a cat, Eva says, no kitten around, Ada says, and the Seuss kitten escapes from the Poozers by jumping into Vent #5, well, that vent where he went was sort of a funnel, Antonio reads, that led him down into a frightful black tunnel, with billions of absurd birds clogging the tunnel with tubas, skateboards, cactus, look, Tata, Eva says, the fish from The Cat in the Hat, I was down there three days in that bird-filled-up place, Antonio reads, and the next day Antonio avoids his apartment again, unable to sleep because what if his former wife receives a message from Goth Raver and decides he shouldn't be allowed to see his daughters again or what if his daughters open his backpack and unearth the Goth Raver Extortion folder he has been carrying with him at all times, until at last he's sitting in front of the criminal attorney referred to him by Nicolas's referral, I represent thieves, he says, arsonists, murderers, what the hell are you doing here, so Antonio shares the Goth Raver backstory and hands him the folder, Goth Raver, he says, examining her photos as if they're part of an art project he's expected to admire (he does), I know, Antonio says, I hear about these scammers on these sugar daddy websites all the time have you heard from her again, he says, no, Antonio says, and you won't, he says, if you haven't heard from her by now you won't hear from her, there's nothing for me to do here, be more careful next time, don't take them to your apartment because if they see you have a nice apartment they will be more tempted to scam you—my extra-small studio apartment is a filthy nook, Antonio doesn't say—and make sure they're over eighteen because I've encountered cases where they organize group sex sessions and sneak in an underage girl for extortion purposes as well, now get the hell out of my office, the criminal attorney says, handing back Antonio's folder, I have criminals to represent, and so Antonio exits the criminal attorney's office, wondering where he should hide the folder he has been carrying at all times, and how long he should keep it (just in case), and whether he will keep his promise to quit his beloved website later today (perhaps tomorrow?).

WHEN ANTONIO IX WAS ANTONIO I

Soccer as science fiction, Antonio thinks — science fiction for people who don't read science fiction, Silvina would have countered since Antonio hasn't read much science fiction besides A Lexicon of Terror & Other Stories — soccer as A Lexicon of Terror, Antonio thinks, soccer as science fiction culled from interplanetary war films I used to watch with my father at Cine Los Mayas, soccer as a transport between worlds such that, if soccer indicator = 1, for instance, then location = Bogotá and Los Angeles and time = 1989 and 2014, which, sure, isn't that remarkable, anyone in Los Angeles who possesses even one vivid memory of another city can be in two places / time periods at the same time, but perhaps it would be more remarkable if he adds a discontinuity indicator to factor in the twenty-one-year interlude when he didn't play soccer, in other words if he, after arriving to the United States, age eighteen, would have continued to play soccer every day as he had done in Bogotá, irrupting into the spaces between his classmates on the dusty soccer field at San Luis Gonzaga as if someone had disinterred his undead and he, without knowing it, was both escaping them and squelching them — pass the ball already, Bruja — accumulating red cards and releasing a sizable fraction of the thermodynamic violence apportioned to him by his upbringing, he probably wouldn't be equating soccer with science fiction while running SQL queries at Prudential Investments and waiting for news of his sister, in other words if discontinuity indicator = 0, then soccer <> science fiction, but unfortunately for the discontinuity indicator to ever equal zero he would have to have been a different Antonio, because that version of Antonio (henceforth Antonio II), age

eighteen, had reprogrammed himself to complete his one assignment, to be admitted to an Ivy League, so Antonio II spent
most of his time either solving differential equations for trans-
ferrable math courses, which didn't require him to compute the
language, or listening to transmissions of American English at
the ESL lab at his community college south of Chapel Hill,
learning to compute a new language he liked to believe he knew
but didn't—you also wanted to gain muscle weight at the gym
since you were as scrawny as a—that's neither here nor—you
quit soccer because it made you lose muscle weight, you vain
fuck—yes and later you stopped watching soccer on television
because you wanted to think of yourself as an intellectual ha
ha—so given that discontinuity indicator = 1, then soccer =
science fiction, location = Bogotá and Los Angeles, and time =
1989 and 2014, and yes, what he'd said to Dora about the soccer
linkage between Ada and him was true—as if I was watching
an apparition of myself as a boy playing soccer in Bogotá but
much better, Dora—but what he hadn't told Dora is that after
Antonio VII (father of Ada & Eva) watched Ada on the soccer
field, Antonio IV (intellectual) felt a longing to transport himself twenty-one years back and set the discontinuity indicator
for Antonio II (Ivy League) and Antonio III (bodybuilder) to
zero, and because that wasn't possible he purchased soccer
cleats, shin guards, expensive jerseys from a Spanish team he
didn't know, and transported himself to a pickup soccer game
in Los Angeles, where he discovered, within minutes, that discontinuity or continuity or whatever, time had indeed passed
and Antonio IX (old man soccer) could neither run for long nor
maintain possession of the ball—why are you even here,
nerd?—and what had been remarkable to Antonio VIII
(writer) was how, despite a span of twenty-one years, Antonio IX
(old man soccer) couldn't disconnect himself from Antonio I

(young man soccer), and so as Antonio V (database analyst) creates a spreadsheet to tabulate the other Antonios, linking Antonio IX and Antonio I with a Curved Double Arrow Connector, he's reminded of the essay about the overweight psychotherapy patient who discovered that, as she was losing significant portions of her weight, memories of her life when she last had that weight came back to her—as if my body has a memory, she said to Dr. Irvin Yalom—yes, Antonio thinks, his own body not only has a memory but two twisted ankles due to the irresponsible equivalence of Antonio IX = Antonio I, his left ankle, incidentally, hasn't recovered so a chronic pain appears and disappears in it depending on the weather, time of day, etc., and just as Antonio VII and Antonio VIII and Antonio V had agreed to shut down Antonio IX to avoid further physical injury, his sister began to ununderstand her life, so all the Antonios still in operation reconvened and agreed that, instead of reactivating temporary disruptive erasure mechanisms like binge drinking or nightclubbing in order to not think about what was happening to his sister (and here Antonio omits Your Sugar Arrangements from his inventory of temporary disruptive erasure mechanisms—déjenme por lo menos un joy, carajo—), they decided to call off the shutdown of Antonio IX, allowing him to recalibrate himself by (1) following the instructions of how-to-tape-your-ankles videos, (2) studying the less taxing passing strategies of Modrić and Iniesta in midfield, (3) not following the instructions of how-to-stretch-before-and-after-a-soccer-match videos because stretching reminded him of his mother's yoga classes in the forest and made him feel old, and once the recalibration had been completed, he began to not think about his sister while chasing a stupid ball for an hour and a half, and despite the sports tape on his ankles and the Epsom salt baths afterward and restricting the wrecking of his body to twice a week, he exists in a constant state of strain now, beginning with his left toe, which cramps on him for no discernible reason, his left thigh, which requires a thigh sleeve while he's reenacting a recalibrated Antonio I—there are turns and feints that only occur while stamping across a soccer field, Antonio writes, and perhaps because these movements are otherwise dormant they electrify everything when they reawaken—this new state of strain, paradoxically, at the same time (1) assuages him, (2) extirpates (most of) his impulse to sink himself with his sister, (3) aerates the subspace corridor that links him to his sister, wherever she might be, okay, 5:01 p.m., folks, enough with the SQL queries and the nebulous science fiction associations (last week one of his classmates at San Luis Gonzaga posted a recent photo of Cine Los Mayas, where he used to watch interplanetary war films with his father on Sundays, its windows and ticket booth boarded up), so Antonio removes his oversized circumaural Sennheiser headphones, which have been transmitting Phase Patterns by Steve Reich on repeat, switches off the fluorescence of his cubicle—goodnight, Lucid—rides his Shadow VLX from the Prudential Investments building to the apartment where his daughters live, thinking along the way of the futility of the bodybuilding efforts of Antonio III since Antonio IX has now lost so much muscle weight due to this new recalibrated soccer that he's almost as scrawny as he was at twenty-one years old, and after dinner with Ada and Eva and his former wife—no dinner for me thanks I have soccer tonight—you should have told me I wouldn't have fried the steka yet, monkey—he stretches out his body on the living room floor so he can wrap his ankles with a layer of self-adhesive bandage and multiple layers of sports tape, those are my scissors but you can borrow them, Eva says, can I come watch you, Tata, Ada says, they have no school tomorrow, Ida says, of course, Antonio says, so Antonio transports Ada and Antonio IX to a turf field on Woodbine Avenue, where Antonio tries not to think about the message he received from his sister's attorney informing him that his sister is finally being transported from Milwaukee to Baltimore through an interstate police system that doesn't allow him to know her precise location yet but instead tries to focus on scoring, passing, skirting opponents, including an oversized college student who clearly doesn't know anything about soccer because whenever Antonio has the ball he just barges against Antonio as if the ball belonged to this giant and Antonio was just a nuisance to be shrugged off, and perhaps because this amorphous giant reminds him of El Mono, a classmate at San Luis Gonzaga who resembled an orangutan (and who used to beat up Antonio whenever), Antonio becomes flustered, irrationally angry, and when this awkward blob dispossesses him again by interposing himself between Antonio and the stupid ball, Antonio pushes him so hard that this primate piece of shit falls backward, quit fouling me, motherfucker, Antonio says (later Antonio will consider that if he would have had his metal water bottle handy, he would have smashed it against this guy's face), I call the fouls, the organizer of the pickup game says, we don't do violence here, we don't want people like you here, you're out, but he's been fouling me all night, Antonio says, embarrassed as he exits the field because he'd forgotten Ada was watching him, what happened, Tata, Ada says, that moron kept fouling me, Antonio says, they should have kicked him out, Ada says, that mnemocartographic dunce, Antonio says, trying to lighten the mood on their drive back to where his former wife will shake her head at him — no milk for you, little boy — that wocket in the pocket, Ada says, that zelf under the shelf, Antonio says, do you believe in ghosts, Ada says, no nobody has seen them, Antonio says, the caretaker at this church told us that it was built over a cemetery and they have footage of ghosts, Ada says, we would have heard, Antonio says, ghosts are like Jesus or god, made up, imagine if I say I'm going to invent a strange creature called Snæborg Ocampo, and then I say oh but Snæborg Ocampo is invisible, ah, Ada says, I understand, we humans have a need to believe someone is watching over us, Antonio says, but there is someone watching over me, Tata, Ada says, you and Mama.

ANTONIO'S MOTHER BY NICOLA CARATI

Your grandmother Martina didn't talk about her upbringing, Antonio's mother says, instead she would repeat the same refrain that her mother died when she was a small child so she had to live with her father, what other refrains do you remember hearing from my grandmother, Antonio says, asking his mother about his grandmother from his father's side during Christmas #6 because Antonio was trying to insert the voices of his grandmothers into a novel set in Bogotá, recording his mother while his former wife and his two daughters tried to sleep in his mother's guest room in Sioux Falls, rewinding his 1:46:43 recording of his mother and listening to her saying your grandmother Martina didn't talk about her upbringing, just as neither Antonio's sister nor Antonio ever talked about their upbringing, drawing flowcharts of his mother's associations in his 1:46:43 recording of her as winter #8 comes to an end without news of when and how his sister will be transferred from Milwaukee to Baltimore, tracing his mother's shifts from one anecdote to another, starting with Martina, the ice cream enterprises of her brother Lucho, the humorless enterprises of her brother Francisco, Lucho's wife saying to Lucho you're going to change or you're going to change because I'm not divorcing you, her brother Francisco who calls her now that his family is also falling apart, all of it in the first 19:28 of his 1:46:43 recording of his mother sitting across from him at her dining table during Christmas #6, his daughters sneaking into the living room to pirouette for them like child actors performing the role of daughters who, like his own daughters, had already attended dance performances choreographed by Merce Cunningham, Sasha Waltz, Martha Graham — my favorite was the dancer with the metal wings going rarr rarr, Tata — the phone not ringing in his mother's kitchen with news of his sister, who before Christmas #6 had severed all communications with his mother after she'd conjoined reality and irreality for the first time, in other words this was his mother's first Christmas in Sioux Falls without his sister either there in person or calling her twice a day, the imaginary Christmas lights flickering on his mother's Christmas tree while he recorded his mother talking about her own upbringing, yes, he can invent Christmas lights flickering behind them and he can invent a family trip on Christmas Eve to a Mormon temple where hundreds of teenagers listened to a handful of teenagers onstage strumming about the lord their savior, but this kind of invention equates to a noninvention because during Christmas #6 his mother had indeed decorated a Christmas tree with flickering lights, and they did take a family trip downtown where they chanced upon a teenage Mormon temple, he just didn't think of either while listening to his recording of his mother at work until he wondered whether he would need to describe the setting of his recording session if he were to write about it, as he's planning to do whenever he's able to write again, or describe the days before and after he recorded his mother during Christmas #6 in Sioux Falls, where his mother still lives with her American husband, and as Antonio listens to his recording of his mother, he decides to prolong his time with his mother's voice by (1) drawing flowcharts of her associations, (2) transcribing her recording in the original Spanish, (3) translating his transcription of her recording, (4) calling his mother after steps (1) to (3), although unfortunately these calls probably won't last 1:46:43 but less than 1:00.

—

None of us wanted to play cards with my brother Lucho, Antonio's mother says, except yes he would convince me, late at night during the school break he would tiptoe to my room, at midnight he would knock on my door, Leonorcita, he would say, Leonorcita, yes what's the matter, let's play cards, he would say, no because you're going to cheat and then we'll fight and then Mom and Dad will punish us, I promise you I won't cheat, he would say, and so he would come into my room and we would play cards, but with money, he would say, how old were you, Antonio says, eight or nine perhaps, and so when I didn't have money, we're talking cents here, I would say I can't play with money I don't have any money and he would say don't worry I will lend you some, and if you win, you return it to me, and if you lose, you owe me for next time, no I don't have any money, and he would hand me five cents and say there you are so you can play, and I knew he was going to win because he always cheated so I would ask him to stand up and of course he'd hidden cards on the side of his shirt, he was an artist when it came to tricking me so he could win, and in the end of course we would quarrel, you're a cheater you're always cheating, don't shout, he would say, don't shout, until Mom and Dad would discover us and fiiiit, they would send us to bed, but before leaving my room he would attempt to charge me, remember I lent you this much and now you owe me this much, he would say, no I already told you no, and later yes, he would rent his comic books, but not so that he could then buy chocolate for the poor, as my mother told you, but because Lucho loved money, all his enterprises were so that he could amass money, everything he did was so that he could have more money, even if he accumulated it little by little, that was part of the fun for him, he'd always been that way, I know because I was the one who spent the most time with him and he always wanted me to join his enterprises like for instance he convinced me to make ice cream with him so we could sell it, but without Dad finding out because he'd forbidden us, and so Lucho would say okay but you have to contribute to the investment for the materials, for the coconut, for the, well, Mom would give us the milk and the sugar but the coconut yes, we had to buy it, and so we were supposed to invest half and half, and so we would make the ice cream, place it in the freezer, and then we would tell the kids in the neighborhood that we had ice cream but to not come when Dad was in the house, but sometimes Dad would park inside the garage so the kids didn't know Dad was home and they would come and call out ice cream, señorita, and Dad would admonish us but later he would forget and we would restart our business, and Lucho would do the accounting for every ice cream, how many we'd made, how many we'd eaten, and if we'd eaten any he would try to charge us, although between me and him we were allowed one per day, but of course we would eat more than one per day, and so Lucho would chase me and my brothers around the house trying to charge us for the ice cream we'd eaten, yes, Lucho was something else, Antonio's mother says, and as Antonio translates his transcription of his mother he remembers playing cards at a tournament with his uncle Lucho at the Colombian Social Club in Miami, which consisted of a converted garage in an alley, playing cards as a team when Antonio was fifteen or fourteen and his uncle Lucho flashing him severe looks whenever Antonio would bungle his hand because goddamn it he should have known those cards had shown up already, flashing him severe looks that Antonio must have enjoyed because, unlike the severe looks of his father, Antonio knew they weren't a prelude to him being kicked or shouted at but that afterward his uncle Lucho would guffaw with him about winning, losing, not drinking again during tournaments, and so when it was time to share the ice cream earnings Lucho would say no you're in debt with me, Antonio's mother says, you ate too many ice creams so we don't have any earnings left, all the earnings Lucho would take for himself, but with him it was always amusing, always he's been funny and inventive and charming, and so I didn't join his ventures for the money but to spend time with him, to share these moments with him and he's still the one that calls me the most, when he heard what was happening to your sister he called me immediately and he checks on me every week, the rest of your uncles don't like to bring it up.

—

God will punish you, my mother would say, the lord said that what you inflict on your mother and father will return to you fivefold, so now you know what awaits you in life, my god what's going to happen to me, I would say, what will I have to endure later in life, everything magnified through a child's imagination, of course, if I'd said to my mother, for instance, I am running away from this house because I can't stand it here anymore because my parents are unjust, and my mother would reply your words will be punished by god because a son or a daughter can't say this to her parents, and later the nightmares I would have my god what's going to happen to me, what will I have to endure later in life, and I would try to find in the bible where it said that I was going to be punished and I couldn't find it, but my mother always invoked divine retribution whenever we did something wrong because hers was a religion of torture, of punishment, not of spirituality, that's what I remember the most from being a child my mother accusing me, pointing with her finger at everything that awaited me as a consequence of my actions, her voice trailing off so Antonio rewinds his recording of his mother and tries to soothe her as if she's his own child — sana sana / culito de rana — don't worry Mom god doesn't exist he won't punish you for trying to run away from your house just like I tried to run away from yours when I was your age — rewinding his recording of his mother to trace what had prompted his mother to begin talking about divine retribution, right, okay, his question to his mother had been what refrains do you remember hearing from your mother when you were growing up, which was the same question he'd asked her about his father's mother because Antonio had been trying to insert the voices of his grandmothers into a novel set in Bogotá, and as he listens to his mother saying that god will punish you, that the lord said that what you inflict on your mother and father will return to you fivefold, he wonders how his own daughters would answer the same question about refrains, worrying that perhaps their answer would be just as bleak — Tata always said either way we're all going to die — yes but Mama ordered him to stop saying that so he snipped his refrain to either way we're all going to — or Tata would sometimes say don't forget to bring a towel, which years later we found out was a refrain from a pot smoking character called Towelie in an asinine cartoon show called South Park — but no, Antonio will not worry for too long about their answers because tonight, as his tasks as a database analyst come to an end for the day, he will record his daughters and ask them what expressions do they think they will remember from growing up with their mother and father, starting with Eva, what I don't get it, Eva says, what will you remember your Mom saying to you, that she always loves me, Eva says, no the kind of things she would say to you, that she loves me, Eva says, what else, that she will never go away, Eva says, what about funny things, once she said Tata eats like a pig, Eva says, okay what about phrases Tata says to you that you will remember, that he loves me, Eva says, what else, another thing that's super funny is when you say Mama's butt is base, Eva says, and that's it, his recording of his youngest daughter Eva lasts 4:13, and as Antonio rewinds his recording of Eva he wonders if she's simply too young to understand what it means to remember the past, to blur, avoid, recast aspects of the past — what child would believe you if you told her that forty years into the future her head will carry thousands of vague voices at the same time? — and perhaps if someone would have asked Antonio as a child what expressions do you think you will remember from growing up with your mother and father, Antonio would have never guessed that his answer, forty years into the future, would be I don't remember any expressions from either my mother or father — I love how many times you've said my Mom had an expression, Stephen Colbert says to Vice President Biden — remember nobody is better than you, Vice President Biden says, but you are not better than anyone — and then Antonio records Ada, who says, in response to the question about expressions she will remember from her mother, Ada no, Ada says, what else, Ada sem, Ada says, what else, Ada můžeš sem na chvíli přijít, Ada says, what does that mean, Ada can you come here for a second, Ada says, what else, Ada můžeš sem na chvíli přijít, Ada says, what does that mean, Ada come clean your room, Ada says, what else, Ada come eat the phone is on the plate, or Ada stop it, or Ada go brush your teeth, that's all I can think of — I never say come eat the phone is on the plate that's what my mother used to say to me, Antonio's former wife messages him — what does it mean, Antonio says — it doesn't translate well it's like saying there's a phone call waiting for you at the table why are you asking all these questions, Antonio's former wife says — and unfortunately Antonio tells his former wife about his question and Ada's quotidian answers to his question and his former wife texts him a sad emoji and stops responding to his texts, refusing to tell him how to transcribe the last three Czech phrases Ada had said to him, okay now the same question but about your father, Antonio says, gooooool, Ada says, what else, go score some goals today, Ada says, what else, cut cut cut, Ada says (Antonio has hired a private soccer coach for Ada, an Italian coach who likes to say cut cut cut with a heavy Italian accent, meaning cut to the right, cut to the left to skirt defenders), you sing a lot of songs, Ada says, what else, Eva come play the game with us, Ada says, what else, Mamo where are my glasses, Ada says, Mamo where are my quarters, snoring we took a video of you snoring, snoring is not a refrain, Antonio says, I know, Ada says, perrito / perrito / perrito pierninuska, or move up, move up you say that a lot when I play soccer, what else, you have to use your body when you're defending, Ada says, you think you will remember these when you grow up, Antonio says, definitively, Ada says, okay let's forget about expressions and think about moments, Antonio says, you are playing with Perrito and Perrito pees, or you're going to the bathroom and you go tpppppft, or you are drawing numbers on my back before going to sleep, or you are reading me a bookie, or you are slapping Mama's butt, or you're looking for your glasses, for your quarters, for your keys, when I took the money from the table, but I didn't yell at you for that, Antonio says, because you would be mad at me and that was after the time you said that if I don't get good grades you will ground me that was mean, Ada says, what else, what I will also remember for the rest of my life is my first goal and the car going beep beep beep after the ball went through the goalie and hit that car, Ada says, and unfortunately Ada's erasures are already happening, Antonio thinks, because during dinner a few weeks ago Ada had accused him of not attending her soccer games and his former wife had to intervene and correct her by saying no, Ada, your father has only missed two games ever because he was out of town due to his job, and Antonio had to remind Ada of being there when she was four and she scored her first goal and the car going beep beep beep, which is probably the reason why she brought up her first goal when he asked her about moments she will remember from growing up with her father.

—

We barely saw Dad, Antonio's mother says, sometimes we only saw him on Sunday afternoons because he worked a lot, though we would share moments with him here and there, he would call home at around nine, nine thirty to say he was coming and so all of us would sit around the table to share with him that moment when he was going to have dinner, and so he would order, well, it was already known that a huge slab of meat had to be prepared for him, a platter of meat with rice and lentils, and he would cut us a piece of meat and feed it to us, no we already ate, we would say, open your mouth and eat, he would say, because he had this notion that in order for us to grow we had to eat meat otherwise we weren't going to grow, and he would say to save money your mother doesn't give you enough meat, which was true, and so Dad would buy meat and would feed each one of us to make sure we ate meat, yes, at home we had abundant food, that was the main preoccupation, but it was true my mother would put some money aside to buy herself jewelry that she would never wear because either the maids stole it or something would happen because the jewelry would disappear, and so Dad figured it out so he decided to start buying the meat, which was the only food item he would buy himself, well, meat but also cheese from Cúcuta, his home-town in Norte de Santander, and so he would come home with his cheese and those tasty square crackers from La Universal, and so we had to sit around him at the table, each one of us had to eat a slice of meat that he would feed to us like birds, a slice of meat plus the square crackers with cheese from Cúcuta, and Mom would say but they already brushed their teeth, Víctor, they can brush their teeth again, he would say, open your mouths, eat, there you have cheese and a glass of milk, but we already ate, Dad, we're full, bah, at this hour you must have digested your food already, because we would eat at six, six thirty, and here Antonio rewinds his recording of his mother because this is his favorite part, his gruff grandfather feeding meat to his mother, to Uncle Francisco, Lucho, Hernán, Víctor Roberto, his gruff grandfather who changed everyone's life by becoming an American citizen and providing green cards for his children and his children's children — your grandfather memorized the English dictionary and studied day and night so he could pass the medical exam in North Carolina, Antonio's mother said — who paid for Antonio's plane ticket to New Haven because Antonio couldn't even afford a plane ticket from Chapel Hill to New Haven, and Mom would say but they already brushed their teeth, Víctor, Antonio's mother says, well they can brush their teeth again, open your mouths, eat, and Mom had us trained and would say don't take away food from your father he arrives tired from work, but we don't take anything from him he gives it to us, no, open your mouth, my dad would say, and he would feed us one by one, so we would eat and finish the square crackers, okay, it's late and you have to wake up early, so we would go to our room, yes, that was the part of the day we had to share with Dad, that was sacred to us, for Dad it was sacred, in other words we couldn't skip it, everyone come sit down, he would say, and we would all come to the table to be with him.

—

Dad was addicted to stress, Antonio's mother says, in other words he would function better under stress, and so in the morning during the week Mom would start with her recitation of Víctor, Víctor, it's 7:25 already, your daughter has to be at school at 7:30, which was a problem because from our house to the school it was twelve or fifteen minutes by car, but Dad would leave at 7:25 and I would say my god we're not going to make it, this is so embarrassing the nuns are going to reprimand me again, every morning the same story, bah, you don't have to worry I will speak to the nuns, my dad would say, and so he would sit me in the car and he would say okay now hold on, there was no safety belts back then, hold on, and we would speed out of the house all the way to Maria Auxiliadora, my elementary school, hold on, he would say, and he would speed us there, because he always liked to speed, running red lights, yellow lights, and when he would see a red light he would look on one side, on the other, and he would say hold on and zoom us through, and so I would hold on and go zssssisst with the wind on my face, and the nuns would reprimand him, of course, and he would appease them by bringing them medicines, by offering them free medical consultations, yes, tomorrow I will come on time, madrecita, you know that I'm busy, but why don't you just put her on the school bus so the girl doesn't have any more problems, yes, madrecita, tomorrow, madrecita, until finally I would cry and say I am not going to school I am too embarrassed of always being late, and so eventually I was allowed to go in the school bus, but that was years later when I was in sixth grade, and here Antonio pauses his recording of his mother, closes his eyes and sees his mother and his grandfather speeding across Bogotá—grandpa?—yes what want do you want I don't have any money—I understand now why you wanted to drive my mother every day that was your special time with her—good for you go water your fertile imagination elsewhere and leave me alone—do I remind you of you?—you're studious like I was, sure—I see an umbilical cord like a fire hose connecting you and me across the universe—stop reading your mother's quack therapy recipes and go back to your database job—and so my Mom would say Víctor, it's 7:25 already, Víctor, it's 7:20 already, all right woman I know leave me alone, every morning the same story, let me finish my coffee, you already had like four, Víctor, goddamn it why do you have to be counting my coffees you're not the one having them, from when he would open his eyes he would drink his coffee, black and concentrated in espresso cups, and he would drink the last coffee on his way to the car so the domestics had the coffee ready for him at the door, here's your coffee, Dr. Hernández, and it was all a pretext, later I understood it, because when he worked here in the United States it was the same story, he had to be at work at eight in the morning and if it would take him fifteen minutes to get there he would leave ten minutes prior, and so he would have to speed there, because he was addicted to stress, that's when I understood it, but Mom was like a clock, every morning repeating Víctor you're going to be late, Víctor, they were like cats and dogs, that was their dynamic, that's how they courted each other, that's how they fell in love, how they married, how they raised seven children, and that's how they lived until Dad died.

—

You can't live here anymore, Dad said, you can't continue to disrespect the rules of this house, your siblings, your mother, you've been given many opportunities but you've refused to change, and so Dad expelled my brother Víctor Roberto from the house, and yet despite our fights with Víctor Roberto, because yes he was always inciting us and fighting with us, plus he was the only one who would dare talk back to Dad, we missed him, our oldest brother, when is he coming back, we would say, when is Víctor Roberto coming back, and Víctor Roberto hasn't forgiven us because he felt that he was expelled from the family, when what he needed at the time was help from us, but in those days psychological help just wasn't something families sought out, I think he started doing drugs and his personality started to change, although he was always hyperactive, extremely intelligent but inconstant in his pursuits, he knew he was intelligent but he wouldn't put his intelligence into practice (and here Antonio makes a note to ask his mother more details about Víctor Roberto's pursuits because he vaguely remembers hearing over the years that Víctor Roberto either piloted jet planes or designed jet planes or rockets but was thrown out of the military for misconduct (and here Antonio decides not to pursue a potential linkage between Víctor Roberto being expelled from everywhere and his own history of being thrown out of his elementary school, his high school, his former apartment where he used to live with Ada and Eva and his former wife, thrown out of so many places that Antonio has wondered if that's the only way he feels most at ease, and what he also remembers about Víctor Roberto is that the domestic at the apartment where Antonio lived with his mother had instructions not to let Víctor Roberto in if his mother wasn't there, and years later, when his grandfather, Dr. Víctor Hernández, died in Chapel Hill, North Carolina—goodbye Grandpa, thank you for everything—Víctor Roberto flew to Chapel Hill and apparently checkbooks and important papers from his last will and testament disappeared in his wake)), and so Víctor Roberto had a lot problems with Francisco, Antonio's mother says, because Francisco was the perfect son, and Mom would always compare between Francisco and Víctor Roberto, Dad never compared between us but Mom did, because for Mom Francisco was a reflection of her Italian side of the family, oh so you're the perfect child, Víctor Roberto would say, you're the blue blood, and so they would fight each other all the time, and by the time they became adolescents these fights became frightening, and Mom couldn't control them anymore because they were men now, and I know Víctor Roberto thinks we were relieved when he was gone but that wasn't the case because we missed him, he was our oldest brother, he would occupy the corner of the dining table, next to Mom at the head of the table, as the oldest he would sit next to her and the rest of us would have to accommodate ourselves whichever way, and so to always see him in that seat, which Francisco occupied after Víctor Roberto left, no, we would say, Francisco shouldn't be sitting there, that's always going to be Víctor Roberto's place, I was always the one fighting about it and I would tell Mom don't allow Francisco to sit there that's Víctor Roberto's place, Víctor Roberto isn't here anymore, Mom would say, he isn't here now but he's going to come back, I would say, and Mom wouldn't say anything and Francisco continued to occupy Víctor Roberto's place, which I felt was an injustice, and later when I studied constellation therapy I learned that when someone is excluded from the family system, the family system undergoes a distortion (and here Antonio decides to order books on constellation therapy to check if they yield any associative threads of interest, although the titles of Bert Hellinger's constellation books (Laws of Healing, Love's Hidden Symmetry, Looking Into the Souls of Children) grate on him, a cynical Colombian with a penchant for being thrown out of everywhere), even more if Francisco took over Víctor Roberto's place, as if Víctor Roberto didn't exist anymore, as if Francisco had become the most important, yes, Francisco did feel he'd become the most important in the family, and that Víctor Roberto wasn't there anymore was a great sadness for us because as a family we were really close, all of us during lunch, dinner, vacations, and all of a sudden he was gone, and to this day Víctor Roberto hasn't escaped this state of feeling rejected, of feeling we all rejected him, to this day he speaks as if we all rejected him, and so I think this was a great sorrow for my Mom but she couldn't deal with him alone, she needed help from Dad but because Dad worked so much he couldn't be at home more often, and so that was the only option Dad had, to throw Víctor Roberto out, and because Dad had come from studying in the United States where children leave the house when they turn eighteen, perhaps he felt it was okay, but in Bogotá this wasn't part of our tradition, children left the house when they married, and so I think life marked him, to me this marked Víctor Roberto, who was the smartest one of us, to this day he continues just as irresponsible, complaining and blaming us for his misfortunes, never coming through in life.

—

I did fall in love with somebody else, Dad said, but my family was more important, I wasn't going to allow my children to be unhappy, to live far away from me, and for me that was more important than the person I'd met, and I don't regret it because I had you near me, and it hurts me that your mother somehow felt it, although I don't think she ever found out, she must have felt that I had found someone else, and as Antonio rewinds his recording of his mother he wonders if his mother was recasting this anecdote about her father, turning it into a moral tale of familial love and sacrifice and so on to remind him of his responsibilities as a father, and yet he doesn't call her to ask her about this anecdote because he barely talks to his mother, hasn't called her on any of his (1) to (3) cycles as he had imagined he would do when he started listening to his recording of her, has barely talked to his mother since the time when he decided to leave his former wife and his mother sided with his former wife, who at the time was pregnant with Eva, and of course in retrospect he can see that his mother was right, he should have ignored his misgivings about being a father again and stayed with his former wife while she was pregnant, but six years ago, and this he hasn't forgotten, the feeling of being trapped in a life he hadn't chosen overwhelmed any consideration about a child he didn't yet know (and here Antonio searches for the emails his mother had intended for his former wife back then but inadvertently sent to him instead — even though my son is a great father to Ada with his attitude he is losing his rights to be a father of the new baby, his mother wrote, unfortunately my son is not giving himself the opportunity and prefers to follow the path of his father — no, Antonio thinks, he can't stand to read these emails again, they are still too painful), and so I asked Dad if he fell in love with someone else when he came to the United States to study, Antonio's mother says, yes, Dad said, but why does that time come to mind, because when you came back you would play romantic songs, and I was very little, I must have been five, four and a half, and I remember you would play a song called el reloj — reloj / detén / tu camino — Dad had brought back a record player and music, in those days it wasn't common yet to have a record player, and he would play that one record over and over, he would arrive home and to relax he would play that song, and later, when I was much older, I would sing that song, and he would say to me oh shut up already you're out of tune, and I would say let me sing I sing because I like the song, no, no, you're out of tune quiet down, I never heard him sing again, only that one song back then, when I was so little still.

—

I wrote Dad a letter, Antonio's mother says, after that surgery on his pancreas when he almost died I wrote him a letter telling him that he'd been given an opportunity to change his life, that he could have been gone just like that, that all that money he'd amassed he wasn't going to be able to take with him, and that it was about time that he share with us what he felt, who he really was, and when he was at the hospital, for a month he was at that hospital, he would ask my mother to read him my letter every day, read me my daughter's letter, he would say, and she would read it to him and tears would pour out, and from then on he changed, in the last fifteen years he had left after that surgery to his pancreas he became more loving, more worried about his grandchildren and his children, he would call me three, four times a day when I came to live in the United States, he became more worried about us, I mean, it wasn't all about him anymore, he was more worried about others, and that's how he began to help everyone, and if someone in the family needed anything, he would give it to them, and your sister when she called your uncle Luis, who still manages Dad's inheritance, your sister told him my grandfather says that if he was alive he would have helped me, because she was calling to ask Luis for a donation when she had to stop working due to her condition, and so in her desperation she would tell Luis that she was speaking to your grandfather and that your grandfather told her he would have helped her if he was alive, and this was true, Antonio, he would have helped her.

—

My grandmother the nurse quarreling with my grandfather the doctor on the stairs of a hospital in Bogotá before they even had their first lunch together, Antonio thinks on his way home from his database analyst job at Prudential Investments, my grandfather Víctor saying to my grandmother Remedios I already found out your name what kind of parent calls his daughter Remedios, my grandmother saying to my grandfather I am not moving to the United States how can you expect me to leave half of my children here, a nurse telling my grandmother to please not leave Dr. Víctor alone in the United States because there's another woman who's trying to steal him from her, my grandmother saying to the teenagers who bag groceries at her local supermarket in Chapel Hill, North Carolina, moo, leche, because she didn't know how to say milk in English yet (Antonio's mother laughing as she tries to imitate her mother saying moo, leche—you weren't embarrassed that they didn't understand you I would have been so embarrassed, Mom—bah tarados who don't know Spanish they should at least know the meaning of leche—), my grandfather the surgeon phoning my grandmother the mother of seven children to say he was coming home and everyone rushing to clean the house because he was a militant man of sanitation, inspecting everything to make sure it was in order when he arrived home, my mother saying your grandmother never spoke ill of your grandfather despite his bad temper and his numerous flaws, we never thought of our father in negative terms that was just our life, how we coexisted with Dad (the summer before starting college Antonio lived with Grandpa the surgeon and Grandma the housewife and Grandpa would yell at Antonio for playing his music too loud and Grandma would yell at him for not washing the blender after making his protein shakes and on Saturday mornings Grandma would wake up early and drive to the garage sales in the neighborhood, proudly bringing back an ancient bowling bag for Antonio, for instance, and because he was still a teenager Antonio would put on his headphones and not talk to his grandmother for days, or until she issued him an ultimatum (Antonio likes to believe he learned English by watching Jerry Lewis marathons on his grandparents' television)), my mother not including in her narrative that because of what her parents were like she decided against moving to the United States with them, finding an excuse to stay in Bogotá by marrying a man she barely knew, a man with whom she would have two children, Antonio and Estela, who would both grow up to prefer that this man didn't exist, who have severed all contact with this man so as to pretend he doesn't exist (Estela when she was eleven, Antonio when he was eighteen), and as Antonio arrives at the apartment where his daughters live he's resigned to the possibility of encountering this man in his sleep again, as he has done for more than twenty years, although in his sleep Antonio doesn't play basketball with him on his grandmother's patio, as he had done with this man, nor does Antonio play chess with him at a second-rate tennis club on Sundays, as he had done with this man, nor does he watch interplanetary war movies at Cine Los Mayas, no, in his sleep the scarred lunar landscape and the catastrophe around him is always the same, or at least he prefers to remember it in this vague one-version way instead of as an accretion of variations on the same impulse, he hasn't written down any of his encounters with this man so as to make them less concrete, more forgettable, and although he can't re-call anymore if his first encounter with this man in his sleep frightened him twenty years ago, by now his encounters with him have become yet another image he has to contend with, in other words while he's awake, if he happens to remember his encounters with this man on a scarred lunar landscape, he isn't frightened or traumatized or saddened, absolutely not, one can get used to anything (except to watching The Exorcist), and even if he knows there's likely a correlation between the brutality of his encounters with this man while he's asleep and his outbursts while he's awake, what is he to do except hope none of these outbursts overturn his life irreversibly, and per-haps this is one of the reasons he has begun playing soccer again after not playing soccer for twenty years, because he has always associated soccer with violence, the mad sprints on the wings, the unhinged tackles, the name calling, the red cards thrown back at the referee's face, and perhaps soccer not only depletes him of the energy that fuels his violent outbursts but brings him back to those years in Bogotá when he would propel himself down the soccer field every day while his sister was discovering that when she was little the man known as her father had committed repugnant acts against her that would roil her life and her reason despite her attempts to pretend this man didn't exist, and as Antonio falls asleep he's resigned at experiencing the terror that comes with his encounters with this man, yes, just because he's used to these encounters doesn't mean he doesn't still experience terror, terror like in those horror films he doesn't watch because why would he want to feed material to the landscape around his encounters with this man — feed your violence, you swine — terror like when he witnesses what he does to this man in that scarred lunar landscape, the man approaching him, an ax in Antonio's hand.

TIME PASSES BY VIRGINIA WOOLF

The wind, Antonio reads, sent its spies about the house again,
they're summoning you in the other room, Ida says, numbers,
Ada says, sparkling water with ice, Eva says, what power could
now prevent the insensibility of nature, Antonio says [in a mock
horror voice], lights off, Ida says, one more page, Mamo, Antonio says, this side, Perrito, Ida says, my side of the covers has all
the amenities plus free lectures on literature, Mister Perro, Antonio says, if he chooses your side of the bed there will be
chicken drumsticks for dinner for a week, Ida says, but what
after all is one night, Virginia Woolf says, why are you doing this
to me, Antonio's father says, say to your son I am not afraid
of you, Peter Ström says, your phone contains a recording of
your sister, Arturo says, don't need to hear it, Antonio says, open
your iTalk app and press aaaa, Arturo says, leave him alone his
visit to his sister's house in Baltimore has been erased already,
Antonio's mother says, the red button on your iTalk app that
says aaaa, Arturo says, your tooth implant looks beautiful the
bone has regenerated, Dr. Sze says, your sister has been delivered
to Baltimore City jail in Baltimore, Thomas Saville says, we're
waiting for her to be transferred to the Spring Grove State Hospital in Catonsville, Maryland, 3:16 a.m., Antonio's phone says,
no chance of falling sleeping again, Arturo says, but the stillness and the brightness of the day were as strange as the chaos
and tumult of the night, Virginia Woolf says, here's the living
room where Ada used to dance to Ravel's Une barque sur
l'océan, Nicola says, running across it in her pink ballet uniform,
Dr. Adler says, the Blood Bank out the window, Hershleder
says, two men loading plasma into a truck, Katerina says, a

truck that will traverse a valley that will resemble the X-rays of your tooth implant, Arturo says, Bovary's multilayered hat according to Nabokov, Jules Jakobsdóttir says, that vent where he went was sort of a funnel, Dora says, that led him down into a frightful black tunnel, did my mother send you to ogle me do you want café con leche, Estela says, or do you want to rest first or rent a movie to distract yourself, what movie do you want to see, Antonio says, Iron Man we can buy it at Best Buy, why don't we rent instead of buy, Antonio says, I want to see it on the television screen, can't you connect the computer to the television, Antonio says, yes but I need the cables, what cables, Antonio says, you know what cables don't be a moron, I wouldn't know I don't have a television, Antonio says, yes you do you hide it from your daughters, I don't have a television, Antonio says, the one in the closet in Ida's room, ah that old mammoth I threw it away already, Antonio says, see I remember everything I'm not crazy the government says that the technology in Iron Man equals the technology deployed through (sorry for the interruption) satellites Barack Obama says that if we [in a robotic voice] don't. leave. this. filthy. house, and don't tell me it isn't a filthy house there's radial frequencies from satellites with lasers that come from the solar system in other words the sun therefore there's abundant vegetation as in a neighborhood park due to the abundant solar energy therefore there's forest animals also, how many hours a day does Barack talk to you, Antonio says, twenty-four hours a day Barack isn't the one who talks to me the CIA talks to me from the Pentagon which controls the armed forces Barack is the leader of the government that controls the CIA they're doing to Obama what they're doing to me sorry. for. the. interruption, which means he's a CIA trainee which means that (stop looking at me sexually) you have to have psychological training from your sister so you can feel better about yourself otherwise Ida and my mother are going to shred you psychologically, they called from Robert Half they're about to cancel your temp contract you will lose your health insurance so we need to talk to them, Antonio says, I'm sorry I'm the one who needs to talk to them it's as if the CEO of Prudential Investments had made a mistake you report to the CEO of Prudential Investments, no, Antonio says, don't tell me that who do you report to, I work in a group called sales and marketing headed by Morton Stephenson, Antonio says, why are you lying to me, why would I lie to you, Antonio says, you don't speak to the CEO every now and then, no, Antonio says, he doesn't call you Guatemalan Superstar yes he calls you Guatemalan Superstar if he doesn't do it to your face he does it behind your back because it's a joke by Barack Obama, if there's no medical certificate justifying your extended medical leave they will cancel your temp contract, Antonio says, I abandoned my job because I have four felony charges pending and according to the instructions given to me by the American government I can't return to work because the client is a media company that has invaded my phone and chases me through the radial system in my car those pieces of shit charge eighty-four dollars an hour for me imagine the margins that's why Robert Half hasn't thrown me out yet this is privileged information (don't interrupt me) if you tell that bitch of my mother I will deny it because there's no invoice to prove it you're quite smart to be working at an investment firm so they can't invade your personal life because it would affect the Federal Reserve System of the United States, they called and said unless you provide them with a medical certificate they're going to cancel your contract, Antonio says, I don't have a certificate I have a legal issue that I can't comment about, I understand but if you don't talk to them they will cancel your contract, Antonio says, if I go back and talk to them and say I have legal issues pending the manager will say what legal issues and I will have to tell her I can't talk about it so she will run a background check on me and she will find out I have four felony charges pending and Robert Half will share it with all their clients so what my lawyer is doing (let me finish) he's saying (no, you're in my house, and I adore you, Toñito, but this is the first time you've been here, and I thank you that you're here) but my lawyer is doing the same thing your CEO is doing to your marriage he's not giving you a raise because you've made the wrong decisions he will spy on you and they will steal your psychiatric files they will know your psychological problems caused by that bitch of a mother by the lies and bribes of Ida who impregnated herself for money they're going to say if you're so smart with your two years at Yale we want to see how you come out of this problem now if you betray me and say to Robert Half [in a little girl's voice] my sister has four felony charges and I am a moron who works for the CEO of Prudential Investments and I travel to the Federal Reserve and I've seen all the hot women in Baltimore and my sister when she's fit she's more beautiful than any stripper from the Gold Club and more intelligent than any of the strippers from the Gold Club and because I am a moron I allowed myself to be taken in by Ida who's the biggest criminal in the world because there's rumors she killed her grandmother I am Antonio Jose Jiménez I am a moron who allowed himself to be conned by my mother who's a bitch [in an angry voice] who sucked my dick when I was an adolescent to destroy me for the rest of my life you think my mother didn't touch me inappropriately when I was little and I don't remember she touched me inappropriately and left me on the floor, naked, yes, my mother, and the American government blocked it from me they're so advanced in their military technology they blocked my brain I had forgotten until now that I'm stuck here in this filthy house receiving secret information from the American government I sound crazy I know it sounds crazy because they're so advanced nobody can believe it so they recommend that we see Iron Man because it isn't a technology invented by Iron Man but by the American government I hope you understand the logic and don't think I'm crazy because the logic of my legal situation (sorry. for. the. interruption) is what I do need you to understand and why I can't call Robert Half do you understand why, no, Antonio says, your logic has limits, or you're tired, stop looking at me sexually, you filthy rat stop looking at me sexually I call you filthy rat not to insult you but because you've lived like a filthy rat being the best father in the world that's why they've promoted you like the filthy rat that is Ida who has abused you psychologically like my mother, the problem with Robert Half, Antonio says, is that without their contract you won't have health insurance and that's a considerable problem, I don't need to see a doctor and you can threaten me a thousand times that you're going to commit me to a psychiatric institute but as long as the police find me sane they can't commit me to a psychiatric facility, and what happens if they don't find you sane, Antonio says, my lawyer has the medical records I am not crazy I just have mood swings, nobody is saying you're crazy what did your lawyer say about it, Antonio says, stop patronizing me, I'm asking you a question because I need to understand, Antonio says, why are you here is it because my mother has nothing else to do or because you want to talk about your divorce with Ida, why would I want to talk about my divorce with Ida, Antonio says, because you have to divorce her otherwise you will never get promoted they're going to steal your psychiatric exams and they're going to see you're a moron that allowed his mother to suck his dick and nobody defends him why doesn't anyone defend him because they're jealous that you're handsome and intelligent and because we come from a racist family, why did your lawyer call 911, Antonio says, because he was drunk the police felt bad I sent him a text saying if the rest of the Guatemalans called him to please not answer the phone he said calm down we'll talk next week he's a nice guy, why would a nice guy call 911 on you, Antonio says, because he had enough of my antics he knows I'm normal why didn't the police take me to a psychiatric institution it's a mind game until you catch up to the big leagues, bro, you're not going to get it, what's going to happen if someone else calls 911 if you're being antic at the supermarket for instance, Antonio says, you said antic, that's the word you used, Antonio says, psychological antics like what I'm doing to you right now, I'm concerned about your current state, Antonio says, why are you concerned, I'm concerned that you are having, Antonio says, that you are in a situation that you are not well, please leave this instant I hope it goes well for you I can throw you out of my own house, I know you can throw me out, Antonio says, why don't you leave then, why would I leave I'm giving you my opinion, Antonio says, you can go now, I am not going, Antonio says, leave or I'll call 911 so they can remove you, call 911, Antonio says, if you start behaving like my mother I won't tolerate it you will leave the house I will call the police, I don't know what you mean, Antonio says, do you want to go out and eat something, yes I'm hungry, Antonio says, stop crying as well, I'm not crying, Antonio says, stop crying the worst that can happen is that I lose my lawyer I can get a court appointed lawyer I can retrieve my psychological files Obama is tired of your psychological antics and says that if you don't believe me that he protected you while you were at Yale and you're a moron who believes my mother who sent you that means you're letting yourself be manipulated by my mother which means you can leave my house (sorry for the interruption) I don't want to suck my mother's vagina or lick my father's penis for the rest of my life that's why I prefer to be alone I say this metaphorically you know I haven't seen my father since I was eleven he barely did anything to me but because my mother is a crazy perverted woman that was raped by her brother she comes here to screw us up and my father barely shouted at me and he hit you and my mother sucked you so you will have the same psychological problems as her for the rest of your life the government blocked it from me so I wouldn't be traumatized unlike you who's a man and if you don't want to believe me that the government can do it, don't believe me, that's your problem, you will end up an embittered old man, alone, I am a spy for the American government that's why they can't take me to a psychiatric facility, let's take a time-out, Antonio says, I've overwhelmed you already, yes, Antonio says, speak, the Censor says, for you have summoned me, I don't want to remember any of this, Antonio says, you misunderstand the nature of my role, the Censor says, the Censor censors, Stanley Elkin says, I disguise, the Censor says, not erase, disguise as blanks, Antonio says, up to you what the disguise will be and not up to you do you understand, the Censor says, is this your first day of high school too, Antonio says, yes but I'm already in the honors program, Silvina says, me too, Antonio says, coincidence, Silvina says, that strange machine, open your iTalk app and press delete, Arturo says, aaaaaaaa, Dr. Sze says, through the open window the voice of the beauty of the world came murmuring, Virginia Woolf says, too softly to hear exactly what it said, el panadero, the ambulatory salesman says, la vitamina.

WHEN ANTONIO'S MOTHER STAYED

After I confronted your father, Antonio's mother says, he ran to his parents and acted like he was the victim, and his parents, who were like my second parents, sided against me, claiming that I was slandering him, and that how could I possibly believe what a child was saying, but your aunt Sofía called me and said Leonora I have to tell you something, because I wasn't well, Antonio, and here Antonio pauses the recording, unable to continue, trying to compose himself because in less than an hour he has to playact at being a database analyst instead of a novelist who insists on spending his mornings listening to recordings of his mother as he awaits news of his sister, composing himself as he recalls his mother, drained of life, seeing her own body on the sofa from above and feeling a pull toward the light, a consoling light, Antonio's mother had said to him when he was still a child, a peaceful light, a light that over the years he has interpreted as god, as the light at the end of the tunnel from the New Age death literature, peace at last, etc.—out-of-body experiences can be induced by delivering mild electric currents to the temporal parietal junction in the brain, Bessel van der Kolk says—as the outcome of the electric currents Antonio's grandparents were inflicting on his mother by pretending his sister was lying, and as I was ready to leave this world, Antonio's mother says, because I wasn't well, Antonio, I'd become a skeleton by then, my face was covered in boils, I remembered the school bus would be dropping off you and your sister soon, and so I panicked because who would open the door for you, who would take care of you if I was gone (for years Antonio has been seeing the ghost of his mother battling to return to her drained

body so she could open the door for them, for years Antonio has
not thought about the ghost of his mother until today (and because he's a parent now, has been one for eight years, he's on the
one hand relieved that he can see himself emulating his mother
in that moment, and on the other hand he suspects that if he
were to discover someone had been harming his daughters in
his own home, he wouldn't feel a pull toward any goddamn
light, he would simply abdicate reason and knife the culprit)),
when did you confront that individual, Antonio hears himself
say in the recording, when we were still living in that house in
Mirandela, Antonio's mother says, that's strange because my
sister told me years later, Antonio says, when we were already
living at that other apartment, yes she told you because a sexual
education class at school reminded her, Antonio's mother says,
oh so she told you beforehand, Antonio says, yes what happened
is that she blocked it out, Antonio's mother says, and how could
she not since your father accused your sister of being a liar,
you're demented and so is your daughter, he would say, and
your sister would hear it and she would say I'm not crazy, Mom,
no, Estelita, I believe you, I am going to defend you, I know
what could have been happening, and it pains me that I wasn't
more alert, and from then on, as soon as she told me, I began to
sleep in your room, I was there with both of you, all the time,
and he would tell me you have to come back to our bedroom,
no, I am not moving from here, you're never touching our
daughter again—why did you keep us in that house with that
individual, Antonio didn't ask his mother while he recorded
her—please don't ask me that question haven't I had enough
punishments already?—yes, no—and so when his parents sided
against me, claiming I was slandering him, Antonio's mother
says, your aunt Sofía called me and said I never told you because
my parents forbade me to do so, Leonora, but my brother

touched us improperly, all three sisters, and instead of finding help for him my father thrashed him and sent him away to military school, that's why my youngest sister Lucía can't stand him, you've seen how Lucía treats him, whenever he tries to hug her she screams, so I do believe you, Leonora, and you haven't reminded your parents about this, I said to your aunt Sofía, yes but you know my mother has always been blinded by her love for my brother and my father does whatever my Mom says, but I want you to stay calm because I know you're telling the truth, and if you have to take drastic measures, take them, so I confronted your father again and told him what Sofía had said and this became another scandal with his parents because why did Sofía have to interfere, his parents who were like my parents, Antonio, who disheartened me because I respected them, loved them, when I was pregnant with your sister they asked me to live with them so they could take care of me because my parents were already in Chapel Hill, and so after this new confrontation your grandmother Martina paid for us to see a psychiatrist, who did tests and asked for drawings and said well, perhaps the child imagined it, I don't see anything concrete in these drawings, perhaps the child invented it, I think the best thing to do is for me to help you, because this is too traumatic for you, he said, plus your husband doesn't want to come anymore since he says he's not the one who has a problem, and then this psychiatrist tried to take advantage of me, on top of everything I was going through this psychiatrist abused his role, what was his name, Antonio says, Winston Villamar, Antonio's mother says — dear Winston Villamar, Antonio writes, if you aren't already dead, you son of a bitch, I wish one day you and everyone you know will read my mother's words — I had to run away from his office, Antonio's mother says, and later he called me and said that I couldn't prove anything, that no one was going to believe me, and of course I never returned to his office but for a while he would lurk near the house in his car, he was the most famous evangelical pastor in Bogotá, that's why your grandmother Martina picked him, your grandmother Martina who never accepted what your father did, Antonio, who would come over to visit you and your sister at our new apartment, bringing sweets and acting as affectionate as possible, but whenever I would leave to the other room she would start saying things to your sister, and one day I heard her from the other room saying what you're accusing your dad of isn't true, this accusation stems from your mother not being right in the head and we are thinking of pressing charges so they can intern her in a psychiatric facility for crazy people, and if you continue to accuse your father you're also going to that facility, and so when I heard this, Antonio, I ran over and threw her out, you don't step in this house ever again, I said, I am here to defend my children, I believe what has been happening, and if you ever want to see them again it'll be under my supervision, I am never leaving you alone with my children, leave this house this instant, and so your grandmother stopped coming, whereas your grandfather would secretly stop by and bring you sweets, and later your grandmother would tell me bring the children to me, please, and I would say I'm sorry but I am not taking them to you, you've caused my daughter too much harm, because they should have supported her, Antonio, nobody in that family supported her, and when years later your grandmother Martina was gravely ill, when you and your sister were already here in the United States, I was meditating alone in my yoga studio and your grandmother appeared to me and said forgive me, Leonora, and I said to her I have already forgiven you—dear Grandma, Antonio writes, I haven't forgotten you, I still remember my summers in Cartagena with you, the tiny mallet you would carry in your purse because you loved to eat crab legs by the beach, I still remember you and Grandpa stationed on the beach under your parasol while my cousin Leonidas and I boogie boarded all day, and even though I don't remember you threatening my sister, don't remember much about those years, no, Grandma, I don't forgive you—but your grandmother insisted, Antonio's mother says, please forgive me, Leonora, she said, everything has been forgiven, I said, wondering if perhaps your grandmother's health had deteriorated further, and about fifteen minutes later your father called and said my mother just died and she never had a chance to talk to you because you never came to see her, yes, your grandmother was gravely ill but I did not visit her—I left Colombia when I was eighteen, Antonio writes, and I never saw those horrible people again—so I said to your father I already said goodbye and she asked me to forgive her, how is that possible, he said, she appeared to me, I said, bah, he said, and he hung up the phone, I do remember when my aunt Elena came to exorcise my sister, Antonio says, yes and your sister couldn't sleep for months—Aunt Elena, Antonio writes, you knew what my father had done to you and your sisters and you had the nerve to come exorcise my sister so she would stop accusing him?—your sister would sleep in my room because your aunt Elena had terrorized her, your aunt Elena, who I had to forbid from visiting the two of you as well, and just imagine, Antonio, when your sister started feeling unwell in Baltimore, when she was still working at Fidelity Insurance as a Senior Actuarial Associate and couldn't sleep—more than thirty years later, Antonio writes—she didn't want to seek help because she was worried that they were going to intern her in a psychiatric facility, that they were going to tell her she was crazy.

THE BYSTANDER BY GINA BERRIAULT

Someone shouted at me to grab a blanket or a coat or something
for crissakes, the narrator of The Bystander says, and wrap your
old man up, because after assaulting the woman the narrator's
father liked best, and after running out with nothing on but the
soap from the bath he'd been taking with her, the narrator's
father is standing on the street, shouting imprecations at her,
and although Antonio never remembers the exact phrases that
describe what happens next (The Bystander by Gina Berriault
first appeared in Antonio's life as a reading assignment during
a retrograde narrative workshop, almost twelve years ago, before he'd met Dora or Silvina or his former wife, before his sister
began to ununderstand her life (what had drawn him to The
Bystander and other fictions of ununderstanding if no such
condition had afflicted anyone he knew back then? If Antonio
were a conspiracy theorist, which he isn't, he would suspect
that someone had been planting these fictions near him to
warn him or prepare him for his sister's misfortunes — I am not
a conspiracy theorist, Antonio writes, and fiction doesn't
prepare you for anything — hi Nicola — shut up —)), he hasn't
forgotten the terrifying image of people watching the narrator's
father from windows and balconies, of people at a bar nearby,
laughing at the narrator's father, and perhaps Antonio hasn't
forgotten this terrifying image because of its familiar dream
logic, all of a sudden you find yourself on the street, without
clothes, and people are laughing at you (and here Antonio
searches for his copy of The Unconsoled by Kazuo Ishiguro,
which does not yield any associative threads of interest — the
dream logic of The Unconsoled is calibrated to be logical and

illogical at the same time, Antonio writes—), but to the narrator
of The Bystander, who tries to cover his father with a
blanket—he struck me away with his elbow, Antonio reads,
sharp in my ribs as a crowbar—the dream doesn't end with the
people laughing at his father or with his father being taken away
by the police, no, he, the son, still has to visit his father at a
mental institute—your grandmother Martina claimed your father's forceps delivery at birth impacted his head, Antonio's
mother said—and because Antonio has been hearing about this
forceps theory for years he searches online for forceps + birth,
hoping to debunk his dead grandmother's exculpatory theory—
although rare, the Mayo Clinic says, risks to your baby include
minor facial injuries due to the pressure of the forceps, minor
external eye trauma, skull fracture, bleeding within the skull,
seizures—I brought his suitcase, the narrator of The Bystander says, as the young man social worker had told me in
some huge loft of hundreds of desks and social workers in an
agency building that was probably not unlike the agency building where Antonio and his mother filled out the forms required
to process their request for an involuntary inpatient treatment
for his sister, announcing his and his mother's dark purpose at
the designated window, sitting apart from each other in the waiting room, a young man leading them to a bare room where he
explained to Antonio and his mother the procedure, one form
for his mother, one form for Antonio even though in the state
of Maryland only one written testimony was required to commit his sister to a mental institute, his mother objecting to her
son's use of the word schizophrenia in his testimony, him and
his mother wavering at the question on whether the person they
were trying to commit to a mental institute was at risk of self-
harm, Antonio proofreading his mother's lengthy testimony—her
words, Antonio writes, completely erased from me—my daughter

wrote beautiful letters, Antonio's mother said—nodding his head, trying to appear reasonable—I was leaning my elbow on the counter, the narrator of The Bystander says, smoking a cigarette, demonstrating with that pose my reasonable nature—and if at that moment, when Antonio and his mother were done filling out the forms required to commit his sister to a mental institute, a butterfly would have landed on him or his mother, they would have burst from grief, but no butterfly came so Antonio and his mother continued as before, containing their organs inside their bodies, waiting for the young man social worker in silence, a silence they maintained throughout the morning and afternoon, as if afraid the most innocuous word might weaken their resolve to commit his sister to a mental institute—butterfly—let's not do this anymore—a resolve that originated mostly from Antonio, who, because he thought he needed to be a man of action, had decided they should take control of his sister's circumstances—her dangerous isolation, Antonio writes, which could have aggravated her legal situation—and since his mother had been too exhausted to object, here they were, waiting for the young man social worker, who returned to the bare room and apologetically explained what would happen next, don't worry, he said, she won't be able to read what you've written on the forms and the police will inform you before they're on their way to her house (but of course later the police didn't inform them and they did show his sister what they'd written on the forms), and so they exited the agency building as quietly as they'd entered it, searching for his compact rental car, heads down, focusing on their steps so as to avoid falling flat against the asphalt—like Henri in A Christmas Tale with Catherine Deneuve, Antonio writes—over my arm I carried his raincoat and in my pocket his wallet, the narrator of The Bystander says, containing, under celluloid, a snapshot of my mother taken the year before she died and a snapshot of myself at the age of five, and as Antonio rereads The Bystander in the living room of the apartment where his daughters live, his former wife asks him what's wrong, Antonio, any news about your sister, and instead of telling his former wife that while performing his database analyst tasks at Prudential Investments earlier in the day his sister's attorney had called him to inform him that at last his sister had been transferred from Baltimore City jail to the Spring Grove State Hospital in Catonsville, Maryland, where she would remain until she was deemed fit to continue her trial proceedings, he asks his former wife to please read The Bystander out loud to him, no, she says, I need to prepare your daughters' school lunch for tomorrow, okay, he says, but she takes pity on him and reads to him in the kitchen about Arty, the son, who's visiting his father at the mental institute, the impact of his presence in this alien place made my throat swell, his former wife reads, and I went up to him quickly and laid my hand on his back, the smell of oranges was on his breath, his former wife reads, and that was good, I thought, his former wife reads, if he had eaten an orange then he was comparatively content, what do you think they'll do to me, Arty, his former wife reads, Tata, Antonio's youngest daughter says, numbers, Eva go back to bed it's late, his former wife says, I'll be there in a second, Antonio says, you tell them in the psycho ward they give your father hot chocolate and a little cookie, his former wife reads, why are you reading this, his former wife doesn't say, and perhaps because his former wife is crying he says I'll go do numbers before it's too late, me first, Eva says, that's not fair, Ada says, I'll flip a coin heads or tails, head, no, tails, here it goes, let me see turn on the light, Ada says, head wins so Eva goes first, fifty numbers today, Tata, just ten, twenty-one, can you sing cuando vuelva a tu lado, cuando vuelva a tu lado / y este solo contigo, and once Antonio is done drawing numbers on both of his daughters' backs and singing a song from Eydie Gormé y Los Panchos, he returns to the kitchen, I'm going to bed, his former wife says, so she turns off the light in the kitchen and living room and goes to bed, but Antonio remains in the living room, trying not to think about butterflies, agency buildings, forms filled with tenebrous words, let's drive to your sister's house to make sure she didn't forget to lock up, Antonio's mother said after his sister had been apprehended, I don't want to I'm scared she might still be there, Antonio didn't say to his mother (on the second day of his unannounced visit to his sister in Baltimore, she'd stormed into the guest room where he'd been updating his mother on his sister's condition over the phone and his sister screamed at him to get the hell out of her house (after he switched on his compact rental car and the air conditioner started running, he couldn't hear his sister anymore but she was there, guarding her driveway and screaming at him, her new imaginary enemy, her last family connection)), and so after Antonio called the police department and someone informed him that yes, the deed authorized by him and his mother had been done, his mother insisted they drive to his sister's house, and so they did, parking in his sister's driveway, where the motion-detection light clarified the existence of his sister's house for them, but Antonio did not want to roll down the windows or step out to check if all the doors of his sister's house were locked because what if his sister was still there, waiting to hurl herself at them like the undead, and so the motion-detection light, registering no further motion, expired, and so they remained inside his compact rental car in his sister's driveway, terrified, and so Antonio switches on the lamp in the living room of the apartment where his daughters live and searches for his copy of A Questionable

Shape by Bennett Sims, which he doesn't find in the bookshelves nearby so he switches off the lamp and powers on the flashlight on his phone and searches for A Questionable Shape on the bookshelves in the bedroom where his former wife is already asleep, nothing, so he searches in his daughters' room and finds A Questionable Shape on Ada's bookshelves, yes, he'd forgotten that, during a long holiday weekend, they'd played the game of Can Ada Read the First Page of Whatever Book Tata Picks, A Questionable Shape by Bennett Sims being one of the books Antonio had picked—what we know about the undead so far is this, Ada had read, they return to the familiar—they'll wander to nostalgically charged sites from their former lives, Antonio reads, and you can somewhat reliably find an undead in the same places you might have found her beforehand—and Ada and Antonio had both laughed as Ada tried to read the word mnemocartography—this book contains so many beautiful words, Antonio said—what are you doing, Tata, don't take my platypus again, Ada says, bookie expedition go back to sleep Bunnytown, Antonio says, returning to the living room and thinking that instead of that horrible word his mother had objected to he should invent beautiful words to describe his sister's illness, even though there was nothing beautiful about his sister's illness—from your point of view, bobito—yes, look at these beautiful words from A Questionable Shape, which he'd penciled on its title page, apophatic, for instance, which means to describe something by stating characteristics it does not have—my sister's house did not have a television in her living room with four split screens tracking the perimeter of her house—yes it did—aphasia, for instance, which means inability to comprehend and form language because of a dysfunction in specific brain regions, and which, incidentally, is also the name of a piece of invented nonsense sign language by Mark

Applebaum—dear Mark Applebaum, Antonio jots down on the back of A Questionable Shape, I want to omit myself from the surface of this world by learning to perform Aphasia—Aphasia is a metaphor for expressive paralysis, Mark Applebaum said—when I was in high school I was possessed by an unexplainable fury, Antonio had written months ago on the title page of A Questionable Shape, and it is all coming back to me now—it started around the time my sister was arrested for the first time, Antonio thinks as he angles the flashlight of his phone on the last page of The Bystander by Gina Berriault, the son turning around and seeing his father standing by the window of the mental institute, watching his son go, and I knew then that I was guilty of something and he was accusing me of it, Antonio reads, and it was the guilt of sight, for he was the father who breaks down under the eyes of his son, the father in his last years when all the circumstances of his life have got him trussed and dying, while the son stands and watches the end of the struggle and then walks away to catch a streetcar.

WHEN ANTONIO & ESTELA DIDN'T ESCAPE

After we escaped from that house in Mirandela, Antonio's mother says, your father would drive by our new apartment, and if he didn't see your uncle Lucho's jeep outside, he would ring the doorbell and try to force himself inside, yelling, with the authority he thought he had as a man, you are my wife, these are my children, and on one occasion, when the two of you went with him, that was so ignorant of me, Antonio, that was a mistake, Estela has to come with me because she's my daughter, he would say, and still, I shouldn't have allowed it, but, well, she'd told me what had happened with your father, and since the psychiatrist had said there was no information and I didn't want to probe her too much on whether it was true or not, I protected her though, we are leaving this house, I said, I protected both of you, because you were just as impacted as she was by his screams and his violence, and so on one occasion when we were already living in our new apartment, he came to see both of you — my father reading stories to my sister and me in the living room in that apartment is that memory possible? — yes, no — and he took both of you for the first time, and when your sister came back home she was crying and trembling and she said I don't want to go with that man ever again, Mom, I am afraid of him, and so then she told me he'd slapped her and she had tried to throw herself out of the car, but Estelita something could have happened to you why would you do something like that, because he said he was going to kill both of us so I screamed no, no, and he said he was going to smash the car against a wall, you don't remember, no I don't remember, Antonio says, you were probably in the back seat, I am not leaving you with your mother, he'd said, we are all going to die together, and he began to accelerate his car, and that's when Estela started crying and screaming and he slapped her face, and so she opened the door and tried to throw herself out, and with me she felt the same way, Antonio, when I would drive her to work on the freeway in Baltimore, and here Antonio pauses the recording, unable to continue, closing his eyes and thinking of his sister's trajectory since she left Colombia when she was eighteen (studying actuarial science at the University of North Carolina, working as a Senior Actuarial Associate in Charlotte, Mexico City, Baltimore, visiting him in Los Angeles for his twenty-seventh birthday, buying a house, crashing her car on the freeway one rainy evening on her way back from work, soon after grandfather Víctor passed away — your sister always felt your grandfather was the only one in the family who supported her, Antonio —), and as Antonio takes inventory of how little he knows about his sister's adult life, he wonders if, just as his sister buried what had happened to her, he has buried her along with what happened to her, and if this was the case — of course this is the case how else do you expect me to function day after day? — how can he expect himself to help his sister, or rather, sure, he can expect himself to be a decent human being and help his sister, but then (and here he sees himself driving a truck at night and falling asleep at the wheel after hours of driving and then awakening in a sunny garden — wake up, Antonio —) his habit of burying her would take over and he would bury her and her troubles, wake up, Tata, but perhaps listening to these recordings of his mother every morning is his way to remain alert to his sister's misfortunes — how are we to remain awake to the misfortunates of the world without sinking ourselves? — and so Antonio opens his eyes and rewinds his mother's recording and she's saying with me she felt the same

way, Antonio, when I would drive her to work on the freeway
in Baltimore, and she would tell me Mom you're driving too
fast, I am not driving that fast, Estelita, no Mom too fast, stop,
stop, I can't stop here we're on the freeway, I'm going to jump
out of the car, calm down, please, we're getting off the freeway
right now, when was this, Antonio says, when she had already
had that incident with her neighbors and she was arrested for
the first time, when I stayed for months with her in her house in
Baltimore and I would drive her to work using only city streets,
she couldn't handle the speed of the freeway, Antonio, and that
day I had told her look, there isn't that much traffic on the freeway, we'll get there faster, but then unfortunately we hit a zone
where cars were racing by and I had to follow the speed of the
other cars, and that's when she became desperate, I had to grab
her and say no, no, no, Estela, you're staying in the car, we are
going to get off the freeway right now, and so from then on we
only drove on city streets, and so in retrospect I can of course
see that she was reliving the trauma that she had lived through
with your father, and that the magnitude of what had happened
that night in Baltimore with her neighbors, the violence of it
all, because one of the women who accused her had tried to run
her over, and she wasn't able to defend herself, Antonio, and the
cops treated your sister like a criminal, handcuffing her while
searching her house for weapons, and so this precipitated a return of those events of abuse and aggression that she had buried
for years, and when she told me what happened with your father
on that occasion that the two of you went with him in his car
for the first time, I told him over my dead body you take the girl
with you ever again, you don't take them out, either of them, but
he tried through the law to take you with him, because he was
embarrassed that if neither of his children wanted to see him
what he'd done to your sister might go public, and so he was

able to find a way through the law, but I would always ask you what happened, did anything happen, is everything okay, and I think that one time that he kicked you in your grandmother's house, because you didn't want to pray the rosary or something like that, you were already fourteen, that's when you told me I don't want to go with that man anymore, Mom, and he became furious, I am sorry, I said, if you mistreat him I don't have to support you taking him with you, the day he wants to go with you, he can go if he wants, and so there was a time when you didn't want to see your father because things like this had happened.

WHEN ESTELA CALLED ANTONIO

As if someone had switched on a television, Antonio's sister says, and now I know no one will be switching it off if you enter a subway train, Antonio's sister says, the doctor says there's a high probability you will encounter other people who are also sick due to their minds now I know I am not a strange insect, Antonio's sister says, I am one of those people in the train I am worried my Mom won't accept that I am permanently sick, Antonio's sister says, but I am permanently sick, the volume of the television just increases or decreases, how is the volume today, Antonio says, a murmur because I am resting and sleeping a lot, Antonio's sister says, but when I was isolated in prison I hallucinated, Antonio's sister says, I would see Ida in a bodysuit like a skater in a circus with a zipper for easy access down there I couldn't differentiate between what was real and not real, Antonio's sister says, I could see you and me on the patio of our house in Mirandela chasing our dog Pelusa and calling after her little piggy, little piggy, and here both Antonio and his sister laugh, because in Spanish the word for little piggy, chanchito, is a funny word for adults to say, have they been giving you medicine, Antonio says, an injection once a week they're calling us for snacks I have to go, Antonio's sister says, and so the first call with his sister after more than a year of not hearing from her ends and Antonio sits inside his car outside the apartment where his daughters live, unable to type notes about her call on his phone even though he knows the erasers in his mind are already at work — when I was eight or nine I was babysitting our cousin Jorge and I rubbed myself against him I think inappropriately I told the doctor already I just needed to confess that,

Antonio's sister said—don't worry too much about that you were a child, Antonio said—please don't pull an involuntary confinement on me again, Antonio's sister said—no Estelita never again you sound so well it's so good to hear from you, Antonio said, adopting the soft voice he reserves for his daughters—see? not so hard to be Nicola—yes it is—and a few days later his sister calls again but he misses her call because he's set his phone to silent as a precaution against calls or text messages from potential arrangements from Your Sugar Arrangements, but fortunately she calls again and says please never pull an involuntary confinement on me again, you can't imagine what it was like to be paranoid to begin with and then have the police come to my house, look inside my windows, and arrest me yet again without knowing why, we were worried about you, Antonio says, I interpreted it as an abuse, Antonio's sister says, so I started hallucinating that you had abused me too, you were incoherent and we were worried that something worse could happen to you, Antonio says, don't ever use that word again, Antonio's sister says, don't ever tell me I was incoherent because it's not like I've forgotten, it's not like I was sick and now that I am less sick I don't remember the times when I was sick, I know I was sick but I was happy, Antonio's sister says, I was content, please promise me you won't do it again, I won't do it again, Antonio says, promising and repromising, on their weekly calls, that he will never again set in motion an involuntary inpatient treatment against her, weekly calls, incidentally, that he receives during the weekend, so as to not interfere with his database analyst job at Prudential Investments, although he never tells her please don't call me during the workweek, no, he's not that heartless (or he is but he has learned to modulate the outward evidence of his heartlessness like everyone else), he just hasn't been able to pick up the phone whenever she calls due to conference calls,

deadlines, meetings with marketing—you did cue your sister to
avoid calling you during your workweek by saying let's talk next
Saturday or Sunday, Estelita—I don't recall I'm sorry—and so he
receives her calls once a week during weekends—what a nice
brother you have, Estela—and yet as Antonio remembers his recordings of his mother—but Mama my brother's so little—as he
imagines injecting himself with a potion that will drive him to be
like his former wife, who talks to her sister every day for as long
as he has known her, as his mother's voice inside his oversized
circumaural Sennheiser headphones courses through his body,
intermixing with the memory of his mother's voice when he was
a child, a memory that was erased long ago but that he likes to
believe could be retrieved if one day he chances upon the right
circumstances, as he stretches his banged-up body on the carpet
after catapulting himself against everyone during soccer, as he
discovers his former wife has been talking to his mother almost
every day since his sister escaped her trial proceedings—your
mother needs to talk to someone, Antonio, his former wife
said—he crosses the subspace corridor that leads to that alternative world where he hasn't spent thirty-plus years trying to
abrade his linkage to his sister and there he concludes that, although a call during the workweek would definitely interfere
with his ability to perform his database analyst job at Prudential Investments—who cares about your stupid database job
you imbecile—his sister needs him, and yes, his sister has
needed him many times before, but if years from now he were
to examine a chart of his life (with time on the X axis and crucial moments on the Y axis), he would see a significant spike in
the chart now—how easy it is to miss these crucial moments,
Antonio writes—what would be the consequences of limiting
your contact with your sister to once a week?—she might feel
that she has no support, that no one cares about her, that she's

better off dead—your sister told me she used to punch herself in the face when she was in jail, Antonio's mother said—and so he tells his sister let's talk every day, Estelita, I will block my calendar at work every day for half an hour, okay, she says, and so in between meetings about hidden Markov models and k-means clustering, he receives calls from his sister, calls that connect a Prudential Investments building in downtown Los Angeles with the mental health wing of the Spring Grove State Hospital in Catonsville, Maryland, where Antonio can hear screams in the background every time his sister calls, screams Antonio's mind tries to erase instantly, just as his mind has tried to erase the Spring Grove State Hospital in Catonsville, Maryland, where, per order of the court, Antonio's sister has to stay for a minimum of ninety days or until she regains sufficient aspects of her reason, I'm a vegetal, Antonio's sister says, I walk and sleep, walk and sleep and rehearse what I will say on my trial, don't worry we're not going to trial, Antonio says, although every time he tries to assuage her worries about a trial or about being deported (his sister neglected to apply for citizenship and her status as a permanent legal resident alien could be compromised if her charges were categorized as crimes of moral turpitude) he has to caveat his statements by saying I know it's easy for me to say, from over here, that you shouldn't worry, and I want you to know I am not trying to dismiss your concerns, which are legitimate, but based on my conversations with your lawyer, who has done a terrific job and believes we can obtain a dismissal, I don't think you have to worry about a trial, nevertheless his sister imagines and reimagines the night she was arrested in preparation for her interrogation at her trial, maybe I did have a knife, Antonio's sister says, but how did those people know I had a knife in my pocket—I can see my sister in that hospital bed, Antonio writes, facing a blank wall

and talking to herself like Giorgia does when Nicola Carati's
brother visits her at her mental institute—and in those rare moments on the phone when his sister asks him how he's doing he
hesitates, doesn't know what to say, so instead of saying, for instance, recently I traded my old car out of despair at what's
happening to you—who knows what miseries await us let's at
least drive a nice car for a few years—after my sister called me I
sat inside my new red German so-called luxury SUV outside the
apartment where my daughters live, Antonio writes, thinking of
Hershleder in The Revisionist, who sits on the doorstep of his
house that is no longer his house—and instead of saying to her,
for instance, that at last he'd completed his first novel and it was
coming out in September—why bring up reminders of our different fates?—I can hear it in your voice, bobito—twelve years
writing about Bogotá—do you remember me in those years?—of
course I do—liar—he tells her about Perrito, the new family dog,
about how he'd told his former wife he didn't want a dog because
what difference would a dog make in their lives, about how one
Saturday his former wife said let's just visit this pet supply store
in Santa Monica since one of the animal shelters is having an
open house there, and his former wife tricked him by saying why
don't you pick our dog, you know the girls really want a dog, no,
I won't, he said, but he approached the handful of dogs behind a
makeshift fence on the sidewalk anyway, ven perrito, he said to
one of them, adopting his dead grandmother's voice—Martina
didn't talk about her upbringing but she did talk to street dogs—
water for dogs / here the water for dogs—and Dora's dog walked
over to him and licked his hand, and because Dora's dog looked
so forlorn, and because Dora's dog wasn't Dora's dog but
looked so much like Dora's dog, he said fine, this is our dog, and
so Dora's dog became their dog, and after a week of arguments
and counterarguments about potential names (Pongo, Fifi,

Gmail, Perrito), they agreed on Perrito, which was a fantastic name because every time anyone asks his former wife what's her dog's name she has to say, in her Czech accent, Perito — Burrito? — Perito — and when he would return home from his database analyst job at Prudential Investments, Perrito would run to greet him and pee out of excitement, and so for a while I had to pretend Perrito wasn't there so he wouldn't pee, Antonio says, and we couldn't take him on walks because he was afraid of shadows, plants, men, but he's better now, Antonio says, now he sleeps under the covers with us and prances everywhere, and so Perrito became a safe topic for them on their daily calls, how is Perrito today, Antonio's sister says, oh Perrito is sunbathing by the window, Antonio says, oh Perrito is hiding in Eva's bed, and one day he receives a card in the mail from his sister, a card printed on thin white copy paper with two rabbits on it thanking him for everything, a card he displays in the living room as a reminder that alternative worlds are possible, why weren't you like this with me before, Antonio's sister says, you used to behave as if I didn't exist, Antonio's sister says, I used to dream of going to Los Angeles to live with you, and of course Antonio doesn't have an answer for her, all he can do is say, in the softest voice he can muster, ay Estelita, and afterward hide in a conference room and cry and cry.

ANTONIO'S FORMER WIFE BY NICOLA CARATI

I would always follow her, Antonio's former wife says, my grandmother called me her tail because I would shadow her everywhere, to the point, I remember, she wanted to use the bathroom, but of course I was there, right behind her, okay can I please use the bathroom by myself, she would say, oh, okay, I'm going to wait right here, I would say, whatever she was doing I would follow her, and she would constantly tell me what she was doing, explaining it to me, okay I am spreading the oil in the frying pan, there's so much that I know because she would constantly tell me, like what, Antonio says, simple things, Antonio's former wife says, I am watering the plants right now, she would say, come Ida let's water the plants, I was her assistant, her tail assistant, her shadow, I remember walking behind her, and she would say let's water the plants, how old were you, Antonio says, it went on all my life, Antonio's former wife says, until I was ten when her Alzheimer's started and I'd reached an age when I needed to be away from everyone, and as Antonio reads the words he has transcribed from his 58:44 recording of his former wife, he tries to remember if his former wife ever followed him around as she'd done with her grandmother, not because he wants to fabricate some temporal linkage of great significance between her grandmother and him, no, of course our games from childhood live on, of course our adulthood consists of reenactments, but he, well, he doesn't know why he's trying to remember if his former wife has ever followed him around, perhaps he wants to retrofit her grandmother into his life with his former wife and his two daughters so as to feel more protected—your grandmother is still among us—of course she's still among us I think about her every day, Antonio — just as, when he was a child, he would feel more protected during his imaginary conversations with the Virgin Mary — dear mother of god today I didn't have one bad thought — think of me always — I don't talk about you anymore how could I explain you to others please forgive me — and although he can't remember one specific moment when his former wife followed him around, one of their domestic skits does include her shadowing him from room to room in silence, without touching him, pretending to have a crucial message that she's unable to verbalize along his trajectory inside their apartment, a trajectory he would prolong for her sake by inventing a menial task in the kitchen or the closet, was there something in particular that was your favorite thing to do with your grandmother, Antonio says, just be with her, Antonio's former wife says, watch the news, a soap opera that she would always watch with an apple in her hand, and I would bring my little chair and sit with her, and she would peel the apple and tell me that most of the vitamins were in the peel, there was this couple, she would say, man and woman, and the man would always peel the apple, and his wife would always bicker with him and say but all the vitamins are in the peel you shouldn't peel it, and one day the husband peeled his apple, sliced it for himself, and handed back the peel to his wife and said here's your vitamins, eat them, yes, I liked hearing that story, Antonio's former wife says, but of course Antonio would prolong his trajectory inside their apartment not only for her sake but for his, too, a trajectory that, even after she's gone (and here Antonio's surprised at how easily he can imagine his former wife at their doorstep, the day after their daughters leave them for college, a quaint suitcase on each side, her task done, ready to fly back to Czechia (when did their roles shift? because for years he was the one on their doorstep, ready to flee to

New York or Berlin or Barcelona after their daughters leave),
and it occurs to Antonio that perhaps he has borrowed the image of the doorstep and the quaint suitcases from The Sound of
Music or Mary Poppins, movies he'd watched for the first time
at the Nuart Theatre with his daughters, both movies screened
as singalongs that included a party kit (crown, glowsticks, bubbles) and two hostesses who instructed the audience on how to
use the party kit and what to holler when — the curtains, Maria, the curtains! — and if years from now someone were to ask
him was there something in particular that was your favorite
thing to do with your daughters, he would omit any pream-
bles about the blanks in his childhood and say the singalongs,
Maria, the whole theater singing along to songs that he likes
to believe he probably heard as a child but has forgotten, his
daughters amazed that they're allowed to blow bubbles inside
the theater, the whole theater a gyration of glowsticks during
the underwater songs of The Little Mermaid (and here Antonio
closes his eyes and sees the dark theater lit with glowsticks, sees
a dark dance club called Universe in Chapel Hill, North Carolina, a college town where he lived with his grandparents when
he was eighteen, soon after arriving to the United States (and
here Antonio pauses Górecki's Miserere, removes his oversized
circumaural Sennheiser headphones, and searches online for
the music he'd heard at Universe twenty-two years ago — I've
come down from the violet skies to save the day, a solemn
trance music voice says, I'm about to reveal the tales of your
life — the three-story brick building that was Universe suddenly
switching from white lasers and bass to darkness and silence,
except for the distant sound of spaceships, yes, he will keep his
eyes closed in his cubicle and stand in the dark at Universe,
marveling at a family life that shouldn't have happened to him
but did, his new family next to him at the Nuart Theatre, singing

their songs of the sea)), his daughters hollering the curtains, Maria, the curtains, Ada dressed as the curtains the second time they attended The Sound of Music singalong, and as he thinks of those singalongs he remembers a story about a father crying due to his son leaving for college, and although he doesn't remember many particulars of that story, he remembers wondering what kind of life do you have to live to have a father who cries when you are leaving for college (later that night, after Ada leaves them for her first sleepover, Antonio and his former wife watch old videos of Ada as a baby and he tells his former wife about the father crying for his son and Antonio cries, too, and yet the next morning he considers his reaction to that story and remembers that when he left Bogotá to attend college in the United States, his mother did cry for him—the light left the house after you left, Antonio—and so perhaps the right formulation isn't what kind of life do you have to live to have a parent who cries when you are leaving for college but what kind of upbringing do you have to procure for your children so that they're moved by your tears), a father that says, as he hopes he can say to his daughters, I was lucky to have spent all these years with you—where was I?—ah, yes, but of course I would prolong my trajectory inside our apartment not only for Ida's sake but for mine, too, a trajectory that, even after she's gone—) will continue with her at his side, shadowing him along with Dora, Silvina, his mother, la Madre Dolorosa, his sister, Ida's grandmother, shadowing him and saying, as Ida would say toward the end of their domestic skit, you don't love me anymore.

—

My grandmother was a hamster, Antonio's former wife says, a carryover after the war, I suppose, because back then you never knew what you were going to need so you had to collect everything, to the point that she would buy margarine, keep the con-

tainer, wash it, and store it in her maze of a basement, where
you could find these humongous old wooden closets from before
World War II, which contained her dresses, little pieces of jewelry, buttons, sewing equipment, I could open a drawer and spend
hours looking at these little treasures, do you remember some of
them, Antonio says, I remember my grandmother's feather coats,
Antonio's former wife says, my Mom told me my grandmother
was always beautifully dressed, and her makeup was perfect,
her jewelry matching, no jeans or pants, because women didn't
wear jeans or pants, but I don't remember her this way because
as a kid that wasn't what mattered to me, how I remember her is
in her favorite dress, which unfortunately was plastic, with a lot
of static, which she would wear every day, how do you mean plastic, Antonio says, acrylic, Antonio's former wife says, gray and
green with little flowers, an acrylic dress that would sparkle with
static against her tights when she would undress, and so my Mom
also told me that when my grandmother was younger she would
change three times a day, and she would ride a scooter to town,
whereas when I remember her she didn't ride anymore because
she had eighty-six breaks in her bones, she was limping in one
leg, her knee couldn't fold, so she would just live in her kitchen,
her bedroom, she had a little garden on the side of the house
gated from the dogs, her kingdom, her garden, her world, she
built her little world in our house and didn't leave it, so she didn't
talk about the outside world, the way she remembered it, was
she part of the resistance during the war, Antonio says, I think
she was somehow involved with the antipropaganda newspaper, Antonio's former wife says, and here Antonio pauses his
58:44 recording of his former wife and remembers the massive
World War II history book he'd read on his first trip to Český
Krumlov, almost twelve years ago, back when he was still trying
to avoid traveling to far away countries because he didn't want

to disrupt the world he was trying to build inside his first novel, a world populated with his memories of Bogotá, him playing soccer at his Jesuit high school, for instance, him conducting imaginary conversations with the Virgin Mary, a world so tenuous, so pockmarked already that a long trip to Czechia might relegate some of his memories to the dark corners of a place like the Central Registry in All the Names by José Saramago, where the index cards for the dead are stored, him on a plane to Czechia reading about the impact of the war on Czechia and Poland, and although he doesn't remember any of its contents, he does remember feeling like he was carrying a portable coffin due to its thickness, its black cover, its cast of doomed resistance fighters, so that, by the time his plane landed, the Czechia of his former wife had become the Czechia invaded by the Germans, who had orders to exterminate buildings and people, although over the years the Czechia of the war also became the Czechia of his former wife's parents, who, on his first trip to Czechia, tested Antonio's endurance to Chopin, their favorite vodka: on Monday the mother would serve Antonio Chopin shots and the father would complain about her serving herself too many Chopin shots, leaving the table in a huff, on Tuesday the father would serve Antonio Chopin shots and the mother would complain about him serving himself too many Chopin shots, leaving the table in a huff, yes, Antonio thinks, he'd enjoyed their brand of bantering (neither of his former wife's parents spoke English or Spanish so he'd interpreted their exchange as bantering), and after his former wife's parents became resigned to him being the father of their two granddaughters, they welcomed him into their family, and although he detested the exhaustion that stayed with him for weeks after flying to Czechia, he'd flown there multiple times, toward the end of summer #1, for instance, six months after Ada was born, soon after

he'd called his former wife in Český Krumlov and told her he
didn't know how long he could continue to playact at being father and husband.

—

My grandmother on my father's side was murdered, Antonio's
former wife says, two weeks before my aunt's wedding, while
everyone was preparing for it, back then it wasn't like you just
drove to the store, you had to grow your own pig, make your
own sausages, so they were storing everything in the barn, and
my grandmother happened to need something from the barn,
where someone had been hiding, and this someone smashed
her head with an ax and killed her, and so my dad, since he was
the oldest, had to be involved in the investigation, and when
your mother did her work on my dad, when they were both
staying with us, my dad opened up, and it was scary because my
dad doesn't talk, especially not about his Mom, he just started
talking and talking and couldn't stop, what work did my Mom
do on your dad, Antonio says, your Mom did Reiki on him, Antonio's former wife says, your Mom's theory about my dad going
blind is that he doesn't want to see, which is weird because if
you think about my dad, he's incredibly intuitive, really good
with people, but as far as emotions, he pretends they don't exist,
so many things he pretends they don't exist, kind of like you,
I didn't even know about the head thing, so your Mom didn't
know how it was going to turn out when she was holding her
hands above my dad's head, she said she feels this heavy weight
above him, and she sees his Mom, only the head, everything
else is dark, as if the rest of her body didn't exist, no eyes, just
the head, and she said she sees my dad not wanting to see, and
I was translating her words to my dad, and of course he was
trying to be silly about it, but afterward his face changed and
later he told me that, after his mother's funeral, after she was

buried and everything, the investigation had gone on and on, and the police were so pissed they couldn't find the murderer that they decided to dig up her grave, and my dad had to identify her, and they didn't want to dig everything out so they just chopped off the head, and my dad had to identify his own mother, which you can imagine after six months it's not just bone it's still flesh, swollen, smells, it's partially eaten by bugs, worms are sticking out, and he had to identify his own mother this way, and he did and then passed out, so when I was telling your Mom about my dad losing his eyesight, she said it's all linked to his inability to, I didn't even remember his mother existed, Antonio, I always thought everyone has only one grandmother, I didn't know she even existed because my father never mentioned her—whenever I think about my former wife's father, Antonio writes, I think about Ida flying to Czechia for three days to surprise her father for his seventieth birthday, or I think about Ida during summer #6, driving to the hospital in Prague every day to sit by him while the surgeons decided what to do about his ailing heart—what do you remember most about those days when your father was in the hospital, Antonio said, the traffic, Antonio's former wife said, the traffic because from our house in Český Krumlov to the hospital in Prague I had to drive for two hours, and sometimes I would roll up the windows, turn up the radio, and scream, just as I used to do as a teenager, when my Mom would shut the windows of our house, turn up the music, and tell us to scream or bark or growl, what else do you remember about those trips to the hospital, Antonio said, the phones always ringing at the nurses' station, the sounds of those ancient, stationary phones, now whenever my dad and I hear those phones anywhere we shudder—so you know all this pretending his mother's murder didn't happen, Antonio's former wife says, pretending his mother didn't exist, grieving after the funeral but never again after that, because according to my mother my father and his two brothers met at our house after the funeral and locked themselves in the bedroom for three days, drinking nonstop, and my uncle's wife and my Mom would prepare food, knock on the door, deliver the food and leave, and they would keep drinking, but after that, after those three days, they left the house and didn't grieve again, goodbye, like nothing ever happened, never any pictures of her, nothing, gone, puff.

—

My childhood was a blast, Antonio's former wife says, I grew up surrounded by greenhouses, a walnut tree forest, and so much land that I could vanish and no one would even notice, or I could build my own bonfires and no one would tell me oh you're going to burn yourself, or I could hide behind the trees, or I could venture out to our three detached garages, by my dad's workstation, that was another activity of mine back then, watching my dad fixing things, I think that's why I'm so good at it too, I would spend hours next to my dad watching him fixing and building, and every weekend, since there was nothing else to do, my parents and their friends would meet in someone's house and throw a party, and there would be music, dancing, tons of alcohol, Coca Cola from the black market, and the kids would just roam around the farm, because all of our friends were farmers, what else do you remember about your parents when you were growing up, Antonio says, they didn't worry, Antonio's former wife says, no one checked where I was, they were always busy and they partied a lot, every weekend they would either take us with them or they would leave us with our grandmother, and if they went by themselves they would come back with more guests and would continue the party at our house, what about your Mom, Antonio says, my Mom was the one who played with us because my dad had to wake up at three in the morning or he was on the farm, Antonio's former wife says, he did take us ice-skating though, but my Mom was the one who would always pick up some kids from the other farmers and take us sledding, or hiking, or to the pool, kind of like I do, funny, what else do you remember about your dad, Antonio says, the greenhouses were our primary income, Antonio's former wife says, and there was this plan that consisted of my dad bringing aszparagus seeds from the United States, asparagus, Antonio says, no asparagus is food here, Antonio's former wife says, anyway you added aszparagus to bouquets of flowers, and because back then there was nothing in the stores, and in Czechia, in Czech culture, if you visit someone's house you don't arrive empty-handed, you always bring something, and since there was nothing else in the stores, you would always arrive with a bouquet of flowers, so every morning, at three in the morning, my dad would load these bunches of green thingies, these aszparagus thingies, drive to the bazaar and sell them there, and he would make a lot of money from it, so he would come back home, back then we had no banks, no credit cards, so it was all cash operated, so he would always come home with stacks of money, and my dad would count the money as fast as a machine, always, every morning, by the time he was back at seven from the bazaar, I would be getting ready for school and I would see him at the table counting the money, it was amazing, he can still count as fast as a machine, although no one has that much cash anymore, did your parents ever hit you, Antonio says, never, Antonio's former wife says, my dad I think I remember once when I was maybe six or seven, we were going to a dance class and my Mom drove us there and left us while she went downstairs to the store, hoping they would have something, and we saw that the class was canceled so we went back down to the store but couldn't find her, the car was still outside so we went back inside, but in the meantime she'd left the store and we see her driving away so we run toward the car, it's like fifteen minutes from our house walking, so it wasn't far but it was already 7:00 p.m., but because I was little I couldn't make it, of course the car is faster, and my sister is superfast, and I keep running and running but I can't make it, so I start walking, and my sister leaves me there and runs home, and when I arrive home she tells my parents that I saw friends and left with them somewhere, and because my parents were so worried about me, my dad hit me with a belt I think, I don't remember, I was so confused, you left me there and I am getting hit, so that was the only time my dad hit me, but I know he was just so scared that something had happened to me.

—

My sister was a difficult child, Antonio's former wife says, she didn't sleep, was colicky, cranky, would always cry, the entire house would take turns staying up with her because she only slept during the day, or she only slept if someone rocked her stroller, and when she was two years old Ida was born, and Ida was perfect, Ida didn't cry, Ida was always smiling, slept through the night, and everyone started falling in love with Ida, so suddenly all this attention my sister had for two years went away because everyone was fascinated by how good Ida was and how bad she was, and look how good Ida is and you are such a bad girl, and of course now everyone knows what a mistake it is to say that, but given her personality, her temper, that was just the worst you could do as far as siblings, and I still remember how they would say oh look Ida is eating everything, because if you gave me pork I would eat pork, if you gave me an apple I would eat the apple, I was fat and chubby and I was cheerful and I had red cheeks and I was healthy and she was sickly and skinny and little and she only wanted to eat hard-boiled eggs, so what would she do to you, Antonio says, she would just create situations to get me in trouble, and she would use how naïve I was and my need to be loved by her, accepted by her, because I was so naïve, I wasn't a clever child, I wasn't sneaky, she would use that to manipulate me, for instance she would play cards with me and she would cheat, so I would constantly lose, and she would set up the game so that the loser would have to do chores, for instance we had a sofa bed and every morning we had to take our sheets and fold them, and in the evening we had to spread out the sheets and the blankets again, and the loser had to do it for the other person, and of course if she was cheating, I was so stupid and naïve, she would always win, oh and if you didn't do it by seven you had to do it an extra ten times, so I would have to make her bed a hundred and fifty times, and if I didn't do it she would hit me, or she would break my toys, and her being angry at me was so scary, I hated that feeling, when she was in a weird mood, angry or mad, she would take it out on me the most, or little things like she would lock me in that sofa bed, but I hear that is very common, she would drag me in there by my hair and lock me there, and because our house was so big, even if my parents wanted to intervene, my Mom was either in the kitchen, or cleaning, or doing laundry, we are on a farm, my dad is out working, there's no way anyone would see it happening, unlike in an apartment where it's so easy, you turn around, you see it, you hear it, no one would hear me in this humongous house, and by the time she would let me out we both would rush to my Mom and I would say Mom she locked me in the bed and she would say what, I would never do such a thing, and so who do you believe, I can't blame my parents for not seeing it, my Mom when I asked her about it she said when we would fight and she couldn't take it anymore she would take me to my grandmother and my sister to my grandfather, who was an alcoholic, and she would make drinks for him, light cigarettes for him, he had a bunch of multivitamins, which were very sweet, and she would eat them, hey, we survived, but the scariest incident was when my parents were changing the heating for the greenhouses from coal to gas, and for that they needed a different furnace, so my dad ordered this huge furnace, steel, with a bunch of doors and pipes inside, and it wasn't hooked up yet, it was still standing inside our garage, and there was a party in our house, of course, and the kids were running and playing hide-and-seek, and my sister talked me into going into that furnace and she locked me in there and left, I don't know how long it lasted, it was pretty long because when I came out everyone was leaving, again, huge farm, no supervision, no way anyone could hear me, I could have easily died, there wasn't enough oxygen, but there were these layers of pipes, so I squeezed myself in and around the pipes, up and up, and there was a tiny little window to look inside and see if the furnace was burning properly, and that wasn't latched so I pushed it open and somehow pushed myself through and came out, and instead of going to my parents and saying you know what your goddamned daughter did, I went to my sister and said na na fu fu, look, I escaped.

—

Sometimes after arriving home from his eight hours of SQL queries at Prudential Investments, Antonio lingers on the stairs by the doorstep, unzipping the boots of his work costume and listening to the children's music inside, the lyrics in Czech, of course, a language that, despite reminding him of the garbled, invented language in The Silence by Ingmar Bergman (the white noise of Bergman's train the same as that of the airplanes

on his way to Czechia), soothes him, and as he unzips his reasonable work boots—so friends, Wendell Berry says, every
day do something that won't compute—his database analyst
boots that do compute—there's man all over for you, Didi says,
blaming on his boots the faults of his feet—twice a week I bandage my feet before playing soccer, Antonio thinks, and twice a
week I limp to work because my left foot hasn't recovered from
its previous injury—he considers how his attempts to deplete
his body through soccer have allowed him to momentarily rest
from his linkage with his sister, as if by draining the batteries
of the antenna in charge of receiving signals from his sister he
can be momentarily at peace, and perhaps the Czech language,
which although familiar still doesn't compute for him—Czech
sounds like Russian to me, Antonio thinks, and when I think
of Czech I think of the poems in The Mirror by Tarkovsky's
father—no more dinner for you if you compare Czech with
Russian ever again, his former wife said—has contributed to
his recurring disbelief that he still shares this warm apartment
with his former wife and his two daughters, although if he had
to explain his current living arrangement he would have to diagram a timeline whereas he lived at Home with his former
wife and his two daughters (t1), The Other Home next door to
Home but visited every day after work plus Saturday (t2), The
Other Home next door to Home but was allowed to sleep at
Home three days a week (t3), and in that interval between (t1)
and (t2) he might pause and explain that in the aftermath of
their divorce proceedings his visits to Home consisted mostly
of him taking Ada to the pool at the Jewish Community Center,
the only location nearby where they could spend time together
in the evening during the workweek without his former wife,
the reverberations inside the underground pool facility like
those inside a cathedral or a submarine, the occasional Russian

grandfathers wading into the adult pool, their bellies like float-
ers, the kids' pool empty, the warm water to his chest when he
sat with his legs outstretched, an awkward sitting position, like
someone's wry idea of levitation, alternating between a feeling
of vacancy and an overwhelming desire to produce warm father and daughter memories for Ada, as he'd tried to do in a
one-page memoir piece entitled Fathers Fated, which he'd ad-
dressed to Ada and had set during the first time they attend a
performance of The Velveteen Rabbit—a father in the audience
was crying, Antonio wrote, you didn't notice because you were
pointing at the crocodile on the stage—a piece he'd never tried
to publish because he'd been unable to capture both the wonder of the moment—you placed your finger to your lips as a
reminder of the silence we'd agreed on, Antonio wrote, twirled
your hands above your head like we'd practiced after your ballet
class, shuffled in your seat because you were so little that the
seat would fold in on you if you didn't sit on the edge—and
the disbelief he felt at being a new father—before the show
you ran in the garden outside as if you'd just snatched the
ball from the dachshund you'd been petting, Antonio wrote,
the patter of your slippers on the grass reminded me of nothing and that was wonderful—Ada splashing the surface of the
kids' pool inside a cathedral or a submarine and him splashing after her as Tata Shark—everywhere we went I saw grandmothers looking at us and marveling at a world where fathers
and daughters held hands, Antonio wrote—wonder and disbelief but also an impulse to record their time together—soon
after our first Velveteen Rabbit I purchased my first camera,
Antonio wrote, I needed the evidence that it was possible, that
that father was really me—and yet the videos are also for you,
Antonio wrote, I like to believe that if you ever decide not to see
me again, like my sister and I did with my father years before

you were born, you can watch how we were together and change your mind—and after their pool sessions Antonio would cross the dark laundry room between Home and The Other Home (Antonio abhors overt symbolism in his own so-called fictions, plus the outside world barely exists for him in retrospect so he can't concoct symbols out of blank landscapes, but because he has been crossing this laundry room for so many years, and because the laundry room looks like a dilapidated basement with cables like entrails, storage spaces like coffins, rats like eels either slithering by or trying to wriggle free from their traps, television voices coming from the ceiling threatening one another in a language that doesn't compute for Antonio, an old tenant with a disfigured mouth who wears a homemade plastic raincoat and patrols her washing machine, he has come to associate the laundry room with purgatory), returning to The Other Home, also known as his quaint nook, where he would panfry his meat and tortilla dinner while listening to Michael Silverblatt saying to a group of Oulipo members that as a child he loved math—dear Mr. Silverblatt, Antonio writes, during a rough interval in my life, when I couldn't read or write in the aftermath of my divorce proceedings, I found consolation in the sound of your voice—dear Mr. Silverblatt I wanted your voice to be a father asking me about fractals—yes, sometimes when he enters the apartment where his daughters live he still feels like an intruder, or like a prospective renter being shown an apartment that comes with furniture and a family, or like a character in one of those Christmas movies who is given the chance to watch how his life might have turned out if he hadn't, for instance, abandoned his children as Antonio had planned to do after his second daughter was born, not abandon them, no, leave them in their mother's custody so as to become a weekend visitor, but most of the time he can't linger on his doorstep for too long because his daughters know the sound of his motorcycle so by the time he climbs the stairs the door is already opened and Ada is saying Tata come see my new storybook, and Eva is saying hurry come see the platypus I drew for you, and their new dog Perrito is jumping and peeing out of excitement, and his former wife is preparing dinner for this family of his, which, amazingly, still includes him.

WHEN ANTONIO WAS ANTONIO

One of the secretaries at Mitsubishi called me and said your father was involved with his eighteen-year-old secretary, Antonio's mother says, and that she wanted me to know because he could lose his job because of this dalliance, and since this girl was from Barranquilla, that year he wanted to spend his birthday in Barranquilla, but his plan was to leave us at his aunt's house in Barranquilla and for him to stay at a hotel, and so I said no, I'm not going, if you want to see your secretary I don't have a problem with you driving there by yourself, leave me in peace with my children, moreover, I am going to the beach with your parents, no, he said, you're going to do what I say, and that's when he slapped me, so this is when it happened, Antonio says, because Antonio had heard about this incident years ago but hadn't heard about the secretary from Barranquilla, although he's heard of the other women near the house in Mirandela, whom his father would visit in the evenings, whenever he said he was going for a walk and a smoke around the block (and here Antonio declines to link his father's extramarital activities to his own YSA activities because what would be the point of that? to say to himself see, you can't escape that individual? — I might have contemplated leaving Ida when Eva was born, just as that individual contemplated leaving my mother when I was born, Antonio writes, but I have never contemplated doing what that individual did to my sister and his stepdaughter—), yes, Antonio's mother says, because I didn't obey him, and so I defended myself, and the neighbor started shouting if I hear you're doing anything to your wife my sons and I are coming for you and we're armed, and that's when I called your uncle Lucho,

and Lucho said I am coming there now, I'm getting that son of a
bitch out of there with bullets, and you can't stay there, you have
to leave that house because you've endured too much abuse, and
so collect the clothes you need for the kids, whatever you feel you
need, and you leave that place, so when I told your father Lucho
was coming, armed, he disappeared, that's how I was able to take
you out and escape from that house, well, Estela wasn't there
because she was spending the long weekend in Cartagena with
my friend Blanca, so you were there by yourself, and perhaps because Antonio knows what his mother is about to say in this part
of the recording, he notices her long, dispirited sigh, knowing,
on the one hand, that as a mother she shouldn't display her help-
lessness in front of her child (because if a mother can't pretend
life is worth living . . .), and on the other hand what his mother
is about to say already happened, it's irreversible, and that was
tough on you, Antonio's mother says, because at first, after hearing his shouting, you hid, but all of a sudden you were there, between me and your father, shouting to your father don't treat my
mother like that, and that's when your father hit you—my father
swats me away and my brain activates its emergency erasure
mechanisms, Antonio writes, erasing that moment and, just in
case, everything that came before it—and I said to your father
I told you the day you touch me or the children all of this ends,
you're never leaving this house, he shouted, and since the neighbor started shouting as well, because remember the house didn't
have glass windows, only wire mesh so the neighbors could hear
everything, and I called Lucho and your father heard what I'd
said to him, and so after your father was gone and I was able to
leave our bedroom where he'd cornered me, I went looking for
you and I found you under your bed, trembling, and here Antonio pauses the recording and closes his eyes, trying to remember that moment—and when I am old and alone and banished

from my loved ones, Antonio writes, I will retrieve that bed from storage and wait for the end underneath it—no, he can't remember that moment, although he does remember having nightmares in that bed and his mother coming to assuage him at night, remembers the purple dinosaur that he would clutch in that bed, the Elmo he was scared of, I went looking for you and I found you under your bed, Antonio's mother says, trembling, and I said no, I have not been thinking about you, I've only been thinking about myself, I've been a coward, so I picked you up, picked up some clothes, and I said we are leaving, no more, this will never happen again.

WHEN ARTURO WAS BILL VIOLA

I prosecuted my father, Daria said, although my mother didn't want to press charges so I had to provide my statement alone and attend his trial alone, how old were you, Antonio said, thirteen, Daria said, just seeing my father in dreams terrifies me, Antonio said, although I'm used to these apparitions by now and they don't happen too often, I see my father in my dreams too, Daria said, but I'm most terrified to run into him in this reality so I've told my friends that if I ever ask them for a quick exit they should take me seriously — dear Daria, Antonio writes, you're the most courageous woman I've ever met — I remember waking up late at night and seeing my mother in our living room, Karla said, staring out the window in the dark, like an automaton programmed to power off at night because her owner was asleep and no household chores were needed, and so in honor of this memory of her, Karla said, one of my earliest memories of my mother, Arturo, because my mother is the subject of most of my performances, I reenacted the punishment my mother knew from school in Seoul at a busy street corner of Koreatown in Los Angeles, a punishment that consisted of tilting her body forward and keeping her arms raised (and here Antonio searches online for corporal punishment + Korea + school and finds too many variations on her mother's punishment) — on my father's birthday my mother asked me and my sister to tell Dad that we wanted to leave Tokyo and return to the United States, Hannah said, and so we told him and Dad left the dinner table and locked himself in the bathroom, why did your mother ask you to say that, Antonio said, because she wanted to return to her lover in California, Hannah said, whom she'd met at a playground while Dad was finishing his graduate program—dear Hannah, Antonio writes, I can see myself in your father, locked in the bathroom to conceal his despair, although I like to believe if you and your sister were my daughters I wouldn't have let you go—we had a good time but I don't want to see you anymore, Artemisia from UCLA messages him while Antonio's on a conference call about the geometric distributed lag marketing model he has built in between SQL queries, you treated me well and don't take it personally but it's hurting me, I want to have a healthy relationship not an arrangement, I see the way waitresses look at us and I feel low, I know people are judging our age difference and I can't handle this shame anymore— Artemisia wanted to become an attorney, Antonio writes later that day, so she was studying philosophy when I met her on Your Sugar Arrangements—send me your class syllabus please—what is the mind?—let's watch The Shining at the Nuart Theatre and smoke some jays—goodbye, dear Artemisia—in town for summer break can I see you tonight, Jasmine messages him while Antonio's on a conference call trying to explain to sundry marketing managers the methodology pitfalls of attitudinal segmentation, tonight it is, Antonio replies, although after the Goth Raver incident Antonio should be avoiding these kinds of encounters but instead he just tries to schedule fewer of them, wondering, each time he slips away at 9:15 p.m., whether this will be the night that destroys his life, which of course increases the thrill of these encounters (not only for him but for his arrangements as well since they're slipping away from their dorms or their parents' basement (Vera, for instance, had taken him to her mother's basement through a side door and a dark corridor and when her mother heard them she yelled at them from above and Vera yelled back in the same island language—Vera's basement had a sleeping bag instead of a bed, Antonio writes, but it did have plenty of rugs, scented candles, immense canvases with hundreds of doodles on them, splotched cans of paint—)), I've finalized a plea agreement for your sister, Antonio's sister's attorney messages him, so she will be transferred from the hospital to Baltimore City jail this week, Roger Sessions's Piano Sonata No. 2, Jasmine says later that evening in answer to his question about what she has been playing, play it for me, Antonio says, because they're at the Frates Cafe, where chamber musicians can drop in to play Mozart, Beethoven, Bach, and perhaps because of Jasmine's outfit, which brings to mind a flight attendant en route to Maui (white jeans, blue blazer, handkerchief around her neck), or because of her long black hair down to her waist that Antonio knows she'll ask him to pull later—I know you know I don't need to ask you, Arturo—or because she's petite and smiles too much on her way to the upright piano, too eager to please, removing her blazer and handing it to Antonio, who bows to her, glad to add intrigue to the performance by pretending to be her servant, or because the Frates Cafe brings to mind the cafe in the movie Shine, where David Helfgott, a pianist whose formulae of reality have been distorted, sneaks in to perform Flight of the Bumblebee—I mean, the point is, David Helfgott says, if you do something wrong you can be punished for the rest of your life—the audience is taken aback by the speed of Jasmine's fingers and the severity of her sound, as is Antonio, who hasn't acknowledged just yet that for him this vision of Jasmine plus Roger Sessions equals an onrush greater than those caused by, say, pornographic videos of rural Russian women selling fruit while underneath the counter men lick their legs, and after Jasmine is done rebuking the audience that condescended to her inside this cafe that reminds Antonio of Amsterdam, even though Antonio has never been to Amster-

dam, Antonio and Jasmine drink from a pitcher of cheap sangria while occasionally a scrawny Caucasian American violist
who has no chance whatsoever with Jasmine interrupts them,
trying to impress her with his role as organizer of local concerts, you okay to drive, he says, eyeing Antonio as if suspecting
him of trying to take advantage of her excess of sangria, don't
worry he's driving, Jasmine says, and so Antonio drives her
mother's 1980s BMW to The Other Home, where he, distracted
by the intensity of his desire for her, forgets to cover her
mouth—she shrieked as I imagined an eagle would shriek, De-
nis Johnson says, and it felt wonderful to be alive to hear
it—which culminates in his neighbor banging on their shared
wall and then on his front door, and perhaps because of his disbelief that his neighbor exists (Antonio has never seen his
neighbor), or because Antonio and Jasmine are silent and still
now and isn't that the point (why is the neighbor still banging
on the door?), he takes too long to wrap himself in blankets and
open the door, it's one in the morning can you shut the hell up,
his neighbor says, okay, Antonio says, too unapologetically
(because if his neighbor would have been a man he would be
egging on Antonio instead of interrupting him, no?—dale con
todo, Bruja—), and the next morning, after opening all the windows to air out the place and showering in silence, his empty
apartment seems, as usual, unreal to him—a Japanese pianist
was here last night? and she woke you up twice in the middle of
the night because she wanted to keep going?—I don't believe it
either—and as usual, once he has purged his body of any evidence of wrongdoing, a purge that reminds him of Bill Viola's
Inverted Birth, which he watched at Disney Hall with Katerina,
also known as Uzi Kitten, he crosses the laundry room that connects his building with the building where his daughters live

(a laundry room that every week seems more populated by other people's junk (bicycles with handwritten warning signs, boxes with pictures of electric heaters)), and when his former wife opens the door Antonio immediately knows something's wrong because she doesn't greet him—good morning, Tato, she doesn't say—was there someone at your apartment last night, his former wife says, what are you talking about, Antonio says, the building manager messaged me that there was a noise complaint from your neighbor last night, his former wife says, that's strange, Antonio says, allowing her question no importance whatsoever, and while in the kitchen Antonio continues to pretend that this is all probably due to some irrelevant misunderstanding, his former wife picks up his keys, crosses the laundry room, enters his apartment, returns, and says don't ever talk to me again, walking out and driving away, and once he's sure she has gone he crosses the laundry room, enters his apartment and finds, by his bed, the dog collar he'd fastened on Jasmine's neck (how is it that he remembered to hide the metal leash that hooks to the collar and dispose of the vinyl tape he tied around Jasmine's wrists but forgot to hide the collar?—you and your stupid Bill Viola showers, Arturo—), and that day and the next everything at the apartment where his daughters live is as before except Ida pretends he doesn't exist, although every now and then she asks him a harmless logistical question so as to not alert the children about their rift, and as the days go by Antonio hopes she will resort to her own erasure mechanisms, and because she has given no indication that she's planning to resort to them he tallies what he could offer her to slowly overturn her pretending he doesn't exist, for instance moving to Czechia, or giving up The Other Home, as Ida has suggested several times through the years, although the latter offering terrifies him because The Other Home has allowed him to skirt

the disastrous father / husband reimaging that had been acti-
vated when he married Ida nine years ago (if current role = husband and father, then Antonio = Antonio's father), in other
words by calling Ida his former wife he isn't a husband, and by
having another home he isn't a father (if current role <> father /
husband, then Antonio = Nicola).

WHEN ANTONIO RECEIVED CALLS FROM
BALTIMORE CITY JAIL

The automated system informs Antonio he's receiving a call from an inmate of Baltimore City jail, an inmate called Estela Jiménez, the words Estela and Jiménez a recording of his sister saying Estela and Jiménez, the automated system informs Antonio that the call will be recorded and monitored, if you have questions or complaints about this call please call customer service, to hear the cost of this call, press 8, to accept this call, press 5, to decline this call, hang up, so Antonio presses 5 and the automated system informs him it requires a credit card to fund an account from which to deduct the cost of this call, so Antonio enters his credit card number and funds an account for $10 and the automated system informs him he has a balance of $1.35 because there's a $8.65 service charge, please hold while you are connected, the automated system disconnects the call, the automated system doesn't acknowledge its error because it doesn't register it as an error, unless the automated system contains the appropriate error-handling code, of course, an SQL syntax as basic as if account = funded and call < 0.01 seconds, then error = 1, else error = 0, the automated system doesn't tabulate how long Estela Jiménez has been holding the public phone to her ear due to the automated process of accepting a collect call from an inmate of Baltimore City jail, unless the chief executive officer of the company that owns the automated system also happens to have a sister whose impaired mind has led her to become an inmate of a county jail and therefore he, the brother, has set quarterly company goals to reduce the length of the automated process of accepting collect calls from

inmates at county jails—let us not lengthen the suffering of
those who are already suffering—the automated system doesn't
wonder what Estela Jiménez might be thinking as she waits for
its automated process to complete—has my brother tired of me
already? did he reject the call and the system hasn't registered
the rejection yet? has my brother tired of being reminded that
he's linked to my miseries?—I'm here, Estelita—the automated
system informs Antonio he's receiving a call from an inmate
of Baltimore City jail, you're receiving a call from an inmate of
Baltimore City jail, the automated system says, to accept this
call, press 5, yes, okay, Antonio presses 5, Toñio, Antonio's sister
says, I've just read in Mundo Hispánico that immigrants who
have committed a crime will be immediately deported so I've
decided not to accept the plea agreement because I don't want
to be deported, the automated system disconnects the call, the
automated system doesn't acknowledge its error because there is
no error but a depletion of the $1.35 in his account, and so out-
side of Menotti's Coffee Stop, where he likes to read on Sunday
afternoons because the sun on his face allows him to read for
hours without falling asleep, Antonio waits for the automated
system to link him to his sister again, the automated system informs Antonio he's receiving a call from an inmate of Baltimore
City jail, an inmate called Estela Jiménez, the automated system accepts the $25 from his credit card and the autorecharge
option (how many brothers and mothers and sisters, rushing
through this automated process, end up misdialing their credit
card numbers? how many fathers worry that the long wait on the
other end of the line might change their daughters irreversibly?),
the automated system informs Antonio the charges will appear
under GTL Inmate Phone Services, which he, a database analyst
for Prudential Investments, knows is the kind of data signal
a credit card company can mine by querying a transaction

statement description field, yes, a database analyst can run a simple SQL query with a like %inmate% statement in the where clause to select all records that contain the word inmate in the transaction statement description field, which might lead a database analyst to conclude that Antonio is in jail, do you have a few minutes, a database analyst might say to his database manager, I think the presence of the term %inmate% in our credit transactions might be a leading indicator that a customer won't have the money to pay us back, so I was thinking we could build a test to minimize charge-offs by significantly reducing the credit line of those customers with transactions that include %inmate%, no, a more experienced database analyst might say, the presence of %inmate% isn't enough, to verify they're in jail you will need to run another query to check whether these customers continue to transact after the word %inmate% surfaces in their transaction history, right, the junior database analyst might say, I will need to (a) check these post-%inmate% transactions are a different pattern of transactions as those before %inmate%, (b) exclude post-%inmate% transactions that could be considered recurring payments, (c) verify post-%inmate% transactions are occurring at merchants that would require his or her physical presence, exactly, the senior database analyst might say, plus what if they were in jail but they're out on bond now, we are better off just A / B testing whether %inmate% gives us any significant net reduction on charge-offs, Toñio, Antonio's sister says, I've just read in Mundo Hispánico that immigrants who have committed a crime will be immediately deported, a crime in this case includes domestic violence, DUI, petty thefts, among others, but you're pleading to three counts of public disturbance, Antonio says, which does not fall under the category of crimes of moral turpitude, the kind of crimes that will lead to deportation according to our immigration attorney, that's not what the newspaper says, Antonio's sister says, the newspaper doesn't have enough space to print all the categories of crimes that will lead to deportation, Antonio says, DUI, petty thefts, among others, Antonio's sister says, we don't know what's in the among others category, Antonio says, if they deport me will you come see me, Antonio's sister says, of course, Antonio says, how am I going to live in Bogotá, Antonio's sister says, please don't worry about that I will support you, Antonio says, but they won't deport you, Estelita, I checked with the immigration attorney, I know you're nervous, I would be too, but we're almost there, Estelita, please accept the plea, I'm sorry, Antonio's sister says, I can't do it, no.

WHEN NICOLA WAS ANTONIO

What I don't transcribe I will forget, Antonio thinks as he reviews the metadata of his recording of his mother, which he has been jotting down on his sketchbook and which consists of timestamps at the beginning of threads, his mother's phrases as headlines to these threads, downward L-shaped arrows linking headlines to subheadlines, stars next to significant headlines, checkmarks next to headlines he has already transcribed, and although Antonio suspects that what he doesn't transcribe he will forget, he also suspects that what he does transcribe he will forget, too (already he has forgotten sizable portions of the Bogotá he spent twelve years writing about, for instance), so perhaps he's been transcribing his recording of his mother not to document those horrible days of childhood so that one day he can write about them but to spend these horrible days of adulthood in the company of her voice—I'm tired of encountering mental institutes and lunar landscapes when I'm asleep let's stroll to a carnival with Ada and Eva and wave at the college students dressed like salmons, Ida—one day I will jump-start a mother business, Antonio writes, a business that will warehouse recordings of your mothers so when your turn for the horrible comes you can press a button on your phone and receive not a call from your mothers (because what would you say to them if they called?) but a call with a recording of your mothers saying that when you were little you sold water for dogs—yes, Antonio thinks, what I don't transcribe I will forget and what I do transcribe I will forget—nevertheless Antonio still wants to at least try to retain these moments he hasn't transcribed—what is to be done with moments that have no place of their own in time, Bruno Schulz says, moments that have occurred too early or too late, after the whole of time has been distributed?—what is to be done about his mother saying when you were little the three of us were like a junta, which Antonio hasn't transcribed yet (too fragmentary), or his mother saying Estela was very protective of you, I mean, your sister started to talk when she was eight months old, and one day, when you were still a newborn, you peed while I was changing your diaper on the couch, splashing me like a lawn sprinkler, and I complained and said something like uff, this darn child, and your sister admonished me and said but Mama, he's little, which Antonio hasn't transcribed yet (too sentimental), or his mother saying a man on the street in downtown Bogotá approached me and said your daughter is so beautiful, please be careful someone could steal her, which Antonio hasn't transcribed yet (too foreboding), or his mother saying your sister painted stories and she would ask me to sew the pages to make them into a book just like Eva does, which Antonio hasn't transcribed yet (too heartbreaking), or his mother saying I kept your childhood drawings in a box, but when we escaped from that house in Mirandela the box stayed behind, and I did ask your father to give it back but he refused, so unfortunately I was never able to save your drawings as you've done, Antonio, all those drawings of Ada and Eva on your kitchen walls, and a month after we escaped, Antonio's mother said, thieves emptied that house in Mirandela, taking both televisions, your father's expensive stereo, his collection of Italian shoes, his canvases with his abstract paintings, everything (and here Antonio can imagine Don Jorge, the old neighbor who would hand him toffees through the wire fence, snacking on popcorn and grinning as the thieves loaded their truck with his father's crap), which Antonio hasn't transcribed yet (too unbelievable due to how quickly retribution came to his father),

or his mother saying every time I would tell your sister we have
to talk about what's been happening with your father, she would
say no, I don't want to talk about him (his father had remarried
a woman who came with a fourteen-year-old daughter, and instead of taking this fourteen-year-old daughter to her confirma-
tion classes, his father would take her to a motel), I want you to
know what's been happening to him (he was on the run now),
because you can become entangled with his situation without
you knowing it, Antonio's mother said, because there's people
who could benefit from you intervening (the fourteen-year-old
daughter's therapist had also been Antonio's mother's therapist
in Bogotá, so this therapist had emailed Antonio's mother asking to please call her because she needed help confirming the
accusations against his father), no, I don't want to know, your
sister would say, and that was my fear, Antonio, that by not sup-
porting that fourteen-year-old girl (Antonio's stepsister), or the
newborn (Antonio's half sister), that Estela or any one of us in
the family might suffer repercussions, even your daughters,
Antonio, so I would insist and she would refuse, to this day I
can't talk to her about what's been happening with your father
in Bogotá (even if Antonio landed in Bogotá, located his father
wherever he was hiding (his aunt Elena, the Exorcist, knew where
he was because Antonio contacted her before, when he was trying to talk to his father—I didn't do anything wrong that girl
seduced me she was mature beyond her years, his father said—the
first time I'd spoken to that man in twenty-one years—), and
knifed him so he would cease to spread misery, the misery
across generations, according to my mother's constellations,
wouldn't end—how else will we make it end, Mother?—we
must bring the perpetrator into the fold—no—), please, Antonio's mother said, there's an energetic entanglement due to what
has been happening with your father, no, my daddy didn't do

anything, my daddy this, my daddy that, as if to submerge that part of her pain, because she had too much already with what was happening to her in Baltimore, and so it came to a point where I told her yes, it happened, he wrote you a letter confessing and apologizing, and I read it, I couldn't remember, Mom, your sister said, I thought nothing had happened, and I think because your sister was in so much pain, she mixed everything up, blocking out what had happened to her so many years ago, enough, Antonio thinks, it's 9:01 a.m. already, time for SQL queries, proc means, nested where statements, so Antonio removes his oversized circumaural Sennheiser headphones, which have been transmitting his mother's voice for months, buries his sketchbook with the metadata of his recording of his mother under his Prudential Investments binders, runs his first batch of SQL queries, tries to read The Unnamable online, receives a call from his sister's attorney, who informs him his sister has at last agreed to a plea for three counts of disorderly misconduct, twelve months of outpatient treatment, twelve months of probation, and a commitment to leave the state of Maryland and never return—this has been one of the most rewarding cases of my career, his sister's attorney says, to see your sister recovering—runs his second and third batch of SQL queries, packs his sketchbook that contains the metadata of his recording of his mother, the metadata of his recording of his former wife, the notes he's been jotting down about his arrangements, about his sister, about the (so many) fictions that have been coursing through him for years (Antonio has been unable to write anything of consequence since summer #8, except the story of Dora and her dog, which contained no imaginative writing since it was an almost exact transcription of what Dora told him about her dog), switches off the fluorescence of his cubicle, rides his Shadow VLX to the apartment where his daughters live and where at last his former wife begins to speak to him, we need to talk, his former wife says, after the girls are asleep yes, Antonio says, Tata do Froggie Froggie, Eva says, not today, Antonio says, come on, Tata, Ada says, hey Froggie, Antonio says [in a severe voice], these girls want to talk to you come over here, what?, Antonio says [in an incredulous voice], you're busy eating fly soup? [Ada and Eva laugh], and so Antonio huffs away and Froggie appears and says [in a dumb country voice] hiiii you all doing, good, Ada and Eva say [pretending to be unamused], hey is that a fly cupcake, Froggie says, noooooo, Eva and Ada say, oh, gotta go, wait come back Froggie, Ada and Eva say [in mock alarm], have you seen Froggie Froggie, Antonio says [reappearing as himself], yeah he was just here, Eva says [as nonchalant as possible], huh, Antonio says, didn't see him, dinner's ready, Ida says, knock knock, Eva says, who's there, Antonio says, interrupting cow, Eva says, interrupting who, Antonio says, moo, Eva says, no you're supposed to interrupt him with your moo, Ada says, again, Eva says, time to brush your teeth, Ida says, bedtime, Ida says, I Had Trouble in Getting to Solla Sollew by Dr. Seuss, Antonio says, lights off, Ida says, one by one the lights were all extinguished, Virginia Woolf says, there's a nostalgic appeal to the asinine Frog skit, Antonio jots down on his sketchbook, because Eva and Ada and I have been sharing the asinine Frog skit with one another for almost three years, since the time they would take baths together, do you want to be with us, Ida says, yes, Antonio says, switching on the extractor above the stove so the girls can't hear them, do you want to continue being part of this family, Ida says, yes, Antonio says, we are not teenagers anymore, Ida says, I can't be running after you, keeping tabs on you, and I won't, Ida says, not anymore, but do know I have only so much patience left, Ida says, at some point I will just leave do you understand, yes, Antonio says, and do know that if a butterfly were to land on my shoulder, Antonio doesn't say, I would burst from grief and say how will I ever repay you for everything you have given me, Ida, and thankfully Ida doesn't sit on the slate steps and doesn't explain to him, Antonio Jose Jiménez, patiently and for the thousandth time, that this was no longer his home (it still is), that the locks have been changed for this very reason (his keys still work), that he had to stop coming around here, upsetting her, upsetting the children, any news of your sister, Ida says, yes, Antonio says, pausing to compose himself (and show, with his composure, that what Ida has said has computed with him and that he is capable of complying), if all goes well my sister will be released tomorrow.

ESTELA JIMÉNEZ BY ANTONIO JOSE JIMÉNEZ

When did you start hearing voices, Antonio says, on a Sunday as I drove my mother to the airport my mother was there I'd become a bit paranoid of everything because Cristian had been conspiring against me always sharing my personal information with our coworkers at Fidelity Insurance so I'd ask my mother to come to Baltimore, and she came, and I didn't want her to leave that Sunday as I drove her to the airport that's when I realized there was this situation of voices I don't know if perhaps they started before, little by little or all of a sudden, but the first time I remember was a Sunday as I drove my mother to the airport later I developed insomnia due to what was happening, what was happening, Antonio says, the noises, the voices, I couldn't sleep, I would try to negotiate with them so they would go away some of the voices were independent from my logical self there's a part that's independent, and a part that's subjective that joins your thoughts the independent part says three or four things and then your subjective part fills the rest they're independent thoughts that you didn't think, they say, for instance, I want to shower this afternoon and you didn't think this but the thought was there, independent, almost everything was related to my job the voices were voices from people at Fidelity Insurance, so the first time you heard voices you heard the voices of your coworkers, Antonio says, yes I drove to work what transpired was a negotiation every day trying to negotiate for these voices to leave they wouldn't leave I would drive to the gym and everything it began to escalate because I continued to negotiate and they wouldn't leave that anxiety that they wouldn't leave, that they would stay permanently, that fear began to escalate until I ended up driving to the hospital because I couldn't sleep, that was the first time at the emergency room when you couldn't sleep, Antonio says, the fear becomes part of your thoughts you can't control them you live in a cloud of independent thoughts that you can't control, what would they say to you, Antonio says, I don't remember at some point I wrote them down they were persecutory they would reject me I do remember that during my leave of absence at work I would remain in bed negotiating trying to exit this cloud of thoughts they would tell me we are the, we are the, how does it go, not the incorruptibles, like a group that demands a lot, the untouchables, Antonio says, no, there's a word, I can't remember, like a group that's severe with you that is not going to forgive you I returned to work hearing voices they never went away it's only recently sleeping over at my Mom's house in Sioux Falls that they've been gone completely, when you came here to Los Angeles for that one weekend were you already hearing voices, Antonio says, yes I think I told you the doctor in the hospital told me that it happens to a lot of people these independent thoughts are so intelligent that you think how is it that this can be I used to compare it to a noise coming from an earpiece the doctor said many people think they are being recruited by the government what happens is that you can't believe that this is happening to you did you see the movie A Beautiful Mind, yes, Antonio says, the protagonist thought he was being recruited by the government too in the hospital it wasn't just about voices but about memories, because my memory started to fail me, certain memories that I had that now that I am rested I know aren't true when I was in jail I was convinced that a former boyfriend who was in real estate wanted my house so he plotted with those people who called the police on me the doctor said that that was unlikely the doctor tried to remove me from that cloud that I was in I was surprised by it sometimes it scares me because I only realized it later how can it be that these nebulous memories that aren't true have filtered through, later I had hallucinations in my house I was having them the day I was arrested I'd been having hallucinations for like two days about my neighbor crossing my front door like a ghost these are symptoms of the same sickness, the doctor said, in the hospital they ask you as part of the questionnaire if you have auditory problems, visual problems, in jail it happened that I had a lot of hallucinations, in the hospital as well I was in a solitary cell for too long I don't know if part of the brain becomes agitated something happens to it it starts to produce hallucinations because when I was in the hospital it was the opposite I was always relating to others so the hallucinations went away as if my brain couldn't produce them anymore when I was younger I could be alone and face anything but my brain didn't produce these kinds of hallucinations now it seems that with age, whenever I'm alone, isolated, my brain, dinner's ready, Ida says, we're recording give us a minute, Antonio says, now or never, monkeys, Ida says, I'm hungry, Toñito, Estela says, and so Antonio pauses the recording and Estela and Antonio join their mother, Ida, Ada, and Eva at the dinner table, tell us the one about how Mama and Tata met, Tata, Ada says, don't mind them it's a game they play, Ida says, a game that consists of Antonio inventing scenarios of how Antonio and Ida met, when Mama and Tata first met, Antonio says, Mama was selling mangoes on the side of the road, why mangoes, Tata, Eva says, and I came into her mango stand, her face as red as a lobster, and I asked her where the closest gas station was because I had to pee and guess what she said, whut?, Ada and Eva say, that's right, Antonio says, whut, they're making fun of me I don't say whut like that, Ida says, never, Antonio says, but of course there had been no mango stand or gas station, only a sky cabin in Tahoe where, on the bottom floor, while he was reading a paperback of Catch-22 instead of drinking with the repulsive investment bankers above (Antonio had agreed to the Tahoe trip because his friend Nicole wanted him to see snow), he saw Ida for the first time, ambling as if in penance because earlier she'd forgotten the sunblock so her face was as red as a lobster, and although he doesn't remember what he said to her, or what she said to him, he remembers telling his friend Nicole as soon as she breaks up with that retrograde investment banker you call me, a call that arrived a year later, on a Tuesday—we're at Taco Tuesdays, Nicole said, she's here and she's very single—and she was so striking, this Amazon woman from Eastern Europe, as his mother called her upon meeting her for the first time, jumping around in her suede cowboy boots and her cowboy hat because she was free of the burden of boyfriend and all she wanted to do was dance, and all every man wanted to do was dance with her, including Antonio, of course, and so Antonio and Ida did (just as friends though due to Ida wanting to be free of boyfriends), two or three times a week (in all the photos from those days, which Antonio keeps in his file cabinet inside his cubicle, Antonio and Ida look drunk, Antonio grinning at the camera while Ida's holding a bottle of champagne like a newborn, for instance), until one Sunday afternoon, at a street party, where a Spaniard had been about to succeed in seducing Ida—she's a bit nuts, Antonio said to the Spaniard, I would avoid her if I were you—Ida said I'm horny, and Antonio said that's what friends are for, and so he flagged a cab for them—so glad there was no cameras in that cab, Ida has said over the years—how do you know there weren't any, eh?—and when they arrived at her apartment she said to her roommates, who were watching television, let's order pizza, as if to cover for what they were about to do, which they

did, that day and the next day and the next, for almost two years
electrifying each other before parties, after parties, at his apartment that soon became her apartment—we never did order that
pizza, Ida has said over the years—let's order it now—stopping
on their way to Sonoma, midway, so they could do it again at a
two-star hotel, where the maid walked in on them and stayed
two or three seconds too long before saying excuse me—we
never made it to Sonoma, Tato—and one day it was over, as it
always had been for Antonio, or so he thought, because on the
Sunday she was about to move out, he, for practical reasons (she
was flying to Czechia in a few weeks anyway so why not wait
until she left to break up?—not for practical reasons, Antonio's
mother said, you just didn't want her to go—if you would have
broken up with me while I was in Czechia that summer I
wouldn't have come back, Antonio—but you never made it to
Czechia because we conceived Ada—), changed his mind, covering the walls of their apartment with Post-it notes that said
please don't go, please stay, and so she did.

—

What else do you want to know, Toñito, no but without the
iPad, Antonio says, but it's boring otherwise, come now, Antonio says, nooooo [in a child's voice], put away the iPad please,
Antonio says, hmmmpff, okay let's restart, seeing those ghosts
must have been scary, Antonio says, I'm still scared there's a
possibility I will get deported I would say my god what's going
to happen even my uncle Francisco would cross my front door
as a ghost I was watching a lot of television because the television was always on at a high volume and they would show
movies what we used to do at the hospital is play cards and
watch television or walk through the hallways if we watched a
good movie that would be our only connection with the exte-

rior world I remember watching The Hunger Games the man from Hunger Games the one who plays President Snow I would see him entering my cell like a ghost that is not a ghost that's a hallucination in the cell in the hospital as well, when you were in jail you were alone, Antonio says, yes for a little while I shared a cell with someone but most of the time I was alone I became scared you can waste a whole day looking at these ghosts a woman in my cell would tell me we're going to have a secret you talk to yourself I won't tell anybody because the process of transferring me from jail to the hospital lasted so long there was no connection with anyone you saw what the phones were like sometimes I would spend most of the day writing letters I wrote letters to the judge that's probably why they transferred me to the hospital I wrote that my mother had injected me, that you had participated, that the two of you had kidnapped me they realized this was improbable they became concerned at first my lawyer wasn't sure do you want to talk to your family or not, he said, when I began to regain my reason I said yes after I was arrested the first time the hallucinations went away they returned on my birthday a year later they were horrible I think it was because I was scared I would get deported back to Colombia and I would have to see Antonio Senior again I get along with our cousin Isabel over the internet my Mom has received messages from Aunt Elena that sometimes I'm like how is it possible that they're still defending him you can come and stay with us, Isabel said, our family is very close, but Isabel is still Aunt Elena's daughter, they are still his sisters and nieces no matter how much they offer to help it's strange I know it isn't their fault because of the possibility of deportation a terror visited me the possibility of separation of our family how will I deal with that family over there, so a year after your first arrest you became scared of deportation, Antonio says, it was as if ghosts were attacking me, what do you think prompted it, Antonio says, because I wasn't getting along with you or my Mom I was living in an environment in which Cristian rallied our coworkers against me they lied and said I had complained of harassment which wasn't true he acted like the victim obviously I have a problem that if I neglect rest or healthy eating it's possible this sickness will return I stopped taking sleeping pills the doctor doesn't think the sleeping pills caused the hallucinations I came to realize that at my Mom's house by resting a lot they went away I still have that strange sound, which I've looked for on the internet, there is a sickness, I wrote down the symptoms, the name, white noise in the brain, I think, most of the time it doesn't bother me when I lie down to sleep the brain feels more pressure when I'm walking not as much either way I've become nervous because it makes me feel more predisposed to death there's a word for that, not more human, vulnerable, Antonio says, I don't remember, yes, more predisposed to death, because it's an imbalance of the body, the body begins to get sick is it a symptom of something else is it going to be the case that I will have to leave this world at a young age remember we had that problem with our teeth are these signs that genetically our body isn't going to last like other people who die of cancer when they're forty or fifty that's what I think about here in Los Angeles I have to constantly eat fruit because I feel my blood pressure dropping if I don't eat a certain amount my energy levels don't rise these downswings are too large are they part of some sickness my Mom doesn't hear any noises she doesn't have these downswings it does worry me, Toñito.

—

Tell me about Milwaukee, Antonio says, I was conscious that
the moment that they arrest you for what they arrested me for,
first of all a terrible depression came over me, because I'd been
charged with five felonies, so that's enough for me not to be able
to work ever again in insurance to only be able to work at a
Wendy's or Burger King, places like that, because those charges
show up in background checks now I have three counts of disorderly conduct all the same they won't hire you, I'm not working now because it's too tiring though I was working in an office
after the arrest I had to do these drug tests, exams, I had a problem at work I began to think I was going to end up in jail the
lawyer never told me that there's usually a plea agreement I was
up in the air, scared, I don't know if the lawyers do it to make
you beg, I'm not going to end up in jail, I said to myself, I have
savings, I had saved something like fifty thousand dollars, and
I am going to spend my savings, and I am going to see the world,
and I've spent all these years working so hard to end up with
these charges, and I am going to end up in jail who knows for
how many years, so I started to travel I drove to Milwaukee, I
removed all my belongings from my house later they auctioned
them all away because I didn't pay the storage fees, and so I
drove to Montana multiple times, what did you do in Montana,
Antonio says, drive around, stay in hotels I spent all my credit,
the fifty thousand plus all my credit lines, so when you arrived
to Milwaukee you didn't have any money anymore, Antonio
says, yes I was already low on money toward the end before they
apprehended me I sold my car, I didn't have any money, any gas,
I went to a CarMax and sold my car for two thousand dollars
then they arrested me I was having memory problems I was at a
laundromat, oh, okay, I was sleeping in an immense shelter but
I discovered that I could sleep by the side of the, I became a

member of a gym I would shower there at night I would sleep next to the storage because it was in a basement I slept better there than in a shelter there was a woman who had gone there to sleep too no one said anything it was all bulletproof with cameras and everything I made a little bed next to it I would wake up early I would walk, I started watching movies, at some point I developed this idea that I'd met Brad Pitt when I was young, strange things were happening to my memory, because of what you had done to commit me in the hospital I thought you and Ida were against me so when they called the police at the laundromat I think I had called a man a Nazi, you're a Nazi, I said, they paid you, and you and Ida were Nazis as well who had paid this man to block my way in the laundromat the attendants called the police due to a disturbance the police arrived to check what was happening but there were no charges or anything when they scanned my license I don't know I guess they saw I had a warrant these kinds of hallucinations were already happening to me I was sure you had followed me to Milwaukee I'd seen a girl who looked just like Ida on the train, Ida is following me, I would think, or I would see someone who looked like you from behind my brother is following me they're going to intern me you are Nazis, so I think it was many years of living with so much pressure, of not living close to family, plus the situation with Cristian exacerbated it as he conspired with others at work against me, since we didn't have a more peaceful relationship, or with more people around, so it developed into paranoia I was surprised my memories were so affected I don't know why like I said they are symptoms of a sickness the doctor said there are people who think they are being recruited by the government and that happened to me too I began to research government spying capabilities I even shared some printouts with you because the independent voices were so intelligent that

one begins to fight against it or a part of you says this can't be
so you begin to make up that you're being recruited because you
can't believe that this is happening to you you live a life so full
of discipline, being the best candidate in most of the jobs you
apply for, and all of a sudden you can't control your thoughts,
so you start to think you're being recruited because you can't
believe it's happening to you I imagine that's what happened to
that man, who died already, you can't believe it, which man,
Antonio says, the one from A Beautiful Mind, what do you remember about us as siblings, Antonio says, I remember we used
to play a lot until we were ten or so you grew up, started school
at San Luis Gonzaga, and after that we didn't play anymore,
how about before then, Antonio says, we would play house don't
you remember we would make houses in our beds in our room
in that house in Mirandela you had your bed I had mine I had
a whole set with dolls we would join them with a bridge between
the two beds we had a village on each side you had your own
village on your side we would spend the whole day playing
house, under the table, later they bought me ceramic jewelry
from Bucaramanga and we would play with the jewelry then
you grew up you would play Barbies with me and you would
undress them and I would become upset because that's all you
would do, undress them, I think I stopped playing with Barbies
when I was ten because I was tired of you undressing them, I
think you told me that even though you were hearing voices you
could function and drive to Montana and Milwaukee what was
that like, Antonio says, I would spend most of my time talking
to myself, like answering, I don't remember what I was saying,
I even considered driving to Los Angeles but the involuntary
confinement had already happened but I would say I'll do it for
my nieces, but you and Ida might call the police I don't want to
be interned again, no, I would spend most of my time talking

to myself because the voices were really strong and I wasn't sleeping well, to overcome this, to me it's a miracle, I mean when I walk, when I am walking around now here in Los Angeles and I don't hear anything except the external sounds I'm like whoa, but back then no, I was hearing voices and it was a nuisance, so to not hear them I would talk to myself, so there were different planes of reality, Antonio says, I think I drove to Montana because when I was young I had a good time there, when, Antonio says, when I was twenty-one with a boyfriend named Jonathan we went rafting, but I drove there in winter I began to think I'd gone to college there in winter with snow and he was there with me it was quite a mix-up my first lawyer had become upset had placed a restraining order on me he tried to negotiate so he wouldn't have to do it I had written him like five pages in my memory I was convinced that I had met him in college so in front of the judge I said I knew him from college and I was well-dressed, looked normal, but that wasn't true, when I was in jail I wrote a letter to his associate who had helped me before I apologized and told him I didn't know these were symptoms of a sickness when I was driving in Montana I thought I'd been in Montana with him, with Ronald Reagan and his wife and Amber, this girl from college, I think my mind produced these things I didn't know this wasn't true I would drive while it was snowing I think I crisscrossed Montana twice, and you would stay in hotels, Antonio says, yes but I would spend most of the day driving, and that helped you, Antonio says, because of the charges I couldn't stay calm what do you do when you have these kinds of charges and you think you are going to end up in jail so I spent most of my time driving around as if on holiday a part of me thought perhaps I wouldn't have been this way but I had worked so much, so hard, and life slips away, mortal, I think that's the word I was looking for, when you know that either way you're going to die, look at my uncle Patricio who used to drink, used to get drunk every day, he died when he was eighty-seven years old just like my grandmother who didn't drink, and one takes care of oneself, doesn't drink, doesn't get drunk, and yet ends up with this sickness, without eating pork, or any of those greasy things they used to eat, and life does slip away, Toñito, Tía Estela come read to me, Eva says, we're recording maybe later, Antonio says, Perro, Estela says, don't pet him or he'll pee on the bed, Eva says, our Eva looks just like our Estela doesn't she, Antonio's mother says, go read to them it's late they have school tomorrow, Ida says, milk in the batter, Antonio says, we bake cake, Eva says, and nothing's the matter, Ada says, say mnemocartography, Antonio says, if you go flying on a flying trapeze, Ada says, I will be a tightrope walker and walk across the air to you, Antonio says, quick, Tía Estela, Eva says, before lights-out.

Mauro Javier Cárdenas was born and brought up in Guayaquil, Ecuador, and studied Economics at Stanford University. His debut novel, *The Revolutionaries Try Again*, was published in 2016. He was awarded the 2016 Joseph Henry Jackson Award and was included in the Hay Festival anthology *Bogotá 39: New Voices from Latin America* (Oneworld, 2018), a selection of the best young Latin American novelists working today.